THE SUBURBAN **RACIAL DILEMMA**

Conflicts in Urban and Regional Development,

a series edited by John R. Logan and Todd Swanstrom

THE SUBURBAN
RACIAL DILEMMA

Housing and Neighborhoods

W. DENNIS KEATING

TEMPLE UNIVERSITY PRESS / **Philadelphia**

Temple University Press, Philadelphia 19122
Copyright © 1994 by Temple University
Published 1994
Printed in the United States of America

Library of Congress Cataloging-in-Publication Data

Keating, W. Dennis (William Dennis)
    The suburban racial dilemma : housing and neighborhoods / W. Dennis Keating.
        p.   cm. — (Conflicts in urban and regional development)
    Includes bibliographical references and index.
    ISBN 1-56639-147-4. — ISBN 1-56639-148-2 (pbk.)
        1. Discrimination in housing—Ohio—Cleveland Metropolitan Area.
    2. Afro-Americans—Housing—Ohio—Cleveland Metropolitan Area.
    3. Housing policy—Ohio—Cleveland Metropolitan Area.   I. Title.   II. Series.
    HD7288.76.U52C65   1994
    363.5'1—dc20
                                                                            93-17865

This book is dedicated to the memory of Bernice Lott and Harry Fagan, two of the most inspirational leaders of the movement for racially integrated neighborhoods of Cleveland Heights, the city to which my family and I moved in 1983. Unfortunately, I never had the opportunity to meet either of these dynamic persons.

Bernice Lott was a civil rights leader and president of the Cleveland Heights–University Heights Board of Education. She died in 1983. She was a trustee of the Heights Community Congress, and her memory is honored through the congress's annual bestowal of the Bernice E. Lott award to an outstanding Cleveland Heights resident.

In 1970 Harry A. Fagan became the first director of the Commission on Catholic Community Action, which supported so much community organizing in metropolitan Cleveland in the 1970s. Fagan was instrumental in the creation of the Heights Community Congress and became its director during its formative period between 1973 and 1976. He died in 1992.

Without such dedicated participants, successful social movements for racially diverse communities in the United States could not exist.

CONTENTS

LIST OF TABLES AND MAPS

Tables

Maps

ACKNOWLEDGMENTS

This book arose from my move to the city of Cleveland Heights and my growing interest in the pro-integrative movement, whose participants included many of its residents. The project took shape over many years.

My research assistants and I interviewed many participants in this continuing drama that has spanned more than the past three decades. These participants are too numerous to mention here. Without their cooperation, memories, and suggestions, this would have been a much more difficult and much less interesting undertaking. I also benefited from the cooperation of cities such as Cleveland Heights, Oak Park, Park Forest, and Shaker Heights and many of the fair housing organizations that are profiled herein.

I have been assisted by four able and interested research assistants—graduate assistants Linda Smith, Beth Sawyer, and Becky Jones and law student Noreen Kuban.

I have received support for my research on this topic from the Levin College of Urban Affairs, the George Gund Foundation, and the Northeast Ohio Inter-Institutional Urban Research Consortium. The research results and interpretation of the data are my own, not those of the funders.

In Spring 1991, I took a sabbatical leave to work on this book, partly in residence at the Institute of Urban and Regional Development at the College of Environmental Design at the University of California at Berkeley. This gave me the time to make substantial progress on the book.

I have given presentations of my work-in-progress at several of the annual meetings of the Association of Collegiate Schools of Planning and the Urban Affairs Association and at two International Research Conferences on Housing.

An overview of some of the issues raised in this book was contained in an article titled "Open Housing in Metropolitan Cleveland," which appeared in *Urban Housing: Segregation of Minorities in Western Europe and the United States*, edited by Elizabeth D. Huttman, Wim Blauw, and Juliet Saltman (Duke University Press, 1991).

Many informed participants have read drafts of parts of the book. I am particularly indebted to the following persons who read the entire manuscript and provided valuable feedback: Chip Bromley, Lana Cowell, Don DeMarco, Gerda Freedheim, George Galster, Norm Krumholz, Kermit Lind, and Juliet Saltman. Special thanks go to John Logan and Todd Swanstrom.

I also received invaluable assistance from Michael Ames, editor-in-chief at Temple University Press.

Secretarial assistance was ably provided by Ellen Baumgardner, Jeanie Stearns, and Ivonne Bates.

Finally, my wife, Kay, and children, Bryan and Kelsey, supported me when my absence was required during evening and weekend hours to research and write this book.

PART I

Racial Divisiveness
and Policy Alternatives

1

Race, Housing, and Neighborhoods in the Metropolitan United States

Racial separation and conflict unfortunately are all too prevalent in the United States in the 1990s. Racial divisions continue to cause social, economic, and political tensions. Nowhere is this problem more pronounced than in housing. Housing and residential neighborhoods in the United States remain largely racially segregated. This pattern differs only by degree in different metropolitan areas and municipalities.

This book addresses housing segregation and efforts at housing integration in the suburbs of metropolitan areas. Its primary focus is Cleveland, Ohio, and the efforts over the past three decades (1963–1993) to reduce racial segregation and promote racial integration in housing in the suburbs of metropolitan Cleveland. Cleveland and its suburbs have long ranked as one of the most racially segregated metropolitan areas in the United States (Massey and Denton, 1987, 1988). Since the early 1960s, fair housing activists have sought to change this pattern. Fair housing programs and policies in suburban Cleveland and the fair housing movement in metropolitan Cleveland are compared herein to their counterparts in several other major metropolitan areas.

Changes in patterns of residential integration and segregation and data on racial discrimination in housing in the metropolitan United States over the past three decades are analyzed throughout

3

this book. Some progress toward greater racial diversity in housing and neighborhoods has been made during this period, but for the most part the movement for fair housing has not been able to overcome prevailing patterns of racial separatism. While the enactment and enforcement of fair housing legislation has reduced, but not eliminated, racial discrimination, this has not in itself resulted in significantly more racial integration.

What is the rationale for housing integration and neighborhood diversity? Those who have advocated the importance of achieving these goals, whether white, black, or of another minority group, have argued that racial barriers will be broken through contact in residential neighborhoods, in the workplace, and in schools and other public venues. Through social contact and participation in community life and organizations, racial stereotypes can be dispelled and race relations can be improved. Leola Spann, a black homeowner and housing counselor who lives in Chicago's northwest Austin neighborhood, adjacent to the suburb of Oak Park, expressed this well when interviewed by Studs Terkel (1992: 98): "I think the main thing—and this is sad to say in the nineties—is not knowing each other. That's the key. I think if we ever know each other, we could iron out all our problems." If this could be achieved, it certainly would go a long way toward reducing social tensions. If it were achieved in American suburbs, it would change the pattern of largely white, mostly affluent suburbs surrounding increasingly poor central cities that are populated increasingly by minorities.

To achieve the goal of community integration, affirmative housing policies are required. These include offering financial incentives to homebuyers, landlords, and homeowners for pro-integrative behavior. Such policies go beyond enforcement of antidiscrimination laws to involve promoting broader choices in housing, not imposing mandatory choices (as has occurred, for example, in the fields of education and employment). They are controversial, with whites and blacks both supportive of and opposed to them. Few suburban governments have taken such action voluntarily. Litigation against selected suburbs accused of exclusionary practices has not had the intended effect of persuading other suburbs to adopt affirmative policies to avoid similar legal problems or of leading to federal or statewide legislative action to mandate affirmative fair housing policies.

The lesson of the civil rights era and the subsequent period is that we cannot expect most individual suburbs, which are predominantly white, voluntarily to decide to take affirmative action to promote racial diversity. Rarely is there a political constituency for such a course. In view of the multiplicity of local governments in the United States, the "balkanization" of political power, the conflicting interests of more affluent and predominantly white suburbs and central cities like Cleveland that are increasingly populated by poorer minority residents, and the inadequacy of fair housing legislation to promote much greater racial diversity, it is critical that affirmative housing policies be initiated and implemented at the metropolitan level. Only at the metropolitan level can there be the possibility of forcing or persuading all suburbs, rather than a few, to eliminate barriers to a more open housing market and society.

Regional fair-share housing programs are one possible approach. During the 1970s, the federal government supported such an approach. The *Mt. Laurel* saga in New Jersey, which began in 1971, represents a sustained attempt to have the state courts and state legislatures mandate statewide fair-share housing allocation to counteract municipal exclusionary zoning (see Chapter 2). Efforts to provide more publicly subsidized housing and to promote "pro-integrative" home purchases through mortgage incentives in the suburbs are other key policies.

The central conclusion of this book is that a variety of affirmative race-conscious housing policies aimed at racial and economic integration in the suburbs is required if residential segregation is to be reduced significantly. If this is to be accomplished on a broad basis, then these policies must be adopted and implemented within metropolitan areas through either mandates or incentives that emanate from the federal and state governments. This means that there must be a much stronger political constituency for affirmative policies aimed at greater racial diversity.

The protracted political controversy over affirmative action and related civil rights policies, which has characterized political debate over race since the 1960s, also threatens the possibility for progress in housing. This has great bearing for the future prospects of developing a broader political coalition for fair housing and for the reduction of segregated housing. In a conservative political climate, affirmative action policies have encountered great political and legal resistance. Yet, without such policies, there seems to be little likelihood of greater racial integration in American housing and neighborhoods.

Opponents of affirmative race-conscious fair housing policies claim that they violate the principle of freedom of choice. As exercised by most blacks and whites, however, freedom of choice in housing has all too often led to resegregation. This is explained in part by the historic pattern of whites choosing to live in all or predominantly white neighborhoods. Some have made this choice due to prejudice against racial minorities. Others make this choice without considering the racial composition of a community, while not challenging the segregated nature of such neighborhoods. Others choose their neighborhoods based on such factors as housing quality and price. Given the income differences between whites and racial minorities in the United States, the absence or underrepresentation of less affluent minorities in many suburban areas can be explained by their being unable to afford higher-priced single-family housing.

However, segregative patterns in housing cannot be explained only by the choices made by homebuyers and renters, whether they be whites or minorities. The policies of government at all levels, as well as those of realtors, financial institutions, and insurers, have had a tremendous impact on the racial patterns of housing and neighborhoods in suburbia. Long-standing discriminatory practices, including restrictive covenants, exclusionary zoning and land use controls, racial steering, and mortgage and insurance "redlining," have combined to deny minorities access to most suburban communities (Darden, 1987).

To reverse these practices and promote pro-integrative behavior will require race-conscious policies affecting the private housing market that some will resist as undesirable, politically difficult, or illegal discrimination. Race-neutral nondiscrimination policies are not likely to change patterns of racial isolation and segregation in suburbia. This dilemma is the heart of this book.

Prevailing Patterns of Racial Segregation in Housing

What is meant by "segregation"? Residential segregation indexes for metropolitan areas in the United States measure several factors, including the "exposure" (i.e., probability of interaction) of racial minorities to nonminorities (e.g., blacks to whites) by residential blocks. If segregation were absolute (i.e., "apartheid"), the exposure of blacks to nonblacks would be zero. In contrast, if racial integration were total, each block (or census tract) would have a racial proportion that parallels that of the locality (city, county, or metropolitan region). A related index measures "dissimilarity," that is, the extent to which members of different racial groups are distributed unevenly within metropolitan areas (Taeuber and Taeuber, 1965; Massey and Denton, 1987, 1988).

At the heart of the movement for residential integration and racial diversity in neighborhoods is the hope that interracial contacts will reduce racial conflict and discrimination. Residential neighborhoods are important social contact points for normal interaction. Where white and black neighbors are of the same social class, acceptance by whites of racially mixed neighborhoods is more likely (Helper, 1979).

Despite the civil rights movement of the 1960s, the passage of fair housing legislation (including the federal Fair Housing Act of 1968), and the emergence of an open housing movement fighting for an end to racial discrimination in housing and for greater racial diversity, the United States remains largely segregated in the 1990s. In an analysis of sixty metropolitan areas in 1980, sociologists Massey and Denton (1987) found little change in the pattern of racial segregation that prevailed in 1970. Blacks were twice as segregated as were the Hispanic and Asian minorities. Chicago was the most segregated metropolis in the United States, followed closely by Cleveland. In 1990, Cleveland remained second only to Chicago among the most racially isolated of fifty metropolitan areas (Gillmor and Doig, 1992).

The Evolution of Segregation in Housing and Neighborhoods

Today's patterns of suburban segregation can be understood only within a historical context. The pattern of racial segregation in residential housing and neighborhoods took hold as the mass black migration from the South to northern cities occurred, during and after World War I. This was the era of the formation of black urban ghettos in northern cities such as Chicago, Cleveland, and New York (a pattern later reinforced by the policies of the Federal Housing Administration [FHA]), the use of restrictive racial covenants, "steering" and "blockbusting" by realtors, and redlining by insurers and lenders (Abrams, 1955).

It was also the era of the formation of the first suburbs. Mostly upper-class bedroom communities for commuters, they were either exclusively restricted to white occupants (except for domestic servants) or were predominantly white, there being few black professionals able to afford the expensive homes even if they were allowed to purchase them. Examples of such suburbs include East Cleveland, Cleveland Heights, and Shaker Heights, Ohio (Teaford, 1986: 69–71).

This pattern of racial segregation in housing in American cities and suburbs was decried by those espousing the cause of black civil rights. Gunnar Myrdal (1944), for example, called attention to prevailing patterns of racial segregation, attributable to white prejudice, and to the educational and income disadvantages suffered by blacks. Social critics and civil rights groups were joined by housing reformers (e.g., Abrams, 1955), who called for interracial housing and an end to discriminatory practices. Racial covenants were outlawed by the U.S. Supreme Court in 1948 (*Shelly v. Kraemer*, 334 U.S. 1 [1948]), but this had little effect on the evolving pattern of racial segregation of postwar private housing development in suburbia.

In addition, efforts to ensure racial integration in public housing encountered heavy opposition from the white neighborhoods of central cities, from their political representatives, and often from white public housing residents (Meyerson and Banfield, 1955). Federally subsidized low-income housing was almost entirely limited to central cities. Suburbs were not required to participate in the public housing program and rarely did.

Most postwar new construction occurred outside the central cities and their older neighborhoods. This was due to the availability of inexpensive undeveloped land at the urban fringe, federal housing and highway policies that promoted suburban growth, the redlining of older urban neighborhoods, and the amenities offered in suburban housing and communities (Jackson, 1985).

Whether on the scale of the Levittowns or small subdivisions, most newly built postwar suburban housing was marketed to and sold to white homebuyers. The New Jersey Levittown was limited initially to whites, when it opened in 1958. Only after a lawsuit was filed to deny Levittown and its homebuyers FHA insurance, because of state antidiscrimination policy regarding government-supported housing, did Levitt reluctantly relent, and the first black purchaser moved into this Levittown in 1960. Although a hostile reception met black homebuyers, Levittown did gradually accept a small but growing number of black residents (Gans, 1967: 371–84).

For the most part, black "pioneers" in suburban housing were few in number, beginning their move to suburbia in the 1920s and continuing after World War II in the 1950s. All too often they either faced a hostile reception from prospective white neighbors or were socially ostracized.

The Metropolitanization of the United States

Since World War II, the spatial and demographic patterns of metropolitan America have fundamentally changed. The overall population of central cities has generally declined, while the percentage of their inhabitants who belong to racial minorities in most cases has increased (see Table 1).

At the same time, suburbanization has dominated metropolitan development. The majority of the residents of metropolitan America lives in the suburbs, not the central cities, a pattern prevailing since 1970. In 1980, of the 172 million Americans living in metropolitan areas, 99 million lived outside central cities (Palen, 1987: 110, table 5–1). The 1990 census revealed that a majority (50.2 percent) of the population lives in the thirty-nine large metropolitan areas (with a population of 1 million or more) in the United States, which together contain nearly 125 million Americans (*New York Times*, Feb. 21, 1991, sec. A, p. 1).

This steady exodus to the suburbs has been caused by such factors as the search for newer and better housing, schools, and amenities and municipal services, as well as employment. Suburbs have generally offered all of these, whereas central cities, with the loss of much of their employment base and middle-class population, and with their increasing proportion of poor residents, have steadily declined. Motivated

Table 1. Black Population in Fourteen Central Cities, 1960–1990

	Black Population		Percent Black		Percent Change 1960–1990
	1960	1990	1960	1990	1990
New York City	1,141,322	2,111,783	14	29	107
Chicago	837,656	1,117,753	23	38	65
Detroit	487,174	810,739	29	66	128
Philadelphia	535,033	689,424	26	40	54
Los Angeles	417,207	592,038	14	14	0
Washington, D.C.	418,693	399,604	54	66	22
Houston	217,672	465,433	23	28	22
Baltimore	328,416	446,732	35	58	66
New Orleans	234,931	310,342	37	60	62
Memphis	184,725	346,648	37	54	46
Atlanta	186,820	273,321	38	62	63
Dallas	131,211	314,963	19	26	37
Cleveland	253,108	235,405	29	47	62
St. Louis	216,022	240,644	29	40	38

Source: U.S. Census, 1960 and 1990

not only by suburbia's attractions, many whites have left the central city also because of their opposition to racial change in their former urban neighborhoods (Jackson, 1985). "White flight" accelerated in the wake of the urban race riots of the 1960s in many central cities.

In some cities (including Cleveland), court-ordered desegregation of the public schools added to the white exodus. Even with increasing black suburbanization, most American suburbs remain almost entirely white. The pattern of racial segregation spreading outward as urban areas continue to expand spatially has made the possibility of metropolitan desegregation of public schools very difficult to achieve. The U.S. Supreme Court has ruled out court-imposed metropolitan interjurisdictional school desegregation unless suburban school districts are proven to have engaged in racially discriminatory policies (*Milliken v. Bradley*, 418 U.S. 717 [1974]). This decision was reinforced in the March 1992 decision in *Freeman v. Pitts*. In 1989 the U.S. Court of Appeals ordered DeKalb County, Atlanta's largest suburban county, to go beyond its voluntary desegregation efforts and engage in cross-country busing to overcome racial resegregation due to white flight (Orfield and Ashkinaze, 1991: 144–45). Between 1969 (when DeKalb County's schools first came under review by the federal courts) and 1989, the black population of the schools grew from 5 to 60 percent. Due to white flight in the face of black suburbanization, more than half of the black students now attend schools in which 90 percent of the students are black. In 1992, writing for a six-to-three majority, Justice Anthony Kennedy overruled the appeals court because he concluded that the public schools were not responsible for residential segregation:

> The District Court in this case heard evidence that racially stable neighborhoods are not likely to emerge because whites prefer a racial mix of 80% white and 20% black, while blacks prefer a 50%–50% mix. Where resegregation is a product not of state action but of private choices, it does not have constitutional implications. It is beyond the authority and beyond the practical ability of the federal courts to try to counteract these kinds of continuous and massive demographic shifts. . . . Residential housing choices and their attendant effects on the racial composition of schools present an ever-changing pattern, one difficult to address through judicial remedies. (118 L. Ed. 2d 108, 137)

With this decision, the nation's highest court said that, unless residential segregation in housing is reversed, resegregation of the suburban public schools is not illegal and the courts are powerless to intervene. This makes promoting racial diversity in suburban housing even more urgent, if integrated suburban public schools are to become a reality.

Black Suburbanization

Black suburbanization has grown steadily since 1960 (see Table 2). Its patterns are not uniform. They vary by region and by types of suburbs available to blacks (Logan and Schneider, 1984; Stahura, 1988). In some metropolitan areas, there have been historic black suburban settlements to which blacks have gravitated. In the process of postwar suburbanization, blacks have most typically moved to

Table 2. Suburban Black Population in Fourteen
Metropolitan Areas, 1990

	Black Population 1990	Percent Black 1990
New York City	138,243	12
Chicago	215,166	7
Detroit	132,740	4
Philadelphia	240,483	8
Los Angeles	400,936	9
Washington, D.C.	619,239	20
Houston	145,810	9
Baltimore	169,333	10
New Orleans	120,128	17
Memphis	52,363	15
Atlanta	462,832	19
Dallas	95,803	7
Cleveland	120,214	9
St. Louis	182,538	10

Source: U.S. Census, 1990

predominantly white suburbs. According to P. L. Clay (1979), the majority of new black suburbanites moved into formerly white neighborhoods in older inner-ring suburbs that were being vacated by whites moving into newer suburban areas.

Black suburbanization, whether it involves single pioneers or larger numbers, has encountered much resistance. As occurred during the racial transition of older inner-city neighborhoods, the changing racial composition of a neighborhood raised fears among many whites that the neighborhood would "tip" eventually to a substantial black minority or a black majority. Such fears and related concerns about potential depreciation of housing and real estate values have been exacerbated by racial blockbusting by unscrupulous realtors. Controversy continues over whether a "tipping point" exists and, if so, at what racial ratio. It has been argued that when the black population reaches 25 to 30 percent, racial resegregation is likely, if not inevitable. Andrew Hacker (1992) has gone even further. He argues that white flight begins when the black proportion of the population reaches somewhere between 10 and 20 percent, even when the blacks moving in have the same economic and social standing as whites (Hacker, 1992: 37–38). Only when the white population is 92 percent or more and remains so does Hacker believe that stable racial diversity is possible (Hacker, 1992: 36). Except for the use of "benign" racial quotas, Hacker offers little hope for racial integration in housing.

Despite Hacker's assertions, there is no conclusive evidence of "tipping" being an inevitable result of racial transition (Goering, 1978). However, fear of racial tipping and resegregation of neighborhoods has led to "integration maintenance" policies and even racial quotas in housing projects. These policies were designed to stabilize the racial proportions of the population in order to maintain racial diversity.

Very few suburban communities have dealt with racial transition and its attendant problems directly. With only a few exceptions throughout the United States (including the community case studies examined herein), most suburbs have not adopted affirmative open housing policies to foster racial integration. Instead, most suburbs have tried to avoid the issues of racial segregation and racial transition in housing. Historically, many have used exclusionary practices such as large-lot, single-family-only residential zoning, which inflates the price of housing to exclude racial minorities and low- and moderate-income households generally. Housing prices beyond their income, white hostility, and lack of access to employment have kept minorities out of many suburbs. However, black suburbanization has continued to increase. Many blacks have migrated to the few "magnet" suburbs considered to be receptive to minorities. These have often been suburbs immediately neighboring large urban black ghettos (Clay, 1979). Unfortunately, this process has all too often resulted in the resegregation of these suburban neighborhoods and, in a few cases, entire suburban cities. They have become predominantly black, with little or no further white demand for housing.

Antidiscrimination Legislation, Litigation, and Judicial Enforcement

More than two decades after enactment of the 1968 federal Fair Housing Act, it and companion state and local laws have had little effect on the overall pattern of racial segregation in most suburban housing (Logan and Schneider, 1984; Massey and Denton, 1988; Stahura, 1988). The failure to change these patterns reflects (1) the preference of a majority of white Americans for predominantly white neighborhoods; (2) the reluctance or refusal of the federal and state governments to attack systematically racially exclusionary local land use and residency patterns through either litigation or legislation; and (3) the persistence of discriminatory behavior in the housing market.

Most fair housing litigation during the past few decades has involved only individuals seeking judicial redress for racial discrimination in housing. Their legal victories, while having a deterrent effect on discriminatory practices by realtors, lenders, insurers, and landlords, have not resulted in significant changes to widespread patterns of housing segregation (Danielson, 1976).

Housing "audits" by "checkers" in the 1980s demonstrated the persistence of racial discrimination. Black homebuyers faced a one-in-five chance of racial bias and black renters a one-in-two chance (Galster, 1990a). The most recent data are found in an analysis of housing audits, conducted in 1989 in twenty-five urban areas with significant minority populations (including Chicago and Detroit but not Cleveland) and funded by the U.S. Department of Housing and Urban Development (HUD). Overall, the study found that almost one-half (48.8 percent) of blacks seeking to purchase a home received unfavorable treatment in the private housing market, with housing availability, credit assistance, and sales effort being the key criteria. Black renters (45.7 percent) and Hispanic homebuyers (44.6 percent) and renters (42.7 percent) also received unfavorable treatment (HUD, 1991). In a 1989 national poll, 52 percent of blacks believed that blacks generally faced discrimination in housing, whereas only about 20 percent of whites held this view (Sigelman and Welch, 1991).

Relatively few housing discrimination cases have involved "patterns and practices" charges brought against municipalities or major developers under the federal law (Selig, 1984). Although a few such cases have gained notoriety, they have had little effect on the vast majority of mostly white suburbs and suburban housing developments whose policies have not been challenged in court. Even in the few states (e.g., New Jersey) in which litigation and legislative efforts to promote broader municipal housing opportunities for moderate-income households have been the most pronounced and sustained, progress has been painstakingly slow.

Racially discriminatory practices and patterns continue despite the passage of laws (including the 1988 amendments to the federal Fair Housing Act), litigation, and public education efforts designed to eliminate racial discrimination in housing. Only a few suburbs have openly and voluntarily embraced racial integration in housing and neighborhoods as municipal policy. These include such suburbs as Oak Park and Park Forest, Illinois; Southfield, Michigan; and Cleveland Heights and Shaker Heights, Ohio.

Changing Attitudes toward Racially Diverse Housing

Suburban housing segregation has persisted despite seemingly significant changes in white attitudes toward racially mixed housing and neighborhoods. For example, analysis of national opinion surveys reveals a growing white acceptance of the concept of the rights of blacks to live in neighborhoods of their choice. By 1976, 88 percent of whites supported blacks' rights to open housing, although this level of tolerance varied by region and the extent of white exposure to blacks in neighborhoods (Schuman, Steeh, and Bobo, 1985: 153–56). However, whites were less supportive of governmental implementation of residential integration through open housing legislation (Schuman, Steeh, and Bobo, 1985: 156–59). A similar trend is found in metropolitan Cleveland.

Despite the seeming improvement in white attitudes toward integration, the past quarter-century has been marred by numerous incidents of racial conflict and violence. White opposition to court-ordered school and housing integration continues. A 1990 national opinion survey revealed that white attitudes toward racial minorities, especially blacks, remain decidedly negative (Smith, 1990). Well-publicized racial confrontations in the 1990s in the neighborhoods of central cities (e.g., Los Angeles and New York), in some suburbs (e.g., Teaneck, New Jersey), and on many college campuses have reinforced the sense that the movement toward greater racial harmony that arose during the 1960s civil rights movement may be losing its force in America. The importance of race of political campaigns, including the 1988 and 1992 presidential elections, confirms its persistence as a divisive issue. While greater racial diversity in housing is not guaranteed to end racism or eliminate altogether white fears of blacks, it can contribute significantly to improved racial harmony and understanding and to resolution of racial conflict.

Suburbia and Housing Integration

While central cities seemingly have much more of an overall racial mix than suburbs have, racially integrated urban neighborhoods are still the exception, and integration in those neighborhoods has been very difficult to sustain (Molotch, 1972; Saltman, 1990). This is true in the city of Cleveland, whose east-side neighborhoods are predominantly black and west-side neighborhoods are predominantly white. With the majority of the U.S. population residing in suburbs, little prospect of massive white migration back to predominantly black inner-city neighborhoods (despite the "gentrification" of some low-income minority urban neighborhoods during the past two decades), and the continuation of both white and black metropolitan suburbanization, the best prospects for increased racial integration in housing and neighborhoods lie in the suburbs of metropolitan America.

Support for racial integration is more likely in those suburban cities whose residents seem generally sympathetic to this ideal. This book examines in detail racial integration efforts and policies in the suburbs of Cleveland, Ohio. Cleveland is one of the most segregated metropolitan areas in the United States, as are its suburbs (Massey and Denton, 1987, 1988). Yet it is also the site of some of the most innovative and enduring efforts to promote sustained housing integration, at both the municipal and metropolitan levels.

Differing Concepts of Integration

What is meant by "integration" is itself a controversial question. Integration has different meanings for different racial groups, organizations, and individuals. There are two basic approaches to defining neighborhood racial integration. The first is to measure the "state" of the residential racial mix according to the proportion of minorities to nonminorities.

There are differing views, including black versus white, as to what proportionately constitutes integration. Many whites view the entry of from only one to a small number of blacks in their "neighborhood" (block, street, or larger geographic area) as signifying that their neighborhood is racially integrated. Likewise, some blacks (and other racial minorities) consider that they live in a racially integrated neighborhood if there is at least a small number of whites.

Researchers have used different ratios to measure integration. For example, in their 1967 national survey of integrated neighborhoods, N. M. Bradburn, Seymour Sudman, and G. L. Gockel (1971: 8) defined neighborhoods by subdividing them into three basic categories:

1. Open: those with two or more Negro families but less than 1 percent Negro residents;
2. Moderately integrated: those with from 1 to 10 percent Negro families;
3. Substantially integrated: those with more than 10 percent Negro families.

In documenting the racial patterns of Cleveland and its suburbs, the Cuyahoga Plan (1987) employed the following six categories:

1. Segregated white (0 to 1 percent nonwhite);
2. Predominantly white (2 to 4 percent nonwhite);
3. Modestly (racially) diverse (5 to 9 percent nonwhite);
4. Racially diverse (10 to 39 percent nonwhite);
5. Potentially (racially) transitional (40 to 69 percent nonwhite);
6. Predominantly nonwhite (70 to 100 percent nonwhite).

Neighborhoods within categories 3 and 4 would generally be considered "integrated." Those within categories 2 and 5 might be considered integrated, depending on the actual racial ratios of the population.

Some argue that the ideal racial ratio would be a roughly equal proportion of white and nonwhite households in as many neighborhoods as possible. Another view is that the minority proportion of all or most neighborhoods should roughly approximate the minority proportion of the population of the larger political or geographical unit (city, county, or metropolitan region). Neither ideal is likely to be realized often in practice, even in those suburbs that are the most integrated. The racial proportions of neighborhoods will vary considerably even in such suburbs.

The second approach to the definition of integration in neighborhoods involves "process" rather than the racial proportional representation of the population. Bradburn, Sudman, and Gockel (1971: 5–6) consider those neighborhoods to which both whites and blacks can move and are moving as integrated. If access to a neighborhood is not denied to either group due to racial discrimination, they argue, then housing is "open" and the neighborhood is not segregated. This is not the same as the condition in neighborhoods undergoing racial transition that ultimately leads to resegregation (i.e., predominantly white neighborhoods that eventually resegregate into predominantly black neighborhoods). Stable racial diversity is a long-term pattern of neighborhood racial diversity, not a transitory phenomenon (Galster, 1990b; Saltman, 1990). According to this second approach, the critical factor is that both whites and blacks openly compete for housing in the same nondiscriminatory market.

Housing Integration in Suburban Cleveland

This book invokes both approaches to the definition of integration in analyzing the residential patterns of Cleveland suburbs during 1963–1993. The suburban cities of Shaker Heights and Cleveland Heights are the two best known in suburban Cleveland for their housing integration policies. In the case of Shaker Heights, the policies date from the mid-1960s; in Cleveland Heights, from the mid-1970s. The black population of Shaker Heights in 1990 was 30 percent and in Cleveland Heights, 37 percent. In contrast, the suburban cities of East Cleveland and Warrensville Heights, to which many blacks migrated from the mid-1960s on, failed to manage this racial transition successfully and almost entirely re-segregated in the 1970s. In 1990 their black populations were 94 percent and 89 percent, respectively.

Most of the fifty-eight suburbs of Cleveland located within Cuyahoga County are predominantly white, and the majority do not have affirmative fair housing policies. These suburbs include Euclid and Maple Heights, which do have a growing black population (16 and 15 percent, respectively, in 1990). The city of Parma, Cleveland's largest suburb, has gained the most notoriety for resistance to black suburbanization. Since 1980 it has been under a federal remedial court order requiring it to promote fair housing (Cooper, 1988). Its black population remained at less than 1 percent in 1990.

The black population of Cuyahoga County in 1990 was 25 percent (Map 1). This includes the city of Cleveland, whose "minority" population was in the majority (50.1 percent) for the first time in its history. If the population of the city of Cleveland is not included, the 1990 black population of suburban Cuyahoga County was 12.7 percent.

Cleveland Fair Housing Organizations

In addition to analyzing the experience of several individual Cleveland suburbs with differing approaches to racial transition, this book also analyzes several organizations formed to promote housing integration in all or part of the metropolitan Cleveland area. These include the Urban League's Operation Equality (1966–1973); Fair Housing, Inc. (1963–1971); the Heights Community Congress (1972–present); the Cuyahoga Plan (1974–present); the Metropolitan Strategy Group (1985–present); and the East Suburban Council for Open Communities (ESCOC) (1985–1991). Similar metropolitan fair housing organizations in other metropolitan areas (e.g., Chicago, Detroit, and Milwaukee) are also discussed.

The Legal Controversy over Suburban Fair Housing

Suburban "integration maintenance" policies from their inception have been subject to criticism as being racially discriminatory. Such suburbs as Oak Park and Park Forest, Illinois, and Cleveland

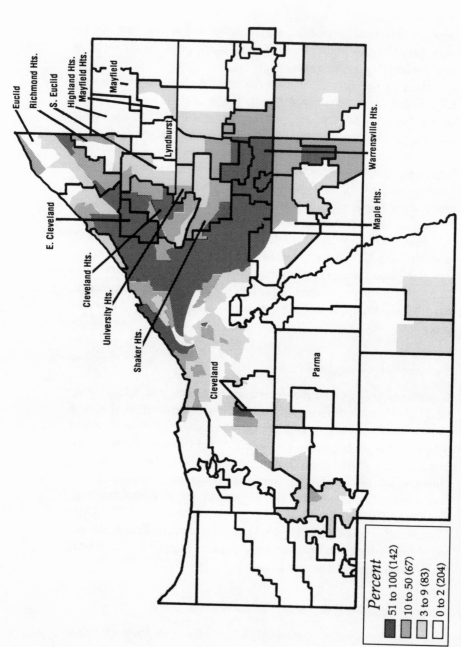

Map 1. Black Population of Cuyahoga County, Ohio, by 1990 Census Tracts

Heights and Shaker Heights, Ohio, have openly sought to maintain and promote white demand for housing in neighborhoods that have disproportionately attracted blacks, using such tactics as providing mortgage incentives primarily to white homebuyers. Some black leaders and real estate brokers have attacked these policies as racially restrictive and demeaning to African Americans. Cleveland Heights, Park Forest, and Shaker Heights have all been the targets of legal challenges by opponents of their pro-integrative policies and programs.

In the 1980s, as the Reagan administration and the Civil Rights Division of the U.S. Justice Department openly criticized and challenged many of the affirmative action policies that had been initiated in the 1960s in response to the civil rights movement's demands for racial equality; integration maintenance in housing became the subject of a continuing legal debate.

In the 1988 case involving Starrett City, a multiracial rental project in Brooklyn, New York, a federal appellate court ruled that racial "quotas" aimed at maintaining balanced racial integration were unconstitutional (Metcalf, 1988). This decision underscored the legal debate over the affirmative marketing policies, undertaken by suburban municipal housing offices and fair housing groups (including those in metropolitan Cleveland), which were aimed at maintaining racial integration in housing. However, these suburban integration policies have not been ruled illegal. In 1992 the U.S. Supreme Court declined to review a Seventh Circuit Court of Appeals decision upholding the right of pro-integrative suburbs to engage in race-conscious affirmative marketing programs, aimed at whites, to promote greater racial diversity in neighborhoods with a high percentage of black residents (*South-Suburban Housing Center v. Greater South-Suburban Board of Realtors*, 112 S. Ct. 971 [1992]).

The Debate over the Desirability of Housing Integration and Black Suburbanization

Legal issues were not the only obstacle to integration maintenance. Since the 1960s, there has not been agreement on the desirability of racial integration. The mainstream leadership of the civil rights and open housing movements has always supported the concept of housing integration, although the main focus has been school desegregation and enforcement of legislation against racial discrimination in employment. However, some black leaders have challenged "integrationist" policies as both unattainable and undesirable. Instead they have championed self-help, separatist, and black nationalist policies (Downs, 1973: 81–83). This debate was particularly heated in the 1960s.

The debate over the desirability of housing integration is not new. Its historical roots can be traced back to philosophical differences between such early black leaders as Booker T. Washington and W.E.B. DuBois. The split within the civil rights movement of the 1960s over Black Power echoed this basic disagreement over how best to achieve black freedom within a predominantly white society. Some advocates of black liberation have feared that housing integration in the suburbs means the perpetuation of black minority status. Black support for living in integrated neighborhoods generally means a preference for racial parity (Schuman, Steeh, and Bobo, 1985; Leigh and McGhee, 1986).

Generally, the higher the income and social standing of blacks, the higher their rating of predominantly white neighborhoods compared to predominantly black neighborhoods (Clay, 1979). This is not always true, however. For example, many middle-class residents of predominantly black neighborhoods in suburban Prince Georges County, Maryland, outside of Washington, D.C., have expressed a preference for African-American neighborhoods (Dent, 1992). Overall, blacks comprised about half of the county's population in 1990, compared to only 14 percent in 1970 and 37 percent in 1980 (Gale, 1987: 185). According to Dent (1992: 25), "The decision to live in a black [suburban] community should not be equated with a desire to live in a one-race world. While many black Prince Georgians say integration shouldn't be a priority, they also say they wouldn't move away if more whites moved into the county."

The movement for black political power has been based in the central cities, as black majorities have emerged and participated in the election of black mayors in such large cities as Atlanta, Chicago, Cleveland, Denver, Detroit, Los Angeles, New Orleans, New York, Philadelphia, Seattle, and Washington, D.C. (Preston, Henderson, and Puryear, 1987). The black mayors have not favored the dispersion of the black population or metropolitan policies (e.g., metropolitan government) that would dilute their newly won political dominance in central cities, despite the many problems faced by these declining cities. Likewise, the much more affluent and predominantly white suburbs surrounding these central cities have shown no interest in addressing such urban ills as racially segregated public schools (including those under federal court-ordered desegregation), poverty, and slums (Orfield, 1981).

Black Suburban Dispersal versus Gilding the Ghetto

In the 1960s, it was the liberal civil rights movement that argued for the racial integration of suburban America. Interracial organizations such as National Neighbors (Saltman, 1971) and legal advocacy organizations such as the National Committee against Discrimination in Housing and Suburban Action (Shields and Spector, 1972) led the fight for open housing in the suburbs. The liberal argument for racial, economic, and social integration of the suburbs was based on the inequality between the central city and its minority poor and the suburbs and their more affluent white residents. This inequality was evidenced by such variables as education, income, occupation, and housing standards and prices.

One approach to eliminating this urban–suburban disparity was called "gilding the ghetto" (Fox, 1986: 174–75). Its advocates argued that the central city's slum and ghetto neighborhoods must be rebuilt for their minority poor residents, because those residents did not have either the social mobility necessary for suburbanization or the occupational skills that would assist them in gaining employment in the suburbs; and they would in addition, face racial discrimination limiting their options. The rebuilding of the present neighborhoods would also reinforce growing black political power in the inner city rather than dilute it, as would happen if blacks were to settle throughout the suburban metropolis, always remaining a minority. The gilded ghetto approach assumed massive federal urban aid, beyond that provided for the antipoverty, model cities, job training, and similar programs of the 1960s. Such programs were a response to urban poverty, ghettos, and race riots but received only marginal funding and won little political support (Katz, 1990).

Opponents of the gilded ghetto approach argued that it would only reinforce racial segregation by largely confining racial minorities to the central cities. Whites in suburbia could continue to ignore urban ills in politically protected suburban enclaves, insulated from the inner city. More practically, there was little prospect for a "Marshall Plan" for rebuilding the cities, often called for by such organizations as the Urban League (Tidwell, 1992). For critic George Sternlieb, among others, this meant that minorities would gradually gain control of ever-poorer central cities without the federal or municipal resources to ameliorate the conditions in those cities (Sternlieb, 1971).

By the late 1980s the debate over the gilded ghetto approach had become one over the magnitude and future of a permanent urban minority "underclass" (Auletta, 1982; Wilson, 1987; Lemann, 1991). With a national shift in favor of conservative politics, the persistence of urban poverty, the continuing decline of the central cities, and little suburban support for addressing central-city problems, there is no realistic prospect for a federal gilding of the urban ghettos in the 1990s. This held true in the debate over federal support for the rebuilding of the South Central ghetto of Los Angeles in the wake of the April 1992 riot, following the "Rodney King verdict."

The Liberal Case for Opening the Suburbs to Blacks

The "liberal" position for "opening up the suburbs" was articulated by economist Anthony Downs. His book was published after the March 1968 report of the Kerner Commission (National Advisory Commission on Civil Disorders, 1968), which was released before the assassinations of Martin Luther King, Jr., and Robert F. Kennedy and the election of Richard Nixon as a conservative law-and-order candidate opposed to liberal democratic social programs.

The Kerner Commission warned that "the nation is rapidly moving toward two increasingly separate Americas" and that "within two decades, this division could be so deep that it would be almost impossible to unite: a white society principally united in suburbs, in smaller central cities, and in the peripheral parts of large central cities; and a Negro society largely concentrated within large central cities." The Commission added: "The Negro society will be permanently relegated to its current status, possibly even if we expend great amounts of money and effort in trying to 'gild' the ghetto" (National Advisory Commission on Civil Disorders, 1968: 407).

To change the patterns of housing segregation and substandard slum housing for blacks, the Kerner Commission recommended the passage of a national open occupancy law and reorientation of federal housing programs to place more low- and moderate-income housing programs outside of ghetto areas (National Advisory Commission on Civil Disorders, 1968: 481). The former happened with the passage of the federal Fair Housing Act in April 1968, shortly after King's death. The latter policy has proven to be much more difficult to implement. The Kerner Commission's recommendations were endorsed by the Douglas Commission on Urban Problems (1968).

Downs argued that crisis ghettos—those with the worst indicia of social distress—can be improved only through a strategy of dispersed economic and social integration requiring the opening of the suburbs to low- and moderate-income minorities. He rejected the strategy of ghetto "enrichment" as unworkable (Downs 1973: 115–130). Downs (1973: 26) further cited seven major benefits from opening up the suburbs:

1. better access to expanding suburban job opportunities;
2. greater opportunities for households to upgrade themselves by moving into middle-income neighborhoods, thereby escaping from crisis ghetto conditions;
3. higher quality public schools;
4. greater opportunity for achievement of the nation's housing goals;
5. fairer geographic distribution of the fiscal and social costs of dealing with metropolitan-area poverty;
6. less possibility of future major interracial conflicts due to separation of the races; and
7. greater possibilities of improving adverse crisis ghetto conditions without displacing urban decay to adjacent neighborhoods.

Downs emphasized economic rather than racial integration. He explicitly disavowed the emphasis of the Kerner Commission on racial integration because of the likely opposition of suburban whites to subsidizing black migration to the suburbs. Instead, he advocated enforcement of fair housing laws. He added: "If not enough racial integration occurs to help counter the tendency toward two separate and unequal societies, then [the emphasis on economic rather than racial integration] should be changed" (Downs, 1973: 139).

According to Downs, the achievement of stable racially integrated neighborhoods requires four ingredients "now difficult to produce":

> The first is the ability to convince whites that their majority status will persist in mixed areas in spite of past experience to the contrary. This in turn requires the second ingredient: a workable mechanism ensuring that whites will remain in a majority—such as some type of quota system—that is both legal and credible. The third ingredient consists of minority-group members willing to reside in a predominantly white neighborhood. And the last is some means of persuading whites not actually living in the mixed area to move in from elsewhere so as to maintain its racial balance as vacancies occur. This requires achievement of the first two ingredients. (Downs, 1973: 99)

While noting that quotas were controversial, were opposed by both presidential candidates in the 1972 campaign, and are often deplored by those who theoretically support racial integration, Downs (1973: 99–100) supported racial quotas: "Stable racial integration under present conditions absolutely requires such racial discrimination. Completely 'color blind' policies quickly lead to racial segregation if the area or development concerned is close to a large and expanding concentration of minority-group members." Downs's support for white majorities and black minorities as a necessary condition for racially integrated neighborhoods typifies an approach that offends black critics of race-conscious integration maintenance policies.

To allow for the dispersal of low- and moderate-income central-city residents in the suburbs, Downs supported providing housing allowances and building scattered subsidized housing to allow for more housing opportunities throughout suburban metropolitan areas. In addition, he identified a wide range of policies necessary to achieve economic integration, including subsidies to suburbs, housing developers, and central-city residents who move to the suburbs (Downs, 1973: 161–62). Two decades later, Downs was pessimistic about the prospects for residential racial integration, although he still supported managed racial integration (Downs, 1992).

F. J. Kain and J. J. Persky took a similar approach, emphasizing economic over racial integration in the suburbs as an alternative to gilding the ghetto. They cautioned: "The presence of Negroes in the suburbs does not necessarily imply Negro integration into white residential neighborhoods. Suburbanization of the Negro and housing integration are not synonymous" (Kain and Persky, 1969: 80). They argued that dispersed, small, Negro suburban ghettos would be much more desirable than central-city ghettos.

The liberal approach of metropolitan dispersion of minorities and federal support for lower-income subsidized housing located in the suburbs, advocated by Downs, has not become national policy. Except for a few notable examples, racial and economic exclusion continue to be hallmarks of suburbanization, unimpeded by federal intervention or sanctions.

The Conservative Argument against the Imposition of Integration Policies on Suburbs

In answer to Downs, neoconservative sociologist Nathan Glazer (1987) argued against mandatory measures to open up the suburbs, either to blacks or to the poor (regardless of race). First, Glazer claimed that black suburbanization was already occurring and required no public policy initiatives or incentives. (G. C. Galster [1991] demonstrates, however, that black suburbanization in the 1970s was not synonymous with increased racial integration.) Second, Glazer concluded that suburban opposition (primarily from whites) to either forced and subsidized racial or economic integration would make Downs's policy impossible to implement.

The conservative political and judicial opposition to affirmative action that arose in the 1980s followed resistance to attempts to force open housing policies on white suburbs in the 1970s. During the 1980s, such policies as minority employment and contract set-asides became the subject of legal and political controversy (e.g., *Croson v. City of Richmond*, 488 U.S. 469 [1989]). In 1990, President George Bush vetoed civil rights employment legislation, claiming that it would lead to racial quotas in hiring. The 1991 controversy over the confirmation of conservative black judge Clarence Thomas to replace retired liberal black justice Thurgood Marshall on the U.S. Supreme Court included debate over Thomas's past opposition to affirmative action policies. Court-ordered desegregation remains a highly charged issue almost four decades after the historic decision of the U.S. Supreme Court in 1954 declaring racial segregation of public schools unconstitutional. In a conservative national political climate, federal fair housing policy has been quiescent.

From the conservative viewpoint, race-conscious affirmative housing policies to promote greater racial diversity represent politically unacceptable "social engineering." These policies require the intervention of government in the private real estate market, whether to regulate homeowners, realtors, and lenders or to offer financial incentives (e.g., to homebuyers or landlords). This violates conservative tenets regarding the primacy of the private market. Conservatives also generally believe that such governmental social policies aimed at changing behavior will not work. Both black and white conservatives express these views in arguing against affirmative action policies, which they often equate with racially discriminatory quotas.

Framework for Analysis: The Metropolitan Dilemma and Metropolitan Strategies

The debates over the desirability, feasibility, and legality of suburban housing integration and integration maintenance policies need to be reviewed in the context of this long national controversy over civil rights, affirmative action policies for racial minorities, and the enforcement of fair housing legislation. This book examines the experience of several suburbs, in metropolitan Cleveland and other cities, that have supported racial integration (both successfully and unsuccessfully), tried to ignore racial transition, or opposed black suburbanization. Key factors that determine whether or not suburbs accept or resist racial transition and whether they adopt affirmative fair housing policies include the rate and pace of racial transition, the type of housing stock available and its price, the attitudes of the population toward open housing, the position of the local government and public schools, the role of civic leaders and community organizations, support for fair housing organizations, and the activities of the real estate industry.

In making the case for federal fair housing policy to promote stable racial diversity without violating the pursuit of freedom of choice, George Galster (1990b) argues that metropolitan areawide coordination must be encouraged. He suggests several possible means for accomplishing this. For example, federal aid to states could be tied to the establishment of regional fair housing organizations or to the use of regional planning agencies to coordinate efforts to promote stable racial diversity in municipalities within regions. Another possible federal "stick" would be to require the active support of state and local governments for metropolitan-wide fair housing organizations as a condition for the allocation of federal aid. Galster also suggests such federal "carrots" as housing and development incentives for those local governments that do take the lead in promoting housing integration.

Juliet Saltman (1990) likewise points to the need for coordinated regional approaches to comprehensive regional fair housing strategies. She identifies several examples involving local governments, schools, and realtors that seek to promote stable racial integration throughout metropolitan areas (including Cleveland).

The basic arguments of this book are that racial and economic integration in suburban housing and neighborhoods are desirable; that they will require both mandatory legal and political restrictions for compliance, as well as economic incentives (e.g., housing subsidies); and that they cannot be effective if limited only to those few suburban cities whose governments and residents actively and voluntarily support open housing policies but rather must be implemented throughout each metropolitan area. While the immediate prospects for the formulation and implementation of such policies are as unlikely at present as they were after the turbulent events of 1968 and the warnings of the Kerner Commission, the prospect for ever wider race- and class-based divisions and conflicts between central cities and racially segregated suburbs demands that the issue of racial and economic integration be faced, the *realpolitik* opposition of neoconservatives like Glazer notwithstanding.

This means that there must be strong leadership in support of metropolitan housing integration from the federal government, the judiciary, state governments, and suburban leaders. Mere adherence to existing legislation against housing discrimination and its enforcement by HUD, state and local governments, and the courts will not change basic patterns of residential segregation. Freedom of choice will for the most part lead to suburban resegregation (as is shown in the case studies herein). Affirmative race-conscious housing policies are required. The examples of sustained racial diversity in the suburban communities studied herein do give hope that their achievements can be expanded to a much broader metropolitan level elsewhere in the United States. To avoid ever-deepening racial divisions in the United States, this hope must lead to action.

2

The Open Housing Movement: Metropolitan Dispersion Strategies

The Kerner Commission on Civil Disorders in its 1968 report warned of the dangers of a racially segregated society in metropolitan America, in which a largely poor minority population would be effectively relegated to the urban ghettos of central cities while the surrounding suburbs would remain almost entirely white, excluding not only minorities but the poor. To prevent this trend from becoming permanent, the Kerner Commission recommended a metropolitan dispersion strategy aimed at opening up the suburbs to the urban poor by providing those citizens with housing, employment, and educational opportunities.

The most comprehensive articulation of a nationally supported metropolitan dispersion strategy was made by economist Anthony Downs of the Brookings Institution in a 1971 lecture series at Yale University, later published as *Opening Up the Suburbs: An Urban Strategy for America* (1973). Downs described the patterns of economic and social inequality and racial segregation between American central cities and their suburbs. He explained the prospects for the growing dominance of the suburbs, looking toward 1980 and beyond toward the year 2000.

Downs cited seven benefits from opening up the suburbs— benefits to minorities moving to the suburbs, to suburban residents, and to the country (Downs, 1973: 26). Perhaps the most ominous of these "benefits" was "less possibility of major conflicts in the future caused by confrontations between two spatially separate and unequal societies in metropolitan areas."

Downs attempted to quantify what would be required to achieve the goals that he espoused. His maximum goal was a reduction in the percentage of the poor in central cities from 12.9 percent in 1970 to 6.2 percent in 1980, to be achieved by increasing suburbia's percentage of poverty-level households to 8.4 percent by 1980. He estimated that the provision of 2,375,000 housing units would be required for this addition to the suburban population, of which 578,000 would be new, rather than existing, housing units, requiring high per-unit subsidies (Downs, 1973: 154–58). In addition to the cost of providing subsidized housing, Downs recognized that suburbs would have to bear the burden of increased educational and social service costs required to provide for the needs of newly arrived low- and moderate-income households.

Downs was well aware of the likely opposition from suburban residents and their political representatives to public policies designed to mandate greater racial, social, and economic integration. He emphasized economic rather than racial integration as a goal and accepted the necessity of imposing racial quotas to assuage the fears of suburbanites that greater integration would lead to reduced property values and increasing social problems (Downs, 1973: 99–100).

Downs (1973: 166–70) also set forth six likely criticisms of his strategy and attempted to rebut them:

1. Opening up the suburbs would spoil the hard won "sanctuary" of the middle class;
2. Members of different economic classes do not want to interact with each other and will not do so even if they live in the same neighborhoods;
3. The risk that economic integration will fail to achieve any "positive up-lift impact" upon low- and moderate-income households is too great to justify the tremendous costs and effort required to achieve such integration;
4. The hidden goal of residential economic integration is long-run achievement of a homogeneous society in which all

different groups have been thoroughly assimilated. This is a liberal dream inconsistent with the group pluralism on which America has been built.

5. Even if it is necessary to move many low-income households out of central cities in order to achieve the benefits [identified], having them settle in separate new communities created especially for the poor would be politically easier and more effective than trying to disperse them throughout each metropolitan area.

6. Opening up the suburbs requires continued large-scale building of new housing units on the edge of our metropolitan areas. But mere "uncontrolled sprawl" like that which has dominated past peripheral growth will cause a rapid deterioration of the general environment there. Hence opening up the suburbs on any large scale is not compatible with preserving the minimum desirable quality of environment there.

These problems cited by Downs reflect the fears and concerns of suburbanites. By and large, suburban communities in the United States do not represent social, economic, or racial diversity by choice of the residents, real estate practices, and design by private developers. To change prevailing attitudes and patterns is, as Downs recognized, a tremendous challenge.

In addition, not all members of minority groups favor racial integration, and even those who do may not wish to be "pioneers" or to subject themselves to racial discrimination. Although a majority of African Americans favors racially mixed neighborhoods (Farley, 1978), not all do so. Some African Americans feel that metropolitan racial dispersion strategies will dilute the hard-won political gains of politicians who have attained leadership positions, among which are the mayoralties of many large U.S. central cities since Carl Stokes was elected as Cleveland's first black mayor in 1967. The often harsh exchanges between Detroit's first black mayor, Coleman Young, elected in 1973, and his white counterparts in suburban Detroit typify the mistrust extant between minority leadership in central cities and suburban government (Rich, 1989).

The Federal Government and the Suburban Integration Question

No federal administration has ever adopted suburban racial integration as a policy. Since the advent of the civil rights movement and passage of the fair housing legislation of 1968, federal policies toward enforcement of antidiscrimination laws have varied (Goering, 1986). Generally, the farthest the federal government has gone has been to sue or to cut off or condition federal aid for violation of fair housing legislation. This has occurred only when. violations have been both overt and provable, and even then action has often been taken only after intense lobbying by fair housing organizations demanding federal intervention. Only under these circumstances has the federal government ordered affirmative remedial action to promote racial integration, and there have been relatively few examples. Parma, Ohio, is one such example (see Chapter 8).

The greatest hope for metropolitan integration through federally subsidized housing programs was tied to the two programs created by the 1968 housing law: Sections 235 (home ownership) and 236 (rental). Both provided subsidies to private lenders and developers to promote new, private, limited dividend or profit housing, with much of it to be constructed outside central cities (Rubinowitz, 1974). This hope was reinforced when a federal court ruled that subsidized housing could not be constructed in a predominantly minority area if this reinforced racial segregation (*Shannon v. HUD*, 436 F.2d 809 [3d. Cir. 1970]).

Even though these programs were aimed at moderate-income households and did not involve public housing authorities, many suburbanites and their governments lumped them together with public housing. Just as suburbs historically opposed public housing because of fears of reduced property values and increased social problems, reflecting their fears of poor, mostly minority tenants, so too many suburbs oppose privately owned subsidized housing. Such opposition proved particularly evident among blue-collar suburbanites, whose communities and neighborhoods would be the most likely sites for subsidized housing, as opposed to middle- and upper-income suburbanites who lived in areas with such high land values that the possibility of subsidized housing would be remote (Danielson, 1976: 91).

Suburbs have used a variety of land use controls to make it difficult or impossible to construct moderately priced housing. Such exclusionary land use practices led to many well-publicized lawsuits against suburbs that denied approval for subsidized housing (Danielson, 1976: 90–91, 159–98). Challenging such permit denials project by project and suburb by suburb did not prove to be successful in changing suburban policies generally. In fact, many suburbs adopted referenda requirements for all land use changes, including zoning permits, which often effectively excluded subsidized housing. The legality of this policy was upheld in 1976 by the U.S. Supreme Court in a case from Eastlake, Ohio (426 U.S. 668). Referenda requirements were then adopted by many other suburbs, for example, Parma, Ohio (Danielson, 1976: 99–101).

It was also in 1976 that the U.S. Supreme Court made a key ruling in the *Gautreaux* litigation. This lawsuit began in 1966 when minority tenants of Chicago public housing sued to protest racially discriminatory site and tenant selection practices. Eventually, both the Chicago Housing Authority and HUD were found guilty of deliberately promoting the racial segregation of Chicago's public housing tenants. In fashioning a remedy, the relevant housing market was defined as the metropolitan Chicago area, not just the city of Chicago. In view of the city's refusal to comply with federal court orders to build additional public housing on a desegregated basis in white neighborhoods, an agreement was reached under which HUD would provide minority public housing tenants with Section 8 existing housing certificates, which the tenants could then use to rent apartments in predominantly white Chicago suburbs (Polikoff, 1978; Vernarelli, 1986). Despite a contrary decision in 1976 regarding a metropolitan remedy in a Detroit school desegregation case (*Milliken v. Bradley*), the U.S. Supreme Court upheld a metropolitan remedy in this unusual housing case.

As of 1990, more than half of the thirty-eight hundred families provided with housing under the *Gautreaux* remedy have moved into Chicago suburbs (Rosenbaum, 1991; Rosenbaum and Popkin, 1990). The *Gautreaux* experiment is unique in its use of federal rental housing assistance to promote a pro-integrative policy. In 1992, HUD was considering support for several small-scale experimental versions of this approach.

During the Carter administration, HUD initiated what were called Areawide Housing Opportunity Plans (AHOPs). The AHOPs were to plan for the dispersion of Section 8 certificate holders throughout metropolitan areas with the assistance of cooperating regional planning agencies and suburban municipalities. Another version, introduced in 1979, was the Regional Housing Mobility Program, intended to achieve the same goal. These efforts were intended to determine if the *Gautreaux* remedy could be introduced voluntarily elsewhere in the United States (Vernarelli, 1986: 221–24). Before these programs were implemented, the Reagan administration took office and discontinued them. Advocates of inner-city regeneration also opposed this approach, unless matching funds were to be provided for improving central-city neighborhoods (Hartman, Keating, and LeGates, 1982: 127–30).

State Government and the Suburban Integration Question

State governments have generally been even less willing than the federal government to become involved in promoting suburban integration. In many states, the "home rule" doctrine effectively insulates local governments from state oversight or direction, except where state funding is involved. Those states with housing programs usually operate by local option, that is, they leave it to localities to choose to participate in state housing subsidy programs. The growing political dominance of the suburbs in state legislatures means that suburban representatives can effectively block any state-mandated measures their constituents oppose.

Nevertheless, a few states have adopted guidelines requiring local governments to take regional needs into effect in the implementation of local planning and development standards by increasing rather than limiting housing choices. Massachusetts led the way in 1969 when it adopted a so-called anti-snob law. Developers of subsidized low- and moderate-income housing projects who were denied permit approval by localities could, under certain circumstances, appeal to a state appeals board, which could override the locality and order issuance of the permit (Danielson, 1976: 300–306; Listokin, 1976: 99–107). The aim was to force suburbs to allow for the construction of more affordable housing, mostly rental. It was assumed that this would also allow more minorities to be able to afford to live in suburbia. More than two decades later, the state claims that this has resulted in the development of twenty thousand units, developers having won most of the appeals filed (Lewis, 1992).

California requires every local government to develop and periodically update a comprehensive master plan, including a housing element. Local housing elements are subject to state review. Every city and county is to indicate how it will comply with a regional fair-share housing allocation determined to apportion lower-income households more equitably (California Government Code, Section 65584). Although the state provides a variety of housing subsidies and could withhold them from noncomplying localities, this has not proven to be an effective enforcement mechanism. Moreover, California's fair-share requirement does not address racial patterns in housing. Oregon has a similar state policy, with similar shortcomings (Knapp, 1990).

Only one state—New York—has attempted to override local zoning and land use policy that is exclusionary and also to create a mechanism to develop below-market housing on a major scale. In 1968, New York created a state Urban Development Corporation (UDC) with the goal of developing new towns and housing with a mix of income groups (mostly those of middle and moderate income, that is, above median income and below median income, respectively). It was empowered to override local building and zoning codes if necessary, as a last resort (Brilliant, 1975). The UDC had no specific authority or mandate to expand racial diversity in housing.

Under the energetic direction of Edward Logue, the renowned urban renewal developer, the UDC proposed major developments in several suburban areas. Resistance was particularly pronounced in Westchester County, where Logue's plan foundered, without his even invoking his override authority. In the spring of 1973, the New York State Legislature revoked UDC's override authority at the behest of local governments that were opposed to the UDC's proposed projects, which included below-market housing (Danielson,

1976: 325–32). The UDC went bankrupt in 1975. This experiment proved the difficulty of overcoming the tradition of the independence of localities in the regulation of development.

Suburban Action: Advocacy for Regional Fair-Share Housing

What state-level intervention has occurred to change exclusionary suburban land use and development policies has largely been the result of the efforts of fair housing groups. Perhaps the most notable example was the work done by Suburban Action. Headed by the late leader of "advocacy planning," Paul Davidoff, Suburban Action sought to promote economic, social, and racial integration in the suburbs of the tri-state Connecticut, New Jersey, and New York metropolitan region. Its tactics included legislative lobbying, litigation, and the sponsorship of nonprofit, subsidized low- and moderate-income housing (Davidoff, Davidoff, and Gold, 1970; Davidoff and Davidoff, 1971).

The Mt. Laurel Saga: Court-ordered Fair-Share Housing in New Jersey

New Jersey stands as a singular example of a statewide attempt to mandate fair-share housing. In 1971 the National Association for the Advancement of Colored People (NAACP) sued the small but growing suburb of Mt. Laurel, New Jersey, charging that it was using its zoning and land use controls to limit housing to middle- and upper-income homeowners. While raising the issue of the exclusionary impact of these policies on minorities who might wish to move to the suburb in search of employment, the thrust of this lawsuit was to challenge economic discrimination based upon so-called fiscal zoning.

In 1975 the New Jersey Supreme Court unanimously ruled against Mt. Laurel. It ruled that every New Jersey municipality, whose authority to control land use and development is derived from the state, had an obligation under the state constitution to allow all economic groups access to housing throughout a region. It proclaimed a "fair share" doctrine under which regional housing needs were to be determined, after which a proportional allocation was to be made to localities (Danielson, 1976: 179; Listokin, 1976:

19–21). Later, certain exceptions were made to the doctrine (for example, already developed cities, environmentally sensitive areas, and agricultural communities).

This landmark decision resulted in considerable litigation against New Jersey municipalities, mostly brought by developers under a "builder's remedy." This allowed developers to sue on behalf of the prospective occupants of housing for which permits had been denied by local governments. Subsequent court decisions failed to resolve such difficult questions as what constituted "least cost" housing and how a municipality's regional share of below-market housing was to be determined. In 1983 the New Jersey Supreme Court revisited the issue and issued a monumental decision known as *Mt. Laurel II*. It reaffirmed its commitment to the constitutional requirements that New Jersey localities must provide broad housing opportunities (which it defined more clearly), that the state must determine each locality's regional fair share of housing need, that municipalities must pursue affirmative policies and programs to promote more affordable housing, and that builders would continue to have the right to sue exclusionary municipalities. *Mt. Laurel II* streamlined judicial procedures in order to limit the ability of municipalities to delay judicial proceedings and continue to obstruct implementation of the *Mt. Laurel* fair-share doctrine, although it continued to allow for the exemption of certain localities from its reach.

Mt. Laurel II occasioned a political crisis as local governments rallied in opposition. This crisis resulted in a 1985 legislative compromise, in which the state government finally agreed to cooperate in the implementation of the state supreme court's decision. A Council on Affordable Housing (COAH) was created to allocate regional fair-share obligations to New Jersey's 567 municipalities. The state government agreed to provide additional financial assistance to localities for below-market housing. The applicability of the builder's remedy was restricted, as long as municipalities were in compliance with COAH policies. The New Jersey Supreme Court, in a 1986 decision (*Mt. Laurel III*), upheld the constitutionality of this legislation.

COAH was established with a goal of promoting the development of 145,000 affordable housing units by 1993. By 1992, approximately 25,000 *Mt. Laurel* housing units had been approved but fewer than 10,000 had actually been started or completed (Lovejoy, 1992). A key provision of the 1985 compromise was to allow suburban communities to enter into so-called regional contribution agreements (RCAs), under which they could sell up to one-half of their fair-share obligations to "receiving communities," which would develop affordable housing subsidized by the selling communities. As of 1992, twenty-three RCA agreements involving about three thousand housing units in fifteen "urban aid" cities had been approved. New Jersey's Public Advocate and *Mt. Laurel* proponents have argued that RCAs allow predominantly white, affluent suburbs to escape much of their obligation and that they reinforce segregative housing patterns by keeping most lower-income subsidized housing and its minority occupants in predominantly minority, poor central cities (Newark, for instance). The New Jersey courts have not agreed.

The RCA buy-out provision aside, a study of some of the first *Mt. Laurel* projects developed and occupied in the suburbs indicates that they have few or no minority occupants (Lamar, Mallach, and Payne, 1989: 1256). This underscores the absence of any pro-integrative mandate in the *Mt. Laurel I* and *II* decisions. Greater economic rather than racial integration in housing is the focus of the New Jersey regional fair-share experiment.

Regional Fair-Share Plans

The most promising method of metropolitan dispersal of low-income subsidized housing and households was the regional fair-share allocation plan. Regional fair-share housing allocation plans came into vogue briefly in the early 1970s. The impetus for their emergence included judicial rulings (e.g., *Mt. Laurel I*); the federal government's support and funding (Section 701 program) for area-wide councils of government (COGs), which were given the responsibility for conducting "A–95" reviews of federal grants within the context of metropolitan planning; and the open housing and anti-exclusionary housing movement (Danielson, 1976).

The federal aim was not necessarily dispersal of overly concentrated minority populations and subsidized low-income housing but rather the more efficient allocation of federal resources. It was only during the short-lived attempt in 1971 by HUD, under George Romney, that the federal government appeared to endorse a metropolitan dispersal policy. However, the Nixon administration effectively ended this controversial initiative in Summer 1971 (Danielson, 1976). Richard Nixon's 1973 moratorium on federally subsidized low- and moderate-income housing programs deprived local governments of the resources required for metropolitan dispersal, even if they were favorably disposed toward this strategy.

Fair-share plans were prepared by regional planning agencies. Usually criteria were developed for the allocation of low- and moderate-income housing units. The simplest criteria were to match subsidized units with a suburb's housing stock or population. Additional factors were usually considered, for example, a suburb's income and racial mix; type of housing stock; number, if any, of existing subsidized units; availability of land for development; and tax base (Listokin, 1976).

The COGs or regional planning agencies that prepared fair-share plans did not operate autonomously. They were the creatures of the local governments within the metropolitan area, which voluntarily chose to cooperate, usually to be able to influence the allocation of federal aid among competing localities. Thus, unless the constituent governments themselves decided to address the question of housing and racial segregation, the regional planning agency itself would not do so.

The Dayton Plan

A notable exception to this pattern was Dayton, Ohio. The Miami Valley Regional Planning Commission (MVRPC) and its executive director at the time, Dale Bertsch, gained renown for the most serious attempt in the United States to actually implement a fair-share housing plan.

In 1970, Dayton was a city in decline. Its population of 244,000 constituted 29 percent of the five-county metropolitan area's total of 850,000. While 30 percent of Dayton's residents were black, less than 3 percent of the surrounding suburban population was black.

Almost all of the 3,350 subsidized housing units in the region were concentrated in the central city of Dayton (Danielson, 1976: 251).

In 1970 the MVRPC developed a fair-share housing allocation plan, responding to federal policy. The MVRPC calculated that approximately sixteen thousand housing units were needed to meet regional housing needs. Of this total, more than fourteen thousand were required for lower-income households. The fair-share plan allocated the lower-income units throughout the region, with only seventeen hundred to be located within the city of Dayton. The allocation formula included numerous factors, including population patterns, the mix of the housing stock, the tax bases, and schools (Danielson, 1976: 253; Gruen and Gruen, 1972; Listoken, 1976: 118–20).

The Dayton Plan ran into heavy opposition from suburban elected officials and school representatives. However, it was adopted without dissent in July 1970 by the MVRPC, whose forty-two-member board included only one representative of the city of Dayton. Bertsch skillfully organized support for the plan, largely from interest groups that belonged to the commission's Housing Advisory Committee. On the one hand, Bertsch held out the threat of federally imposed mandates; on the other hand, he compromised by withdrawing a proposal to seek authority to override local zoning to ensure the construction of targeted projects.

Unfortunately, once adopted, implementation of the Dayton Plan was largely dependent on the federal government. Although HUD Secretary Romney was enthusiastically supportive of the plan and cited Dayton as a model, once the Nixon administration publicly turned against his initiatives, he was powerless to deliver. Romney could not provide the subsidies for the projected fourteen thousand housing units, particularly after the 1973 moratorium on federal housing subsidy programs (shortly after which he departed); nor could he deny uncooperative localities other desired federal aid, such as sewer grants available from HUD, without White House support. Romney effectively admitted defeat in June 1971, shortly after Nixon reassured the suburbs that his administration would not impose affirmative fair housing policies upon them. In addressing the U.S. Commission on Civil Rights, Romney admitted: "The Dayton Plan is a great example [of metropolitan fair-share housing

Fair Share

dispersal]. I'm all for it. . . . But to undertake to bring this about through coercive means in my opinion would be self-defeating" (Danielson, 1976: 262).

The Dayton Plan was at least partially implemented despite these obstacles. By 1976 an additional eight thousand federally subsidized housing units had been constructed in the Dayton region, reducing the city of Dayton's share of the regional total of such units to about one-half (Listokin, 1976: 121). However, most of the housing built in the suburbs was occupied by low-income white residents, assuaging suburban fears of a massive influx of inner-city black relocatees.

The other highly touted example of success in COG-sponsored fair-share planning was the Minneapolis–St. Paul metropolitan region. There the metropolitan council was able to expand dispersion of subsidized housing during the period 1971–1975 (Listokin, 1976: 110–12). However, this region's characteristics differ from many others; there was a past history of central city–suburban cooperation, and the Twin Cities area has a very small minority population, virtually eliminating racial dispersion as a divisive issue (Danielson, 1976: 259–60). The other major examples of fair-share plans during this period—Chicago, San Francisco, and Washington, D.C.—were much less successful, particularly in the implementation stage, relying on the voluntary cooperation of the suburbs (in the adjoining states of Maryland and Virginia, in the case of the District of Columbia) and dependent on federal support (Danielson, 1976: 258–60, 265–69; Listoken, 1976: 112–18).

Danielson sounded the contemporary epitaph for metropolitan fair-share housing allocation plans:

> Underlying these setbacks was the lack of any substantial political support in Washington for regional approaches to housing, either in Washington or the metropolitan areas. Suburbanites feared that metropolitan arrangements would jeopardize local housing and zoning controls. . . . [Central] city officials also vigorously opposed an authoritative role for metropolitan agencies in the distribution of federal housing aid. . . . In the absence of support from any major interest, federal action to bolster metropolitan housing plans and programs was foreclosed. Without federal pressure and subsidies, metropolitan hous-

ing efforts lost what little momentum they had been able to generate. . . . And, as in Dayton, almost all of the housing built in the suburbs under metropolitan plans served suburban needs, rather than fulfilling the forlorn hope of using fair shares to disperse blacks and the poor out of the older cities. (Danielson, 1976: 278)

Although regional fair-share plans have not been mandated by the federal government or by most state governments, the idea has not died entirely. For example, in 1988 the state of Connecticut enacted legislation creating a pilot program for voluntary regional fair-share housing compacts. In 1990, twenty-six of twenty-nine communities in the greater Hartford region ratified the Capitol Region Fair Housing Compact on Affordable Housing, which aims to create 5,000 to 6,421 units of affordable housing over a five-year period (Podziba, 1992; Wheeler, 1993). In addition, in 1990 HUD authorized that Section 8 subsidies allocated to Hartford could be used in its suburbs (while 70 percent of Hartford's population belongs to minority groups, only 8 percent of the surrounding suburban population is minority). Because only a small number of eligible households took advantage of this special use of HUD's subsidies, foundation funding was obtained in 1992 to counsel low-income Hartford households about the regional mobility program and to assist participating households (McClain, 1992). However, these experimental programs were not designed to promote greater racial diversity in Hartford's suburbs through the dispersion of below- market housing and households, although that could be a significant result of their successful implementation.

Without a federal recommitment to large-scale subsidy programs for below-market housing, in tandem with renewed support for the regional mobility approach, there is little prospect for achieving far greater metropolitan racial diversity through the construction of subsidized housing on a dispersed regional basis, as proposed by Downs (1973). John Yinger (1986) is pessimistic about the prospects of such a policy working, except for small-scale experiments in receptive suburbs, which may eventually build up much greater acceptance than has existed in the past in suburbs that have generally opposed below-market housing.

A Proposed Fair-Share Plan for Cuyahoga County

The origin of a fair-share proposal to deconcentrate low-income, federally subsidized public housing in Cuyahoga County lies with the formation of Plan of Action for Tomorrow's Housing (PATH) in 1967. PATH's creation followed the issuance of a report, funded by the predecessor of the Cleveland Foundation, that called for racially integrated housing in the city of Cleveland and greater black access to housing in Cleveland's suburbs. When PATH's first director, Irv Kriegsfeld, became director of the Cuyahoga Metropolitan Housing Authority (CMHA) in 1968, he aggressively sought to realize PATH's goals. His attempt to construct thirty-seven hundred new units of public housing in predominantly white wards in the city of Cleveland led to tremendous opposition and resulted in his firing in January 1971 (Krumholz and Forester, 1990: 90–98). Then in 1972 a federal court ordered the construction of any new public housing in Cleveland to be located in predominantly white wards to redress past racial discrimination (*Banks v. Perk*).

CMHA was aided in its pro-integrative efforts by the city of Cleveland's planning commission, under the direction of Norman Krumholz. Krumholz gained a national reputation for his "equity planning" policies on behalf of Cleveland's poor and minority populations. His planners unveiled their fair-share plan in 1970. Based on an allocation of new public housing units equal to 2 percent of the housing units in each of Cleveland's suburban neighbors in Cuyahoga County, each of the fifty-eight suburbs was allocated a specific number of the 4,078 new units proposed to be built beyond the city limits (Krumholz and Forester, 1990: 98). Krumholz explained his rationale:

> We [the Cleveland City Planning Commission] proposed fair share for three reasons. First, as already noted, we wanted to help the Kriegsfeld city proposals [for dispersal]; second, we wanted to demonstrate that every one of the sixty municipalities in Cuyahoga County was in need of some low-income housing to serve its own low-income families; and, third, we wanted to underscore the fact that if all shared equally, the impact on any one community would be slight. It was well understood by everyone that the city lacked the power to impose any such plan on other municipalities. Fair share was proposed only as a basis to begin reasonable discussion. (Krumholz and Forester, 1990: 99)

This proposal raised a storm of protest from suburban officials and "died a quiet death" before ever being considered by the CMHA and the board of Cuyahoga County commissioners (Danielson, 1976: 95; Krumholz and Forester, 1990: 99). The rejection of public housing by Cleveland's suburbs was predictable; almost all American suburbs have excluded low-income housing (Danielson, 1976).

If CMHA were to build public housing in Cleveland's suburbs, it was required under federal law to arrange cooperation agreements with participating municipalities. With the exception of the cities of Berea, Cleveland Heights, and East Cleveland and the village of Oakwood, Cuyahoga County suburbs refused to enter into cooperation agreements and did not create their own public housing agencies.

In 1971 PATH and minority public housing tenants sued CMHA and five suburbs—Euclid, Garfield Heights, Parma, Solon, and Westlake. The lawsuit claimed that the cooperation agreement requirement was unconstitutional because its impact was to allow noncooperating suburbs to exclude low-income minorities eligible for public housing from living in these suburbs. A federal district court panel, despite a contrary ruling by one of its members (Frank Battisti, who later found Parma guilty of fair housing violations), upheld the constitutionality of this provision of federal law in *Mahaley v. CMHA* (1973, 1974), thereby shielding suburban governments from public housing unless they voluntarily chose to cooperate with central-city public housing agencies like CMHA (Danielson, 1976: 177–78; Listokin, 1976: 144). With this legal ruling (upheld on appeal) and the demise of PATH in 1974, the effort to promote a metropolitan fair-share allocation plan for Cuyahoga County died.

The Failed Attempts to Promote Metropolitan Government in Cuyahoga County

An alternative approach to achieving greater racial diversity in suburban Cleveland could have been to try to promote a fair housing policy through metropolitan government. Metropolitan government has long been seen as the necessary antidote to the balkanization of local government in the United States. Governmental fragmentation and parochialism have been criticized on many grounds, including the pattern of suburban exclusion of minorities and poorer citizens through discriminatory land use controls and housing policy (Danielson, 1976). It has been argued that whites, particularly those leaving central cities, take segregative suburban residential patterns into account in choosing where to live (Weiher, 1991).

The movement for metropolitan government has largely failed in the United States, with only a few metropolitan areas having functioning metropolitan governments (Teaford, 1986: 73–74). Cleveland is not among these. It has not been for lack of effort. In 1927 a Regional Government Committee of 400 was appointed to study the restructuring of the government of Cuyahoga County. Eventually, in 1935, a county charter was approved by the voters, only to be invalidated by the Ohio Supreme Court in 1936. Through the efforts of the Citizens League, a Cuyahoga County Charter Commission was finally revived in 1949, but its recommended charter was defeated in a 1950 referendum (Teaford, 1976: 109). A Cleveland Metropolitan Services Commission was then created in 1955, with more than one hundred civic leaders participating. In 1957 to 1958 this commission issued numerous reports, which led to the appointment of yet another Cuyahoga County Charter Commission in 1958. However, its recommended charter proposal was defeated in a 1959 charter referendum. Subsequent attempts to promote a charter form of government in Cuyahoga County were rejected by voters in 1969 and 1970. This effectively ended serious efforts either to create metropolitan government or to reform the structure of Cuyahoga County's government (Governmental Research Institute, 1971).

Throughout this decades-long saga, the issue of racial segregation, particularly in the suburbs, did not arise, and advocates of metropolitan government and of regional approaches to urban problem solving did not argue that they could better address this issue. Even if these efforts had succeeded, it is not clear how or why a metropolitan form of government, which under the U.S. Supreme Court's "one man, one vote" ruling would have been dominated by the suburbs after 1970 as the city's population declined and the county's population increased, would have acted any differently from the suburbs themselves, most of which have remained predominantly white.

While the elected three-member Cuyahoga County Board of Commissioners (which saw its first black commissioner—a conservative Republican—elected in 1980), has been supportive of the Cuyahoga Plan since its inception in 1974, it has not directly confronted its constituent suburbs about changing prevailing patterns of racial segregation. In its 1992 Comprehensive Housing Assistance Strategy, Cuyahoga County barely acknowledged that housing segregation remains a problem and proposed no new housing strategies to address the issue. Fair housing proponents asked the county commissioners to cite the continuation of prevailing patterns of racial segregation in housing and to take steps to redress it in most of the county. They proposed that fair housing impact statements be required in connection with the use of federal housing subsidies in the county, that the county and cooperating suburbs institute affirmative marketing programs, and that federally subsidized housing loans be tracked to ensure that they did not reinforce prevailing segregative patterns. Their proposals were not adopted.

Conclusion

The effort to persuade the federal government to take the lead in dispersing low-income housing, lower-income households, and racial minorities throughout metropolitan areas, as advocated by the Kerner Commission and by Anthony Downs, has largely failed. The *Gautreaux* experiment in metropolitan Chicago is a unique example so far, and it was tied to a broad-sweeping federal court order. Although HUD did support metropolitan fair-share housing plans in the 1970s, it never mandated them as a condition for receipt of federal funding (e.g., Community Development Block Grants). Only a few metropolitan agencies in areas such as Dayton, Ohio, and Minneapolis seriously attempted to adopt and implement voluntary regional fair-share plans to disperse federally subsidized housing. In Cleveland the proposal made by the Cleveland City Planning Commission under Norman Krumholz was never given serious consideration in the face of overwhelming opposition by suburban governments in Cuyahoga County.

At the state level, only a few states (e.g., California, Massachusetts, and Oregon) have acted at all to ameliorate exclusionary local government policies that have restricted the dispersion of low-income housing. Most states, like Ohio, have done nothing to address this issue. Except for fair housing advocates, there is virtually no political constituency at the state level in favor of such policies, whereas powerful suburban (and rural) interests are aligned against state-mandated overrides of local autonomy in land use planning, development controls, and housing policy.

The most instructive examples of the limitations of the political will and ability of state government to deal with this issue come from New York and New Jersey. The original power of the New York Urban Development Corporation (UDC) to override local zoning and the UDC's attempt to develop low-income housing in such suburbs as Westchester County represent the greatest degree of affirmative action ever taken by a state government. The revocation of the UDC's power by the New York state legislature in 1973 and the failure of the UDC's Westchester County fair-share housing plan to win the support of suburban governments in this affluent county marked a major setback to the hope for active intervention by state governments.

In the case of New Jersey, it took two major state supreme court constitutional rulings (in 1975 and 1983) in the *Mt. Laurel* litigation and the political crisis that resulted from the court's 1983 ruling finally to force the state legislature's hand, which resulted in compromise legislation in 1985. Except for the court's interpretation of the state constitution as mandating fair-share housing generally, it is most unlikely that New Jersey's state government would have acted to require local governments to accept lower-cost housing and then provided funding support. Implementation of this legislation has been slow, political opposition remains strong, there has been little indication that *Mt. Laurel*-supported housing will be pro-integrative, and this example remains peculiar to New Jersey.

At the regional level, there are only a few examples in the United States of metropolitan government. Cleveland is not among them. There are no examples of metropolitan governmental bodies in the

United States that are directly tackling the issue of racial segregation in housing by adopting and implementing pro-integrative fair-share housing plans. Yet this is the level of government where such action is most needed. Without a national policy of metropolitan dispersion, the actions of municipal government and the practices of the private housing market will determine whether America's suburbs remain mostly segregated.

PART II

Housing, Race, and Neighborhoods
in Metropolitan Cleveland

3

Cleveland: A Racially Polarized City

Cleveland has gained an unfortunate reputation for its racial polarization, rivaling Chicago in its high level of racial segregation. The past three decades have been marred by race riots, racial politics, resegregation of neighborhoods, racial segregation in public schools and a long-standing controversy over court-ordered desegregation of the schools, racial segregation in public housing, and a continuation of various racial confrontations. Attempts at suburban racial integration in metropolitan Cleveland cannot be understood without a familiarity with the racial history of the city of Cleveland.

The Great Black Migration

Cleveland has not always been racially segregated. While it grew from a village to a city in the pre–Civil War era, it's free black population was not consigned to ghettoized neighborhoods (Kusmer, 1976). As in other northern cities, a small black population was not regarded as a threat by whites. Indeed, in Cleveland there was strong abolitionist sentiment, which included support for opponents of the enforcement of national fugitive slave legislation. A trial in Cleveland in 1859 of persons from nearby Oberlin and Wellington, Ohio, who had freed a captured runaway slave resulted in a much-acclaimed acquittal (Brandt, 1990).

In the late nineteenth century, Cleveland was transformed into an industrial city. Its tremendous growth fueled a massive migration from Europe, which resulted in the creation of urban ethnic villages. While there was interethnic conflict, there was not conflict between these European immigrants and the city's still small African-American population. Just prior to World War I, which curtailed the mass migration from Europe, Cleveland's population of 560,663 in 1910 included only about 8,500 blacks, most of whom lived in four areas of settlement (Kusmer, 1976: 50).

The "Great Black Migration" from the American South had Cleveland as one destination among other northern industrial cities. In only a decade (1910–1920), the city's black population quadrupled (to 34,451 in 1920), and it more than doubled in the following decade, reaching about 72,000 in 1930, at the beginning of the Great Depression. As K. L. Kusmer (1976) details, this dramatic increase in the city's black population led to increased competition for jobs and the creation of institutional racism, discriminating against blacks. Blacks found themselves systematically excluded from restaurants, hospitals, schools, and many kinds of employment. Blacks became more concentrated in the Central–Woodland area, as Italian and eastern European immigrants moved elsewhere. Cleveland's black ghetto began to take shape.

At the same time, racial incidents began to occur. These incidents included violence against black professionals who were attempting to move into such new suburbs as Garfield Heights and Shaker Heights. For the most part, however, blacks were excluded from the developing suburbs because they were too poor to afford higher-priced suburban housing (Kusmer, 1976: 165–70). By the beginning of the Depression, Cleveland's mostly poor, black population was concentrated in the Central–Woodland area on the city's near east side.

In 1945, Cleveland became the first major American city to create a municipal agency to deal with race relations. This agency, the Community Relations Board (CRB), was an outgrowth of the Inter-Racial Relations Panel of the Post-War Planning Council, which had been established in 1943 by Mayor Frank Lausche. The CRB spearheaded efforts to ban discrimination in public agencies and to end segregation in public accommodations in Cleveland. After the passage of a fair employment practices ordinance in 1950, the CRB administered implementation of that law. However, it was not until 1965 that the city council gave the CRB investigative powers. In 1960 the city council rejected a fair housing ordinance recommended by the CRB.

The Civil Rights Movement, the Hough Riot, the Stokes Administration, and the Glenville Shoot-out

Cleveland, like other northern cities, eventually felt the impact of the civil rights movement. The Reverend Martin Luther King, Jr., made his first Cleveland appearance on August 7, 1956. Demands for fair employment practices, especially in the construction trades, and for desegregation of the Cleveland public schools became major issues. The accidental death of the Reverend Bruce Klunder on April 7, 1964, during a protest against the construction of new schools on a segregated basis, spurred the protest movement.

Protest led to demands for political reform. There had been black representation on Cleveland's city council since 1909, when Thomas Fleming, a Republican, had been elected. However, black officials were not elected in proportion to the city's black population and did not have great influence. In 1960, 29 percent of the city's population was nonwhite; by 1965 the nonwhite population had grown to one-third of the city population, as the white postwar movement to Cleveland's suburbs continued. Gauging this growth in proportional black population, Carl Stokes, a black state representative from Cleveland, decided that it was possible for a black candidate to win the mayoralty with a coalition of mostly black voters and supportive white liberals. In 1965, however, running as an independent candidate, Stokes lost narrowly to Democratic incumbent Ralph Locher.

On July 18, 1966, the Locher mayoralty went up in flames with a riot in the city's Hough neighborhood, which lasted several days and required the presence of the Ohio National Guard to restore order. An incident at a bar at Seventy-ninth and Hough streets, in which a white bartender denied a black resident a glass of water, triggered the riot and reflected long-standing tension between a mostly white police force and the city's black population. In the wake of the riot, which claimed the lives of four blacks and resulted in extensive property damage, race relations became more tense, despite the efforts of the CRB. Whereas a grand jury blamed the riot on outside agitators, a community panel identified poor social conditions in black neighborhoods as the underlying cause of the episode.

In 1967, running as a Democrat, Stokes defeated Locher on the basis of an unprecedented mobilization of black voters, with white liberal support. Stokes then defeated Republican Seth Taft to become the first black mayor of a major American city (Nelson, 1987; Stokes, 1973). The Stokes administration undertook to improve the lot of black citizens with affirmative action programs to promote minority hiring by the city, including the hiring of minority contractors. With the support of the corporate community, Stokes also began a campaign to improve conditions in poor black neighborhoods, under the name "Cleveland NOW." The Hough Area Development Corporation (HADC) also was created in 1967, one of the country's first neighborhood-based economic development efforts (Perry, 1987; Tittle, 1992).

However, much of this effort literally went up in smoke in July 1968, when black nationalists and Cleveland police engaged in a shoot-out in the Glenville neighborhood. During several days of armed confrontation, seven persons died and many were wounded, including fifteen Cleveland police officers. Tensions rose when Stokes withdrew white police officers to use only black police officers and volunteers to try to restore order, prior to the use again of the Ohio National Guard. Stokes's actions were praised by black leaders but criticized by whites and resented by the white police (Masotti and Corsi, 1969; Zannes, 1972). The efforts of the Stokes administration to improve race relations and conditions in black neighborhoods like Hough and Glenville were severely damaged by these two destructive events. Cleveland NOW soon lost its funding, and HADC later ended in failure, after the end of the Stokes administration.

Another major initiative of the Stokes mayoralty—the Greater Cleveland Associated Foundation's Plan of Action for Tomorrow's Housing (PATH)—also ended in failure. Prior to Stokes's election, in March 1967 PATH issued a report on housing. It called for greater racial integration of housing in Cleveland's neighborhoods and in the surrounding suburbs (Tittle, 1992). PATH's first director—Irving Kriegsfeld—became the director of the Cuyahoga Metropolitan Housing Authority (CMHA) in May 1968, hired by the CMHA board influenced by Stokes through his appointees.

PATH and Kriegsfeld's CMHA sought to promote a "fair share" housing policy for Cleveland and its suburbs, in which all neighborhoods and suburbs would agree to support open housing available to blacks and to provide racially integrated public housing. Kriegsfeld's attempt to scatter four thousand units of public housing throughout the city of Cleveland, including the mostly white west side, ran into heavy resistance, led by James Stanton, the powerful president of the city council and an opponent of Stokes (Krumholz and Forester, 1990). Kriegsfeld's attempts to persuade Cuyahoga County suburbs to sign cooperation agreements with CMHA to allow for public housing were mostly rejected. Stymied on both fronts, Kriegsfeld was fired in early 1971. Stokes did not seek reelection in 1971, and his endorsed black political lieutenant was defeated by Republican ethnic candidate Ralph Perk. By 1970, Cleveland's black population had increased to 38 percent.

Transformation of the City of Cleveland

In the following two decades, the city of Cleveland was dramatically transformed—demographically, economically, and socially. Three ethnically based mayors—Republican Ralph Perk (1971–1977), populist Democrat Dennis Kucinich (1977–1979), and conservative Republican George Voinovich (1979–1989)—presided over the decline of the city. A second black mayor—Michael White—took over Cleveland in 1990, defeating his black mentor and rival, George Forbes, powerful president of the city council from 1973 to 1989.

Two decades (1970–1990) saw Cleveland's population fall from 751,000 to 505,000 (almost one-third), with much of the loss representing movement to surrounding suburbs. By 1990, half of the city's population was black. The city lost much of its manufacturing employment base (Hill, forthcoming). In the face of this transformation of the regional economy, the Voinovich administration made a concerted effort to redevelop the downtown in order to retain and attract white-collar, corporate employment (mostly suburbanites) and make the downtown an entertainment and shopping center for conventioneers and visitors (including suburbanites) (Keating, Krumholz, and Metzger, 1989).

Within the city, residential racial patterns shifted somewhat, but a majority of neighborhoods in 1990 were still almost totally either black (east side) or white (west side), despite the attempts of the Cuyahoga Plan to prevent racial discrimination in housing. Not until 1988 had the city finally enacted its own fair housing ordinance, after considerable debate and the opposition of many realtors, especially black realtors who opposed adoption of an antisolicitation policy.

The public housing system administered by CMHA, which includes about twelve thousand units, most of which are located in the city of Cleveland, today remains racially segregated. About two-thirds of the units are located in Cleveland's predominantly black east side. The population of public housing is now predominantly black: 82 percent of the resident population and 95 percent of those on the waiting list (Chandler, forthcoming).

For most of this period, the desegregation of the city's public schools, triggered by a 1973 NAACP lawsuit and ordered in 1977 by a federal court, was controversial. There was considerable opposition to court-ordered citywide busing, which was a major political issue in the 1990 school board campaign. White enrollment in the public schools dropped, and many parents—black and white—transferred their children to the parochial school system. Divisive racial politics characterized the school board, which saw its finances weakened, its enrollment fall drastically, its students' performance decline, and its role highlighted in the exodus to the suburbs. The 1985 suicide of the city's first black school superintendent, the firing of two successor superintendents, financial problems, school closings, and the possibility of a state takeover all contributed to the decline of the public schools. Amid numerous public forums on the schools' plight, a biracial reform slate endorsed by newly elected mayor White swept the 1990 election and took control of the school board.

Without greatly improved public schools, the city's attempts to stem its population losses have been greatly hampered. In a 1989 survey of Cleveland homeowners who had sold their houses, 88

schools

percent left the city of Cleveland. The second most frequent reason given for leaving the city (ranking after "seeking safer neighbor-hoods") was enrollment of children in suburban public schools. Of responding Cleveland homesellers with school-age children, 68 percent had enrolled their children in parochial rather than public schools (Bier, 1989b). In a companion 1989 study of home purchasers in Cleveland, 77 percent did not have school-age children and, of those who did, only 44 percent had enrolled their children in the city's public schools (Bier, 1989a).

Like most other central cities not only has Cleveland lost population but the remaining population has become poorer. In 1990 the population of Cleveland living below the federal poverty line reached 42 percent, with the poverty rate in the city's predomi-nantly black east side averaging 52 percent. The rates of poverty in the five poorest east-side black neighborhoods were: 83 percent (Kinsman), 82 percent (Fairfax), 74 percent (Central), 70 percent (Hough), and 65 percent (Glenville) (CEOGC, 1991). Poverty has been persistent in these black neighborhoods and has spread to other black (as well as white) neighborhoods over the decade of the 1980s (Coulton, Chow, and Pandey, 1990). The city has steadily lost most of its middle class, both white and black, in its losing competition with the surrounding suburbs.

The city remains plagued by recurrent racial incidents. Back in 1974, the CRB formed the Collinwood Biracial Dialogue Group to develop a biracial dialogue. Yet in the 1980s the Collinwood neigh-borhood (home to then mayor Voinovich) was the scene of several violent racial confrontations. A 1991 analysis of race relations in greater Cleveland featured attacks on the home of a black family that had recently moved into an otherwise all-white street in South Collinwood (Bernstein, 1991). After CRB intervention, this particular problem was seemingly resolved, but racially motivated confronta-tions have continued.

In 1988, CMHA's desegregative, decentralization effort—to scat-ter public housing sites through the rental of single-family homes—led to a racial confrontation on the west side in which white neighbors attacked a newly arrived black family, resulting in a shooting. A neighborhood-based effort to resolve this conflict in turn led to the formation of "Turning Point," a foundation-funded effort to organize Cleveland's neighborhoods to prevent racial confrontations. Turning Point was sponsored by the Greater Cleveland Roundtable (GCR). Founded in 1981, the Roundtable is a leadership forum of corporate, civic, and religious organizations, which is intended to promote interracial harmony as well as minority economic development.

Despite the efforts of such groups as the Roundtable and Turning Point, the city's CRB has remained the most visible organization with the responsibility for dealing with racial conflict. In 1990 fair housing attorney Avery Friedman lambasted the CRB for its failure to deal effectively with racial conflict and violence, a charge disputed by the CRB, which cited a 40 percent decline in reported racially motivated crimes in Cleveland from 1989 to 1990 (O'Malley, 1991).

Assessing Changing Race Relations

In assessing changes in race relations in Cleveland over the past three decades, optimists would cite the following positive changes: the election of two black mayors, Carl Stokes (1967–1971) and Michael White (1989 to the present); affirmative action hiring and contracting practices by the city of Cleveland, the Cleveland School Board, and such public agencies as the Regional Transit Authority (RTA) and the public housing authority (CMHA), which have greatly increased minority employment and influence (Nelson, 1987; Krumholz, 1990); and some black movement to the city's mostly white west side.

Pessimists, in contrast, would cite white backlash against court-ordered desegregation of the public schools and affirmative action hiring (e.g., the firefighters); racially based political conflict (e.g., on the city council and the school board and in such public agencies as RTA and CMHA); very high poverty and unemployment rates among the city's black population; the high black dropout rate in the city's public schools; the poor social conditions in predominantly black neighborhoods; the continued racial segregation of most of the city's neighborhoods and public housing projects; the lack of high-level corporate advancement by black professionals; and the continued pattern of racial incidents (e.g., tension between blacks and Arab-American shopkeepers over shootings).

Whichever viewpoint is espoused, Cleveland is typical of the "good, bad, and ugly" pattern of race relations prevalent in major American cities. Northern cities, including Cleveland's midwestern neighbors, have all experienced recurrent racial conflicts in the decades following the 1960s riots.

Comparative Changes in Public Opinion on Race Relations

One measure of change is attitudes. Surveys of Greater Clevelanders, including city residents, have shown greater racial tolerance, recognition of continuing racial discrimination, and increased support for governmental intervention to promote civil rights, including open housing.

In 1982 the GCR conducted a dual survey on racial and ethnic relations. A public telephone survey of 928 residents included 501 city residents, of whom 224 were white, 176 were black, and 101 were Hispanic. In addition, a cross-section of approximately one hundred civic leaders was also surveyed. Key findings among the general public were:

- while a majority believed that race relations had improved over the previous five years, an even larger majority believed that considerably more progress was needed;
- increased racial conflict was of greater concern to blacks (40 percent) than whites (28 percent), and suburban whites were much less concerned about racial issues;
- there was little reported social contact between the races;
- about a third of whites held discriminatory attitudes toward blacks.

On key specific issues, black and white responses were as follows:

- racial tension in housing and neighborhoods is a fairly sizable problem: agreed—all (57 percent), whites (52 percent), blacks (58 percent);

- housing integration is a good idea: agreed—whites: city of Cleveland (32 percent), east-side suburbs (37 percent), west-side suburbs (26 percent);
- white people have a right to keep blacks out of their neighborhood, and blacks should respect that right: agreed—whites: city of Cleveland (26 percent), east-side suburbs (23 percent), west-side suburbs (30 percent);
- prefer not to have any blacks in neighborhood: agree—whites: city of Cleveland (32 percent), east-side suburbs (36 percent), west-side suburbs (35 percent).

These responses indicate that only about one-third of whites supported housing integration, about one-fourth of whites thought that whites should be able to keep blacks out of their neighborhoods, and about one-third of whites preferred to live in all-white neighborhoods.

When asked whether housing integration was a good idea in relationship to the racial composition of their present neighborhood, 27 percent of whites living in predominantly white areas agreed, as compared with 60 percent of whites living in racially mixed areas. Among blacks, 68 percent of those living in predominantly black areas agreed, as compared with 90 percent of those living in racially mixed areas. Clearly, both whites and blacks living in racially mixed areas were more supportive of housing integration than were those living in nonmixed areas. A majority of whites reported living in neighborhoods that were 2 percent or less black: city of Cleveland— 66 percent; east-side suburbs—55 percent; and west-side suburbs— 92 percent. The greatest racial mix was in the east-side suburbs, where 20 percent of whites reported living in neighborhoods with a black population of 3 to 10 percent and 18 percent reported neighborhoods with a black population of 11 to 35 percent.

While the 1990 census showed some shifts and changes in the racial composition of suburban Cuyahoga County, the basic pattern that prevailed for the previous two decades continued. The suburban black population was concentrated in the east-side suburbs, where 96 percent lived. All east-side suburbs with a significant (5 percent or more) black population in 1980 experienced an increase. In addition three east-side suburban cities (Maple Heights,

Richmond Heights, and South Euclid) saw their black populations rise from less to more than 5 percent between 1980 and 1990 (Table 3). In contrast, except for Berea (with a black population of 5.3 percent in 1990), no west-side suburban city had a black population of more than 2 percent in 1990.

In 1991 the Citizens League Research Institute (CLRI reported on race relations in greater Cleveland. Its results were comparable in some respects to the answers to questions asked in three previous annual surveys, which included questions regarding race and housing (the questions asked were not exactly the same as those asked in the 1982 GCR survey or similar national surveys, but a rough comparison of the results is possible). The 1991 CLRI survey questioned 793 residents, of whom 559 were white and 157 were black. An overall conclusion was that "neighborhood integration is seen as an important societal goal, but it is unlikely to occur without vigorous efforts by the community's leadership—especially assuring residents that 'things will stay the same' if they make or accept integrative moves." Of all the suburban respondents, a majority lived in a neighborhood (34 percent) or on a block (25 percent) with only one family of a different race, whereas 16 percent reported

Table 3. Black Population in Eleven East-Side Cleveland Suburbs, 1980–1990

	1980 (%)	1990 (%)	Increase, 1980–1990 (%)
Bedford Heights	26.7	52.6	97.0
Cleveland Heights	24.9	37.1	49.0
East Cleveland	86.5	93.7	8.3
Euclid	7.6	16.0	110.5
Garfield Heights	14.2	14.8	4.2
Maple Heights	3.3	14.7	345.5
Richmond Heights	1.1	7.7	600.0
Shaker Heights	24.4	30.7	25.8
South Euclid	2.2	9.1	313.6
University Heights	9.6	16.3	69.8
Warrensville Heights	75.0	89.0	18.7

Note: Not included are several east-side villages with a high proportion of black residents: Highland Hills, North Randall, Oakwood, Orange, and Woodmere.

Source: Northern Ohio Data Information Service, Maxine Goodman Levin College of Urban Affairs, Cleveland State University, Cleveland, Ohio

living in a racially mixed neighborhood that reflected the county's racial mix (73 percent white, 27 percent minority in 1990) and only 13 percent reported living in neighborhoods with equal numbers of different races (CLRI, 1991: graph Q–2). When asked to choose their preferred definition of a racially mixed neighborhood, 35 percent of suburbanites chose racial parity, over one-third (38 percent) chose the county pattern of about three-quarters white to one-quarter minority, and only 18 percent chose an almost all-white composition. However, a majority (55 percent) of blacks chose racial parity, compared to only about one-third (35 percent) of whites, whereas about one-half (49 percent) of whites preferred the county pattern, compared to about one-third (32 percent) of blacks. Only 16 percent of whites and 13 percent of blacks chose mostly all-white or all-black neighborhoods (CLRI, 1991: graphs Q–3 and Q–4).

When asked generally whether they would like their neighborhood to be "racially mixed," 68 percent of all whites agreed (14 percent strongly), compared to a higher black response of 82 percent (28 percent strongly) (CLRI, 1991: graph P–1). Seventy-two percent of suburbanites overall indicated (18 percent strongly) that they wanted their neighborhoods to be racially mixed (CLRI, 1991: graph P–2). What these survey data reveal is that whites generally and suburbanites, who are predominantly white, are mostly in favor of some degree of racially mixed neighborhoods but do not actually choose to live in them. This is particularly the case in the western suburbs, where the average black population in 1990 was less than 2 percent. Unless this ratio of whites to blacks is considered "racially mixed" or "diverse," most whites live in almost all-white suburban neighborhoods in the western Cleveland suburbs.

When asked how likely they would be actually to move into a neighborhood where most neighbors were of another race, only a minority (22 percent) of whites responded affirmatively (CLRI, 1991: graph V–2). In contrast, a majority (55 percent) of blacks were actually likely to move into a neighborhood when most people were of another race (e.g., white). Black support was highest (65 percent) for moving into a neighborhood with racial parity.

When whites were asked what it would take for them to move into a mostly minority neighborhood, they responded as follows: (CLRI, 1991: graph W–2):

Better education for children (60 percent);
Guarantee of personal safety (58 percent);
Belief city services would be better (52 percent);
Belief racial discrimination won't take place (48 percent);
Mortgage incentives (44 percent).

Pro-integrative mortgage incentive programs more realistically require only that whites move into neighborhoods where whites are underrepresented but still in the majority.

When whites were asked what it would take for them to accept people of another race moving into their neighborhood, they responded as follows (CLRI, 1991: graph X–2):

City services would remain the same (62 percent);
Property values would be steady (61 percent);
Crime rate wouldn't increase (59 percent);
Racial strife wouldn't increase (57 percent);
Quality of education wouldn't fall (57 percent).

A majority (51 percent) of whites and suburbanites agreed that they would rather live next door to "a middle class person of another race" than a poor white person (CLRI, 1991: graphs Y–1 and Y–2).

On an encouraging note, only 7 percent of whites said that they would be likely actually to move out if "only a few" persons of another race moved into their neighborhood, and those likely to move increased only to 14 percent if the rate of minority influx was increased to about 25 percent. If the minority influx resulted in racial parity (about one-half minority), however, then about one-third (35 percent) of whites responded that they would be likely actually to move out and about one-half (49 percent) responded similarly when asked what their reaction would be to their neighborhood becoming mostly minority (CLRI, 1991: graph V–1). The rapid increase in the rate of likely white move-outs in the face of higher rates of minority influx illustrates the difficulty of trying to achieve a stable neighborhood racial mix without the neighborhoods remaining predominantly white.

As the following case studies illustrate, after three decades of racial transition and fair housing efforts in suburban Cuyahoga

County, the ideal of stable racial diversity becoming the acceptable norm in practice rather than merely an acceptable hope still remains, for the most part, unattained in metropolitan Cleveland.

The 1982 GCR and 1991 CLRI surveys indicate that white support for racial integration in housing and neighborhoods has grown, although it still remains below that of blacks; but this support has not been translated actively into greater actual racial integration. The 1990 census data show that greater Cleveland, including the city of Cleveland, remains largely segregated, much as it was in 1980 and earlier, although a shift in patterns of segregation has occurred (e.g., greater black suburbanization). Although the black population in many suburbs has grown, its remains largely concentrated in relatively few east-side suburbs. Within the city of Cleveland, most west-side neighborhoods remain predominantly white. In the absence of signs of gentrification in the city of Cleveland, there is little likelihood of whites, either those already living in the city or those in the suburbs, moving into mostly black neighborhoods. In the 1990s the best hope for increased racial integration in housing and neighborhoods lies in the suburbs of metropolitan Cleveland, rather than in the city of Cleveland.

4

Suburban Cleveland:
Case Studies of Suburbs
and Fair Housing Organizations

Suburbanization in metropolitan Cleveland began early in the twentieth century in the east-side cities of East Cleveland and neighboring Cleveland Heights and on the west side in the city of Lakewood. Shaker Heights was developed as an independent suburb in the 1920s. However, metropolitan suburban growth on a large scale really began with the post–World War II development that characterized the United States (Jackson, 1985). As the city of Cleveland's population declined after 1950, the population of the surrounding suburbs in Cuyahoga County grew rapidly, especially between 1950 and 1970, when the county's suburban population increased from 420,630 to 909,730 (a cumulative increase of 116 percent). Suburban Cuyahoga County's growth rate then dropped between 1970 and 1990 to −.0035 percent (basically "steady state"), with the 1990 population being 906,524. This is explained by the region's economic problems, out-migration to outlying suburbs in surrounding counties and elsewhere in Ohio and the United States, and the falling birthrate.

From 1980 to 1990, the black population of suburban Cuyahoga County grew from 9.4 percent to 12.7 percent (an increase of 35 percent). Cleveland ranks with Chicago and Philadelphia as a metropolitan area with a significant increase in the suburban black population in the 1980s, despite no population growth in the metropolitan area (O'Hare and Frey, 1992). However, the pattern of black suburbanization has been skewed. Although the population of the east-side suburbs was 25 percent black in 1990, most black suburbanization has occurred in a few suburbs: Cleveland Heights, East Cleveland, Shaker Heights, and Warrensville Heights, and Oakwood. Other east-side suburban cities with a significant black population in 1990 were Euclid, Garfield Heights, Maple Heights, and University Heights. A majority of east-side suburbs, however, had a black population of 10 percent or less. In the west-side suburbs, all but the city of Berea had a black population of 2 percent or less.

In 1983, using the 1980 census data, the Cuyahoga Plan projected where blacks could live in Cuyahoga County, based solely on their income in relationship to housing prices. With a black population in Cuyahoga County (including the city of Cleveland) of 22.8 percent in 1980, the Cuyahoga Plan estimated that no suburb would have had a black population of less than 11 percent, based on a broad distribution of minorities and an open housing market. The five suburbs that are discussed in detail in this chapter would have had markedly different racial mixes in their populations under the hypothesized circumstances of this study (Table 4).

The primary goal of the many fair housing organizations that have been active in Cuyahoga County since the 1960s has been an open, nondiscriminatory housing market in which blacks (and other minorities) moving to the suburbs will freely explore all possible, affordable options. Overt racial discrimination has been greatly

Table 4. Actual versus Projected Black
Population in Five Cleveland Suburbs, 1980

	Actual (%)	Projected (%)
Cleveland Heights	25	19
East Cleveland	87	28
Euclid	7	20
Parma	0	18
Shaker Heights	24	15

Source: Cuyahoga Plan

reduced in reaction to enforcement of fair housing laws. However, housing audits and complaints filed with the Cuyahoga Plan's Discrimination Complaint Service confirm that covert racial discrimination in housing continues (Galster, 1987, 1990a; Cuyahoga Plan, 1991).

Nonetheless, black suburbanization patterns have not been greatly altered. Blacks in metropolitan Cleveland continue to be concentrated in a small number of east-side suburbs. The suburban cities of East Cleveland and Warrensville Heights have almost entirely resegregated, with 1990 black populations of 94 and 89 percent, respectively. In such cities as Cleveland Heights, Euclid, Garfield Heights, Maple Heights, Shaker Heights, and South Euclid, much of the black population is concentrated in majority or predominantly black neighborhoods. Pro-integrationists fear that, if this trend continues, eventually these racially mixed neighborhoods will also resegregate. Despite the tireless efforts of a succession of fair housing organizations to encourage blacks to consider housing in predominantly white east-side suburbs that have not traditionally been settled by blacks (e.g., the six-city "Hillcrest" area), there have only been small gains. While there has been some black migration to the western suburbs, it has been so small in numbers that it has had little impact so far in significantly changing the racial mix of west-side suburbs. Parma, despite the imposition of a federal court order mandating pro-integrative housing efforts, is the most notorious example of this phenomenon.

Suburban Governments and Fair Housing

Despite the seeming increased support of suburban residents for open access to housing and for fair housing legislation, most suburban governments in metropolitan Cleveland have done little or nothing to promote greater racial diversity. A 1989 Cuyahoga Plan survey found that a majority of Cuyahoga County's suburban governments had merely adopted resolutions supporting the goal of fair housing.

In the absence of state or federal mandates to integrate, elected officials of predominantly white suburbs in metropolitan Cleveland have not acted affirmatively to promote greater racial diversity. This is hardly surprising; those few officials who have occasionally espoused such policies, for example, in Euclid and South Euclid, have found their political careers threatened or actually ended by white voter backlash. This explains why pro-integrative activities have been conducted almost entirely by fair housing organizations operating on a metropolitan basis. The histories of some of these organizations' activities are found in the case studies of the five cities and fair housing organizations in Chapters 5 through 10.

Governmental support for metropolitan fair housing organizations in Cuyahoga County has come from three sources. First, Cuyahoga County, the city of Cleveland, and several suburbs (e.g., Cleveland Heights, Euclid, and Lakewood) that receive Community Development Block Grant funding from the federal government have supported fair housing, primarily through funding of the Cuyahoga Plan and its programs. Second, a few suburbs, most notably Cleveland Heights, Shaker Heights, and University Heights, have used their own funds to support wider pro-integrative efforts outside their borders. A notable example is their creation of and support for the East Suburban Council for Open Communities (ESCOC). Third, the Ohio Housing Finance Agency's first-time homebuyer mortgage incentive program set-aside to pro-integrative movers has been used throughout Cuyahoga County.

Philanthropic Foundations' Support for Fair Housing

Perhaps as important as the public funding sources for fair housing mentioned above has been the support of Cleveland's two leading philanthropic foundations, the Cleveland Foundation and the George Gund Foundation. Philanthropic foundation support for fair housing began with the leadership of the Greater Cleveland Associated Foundation (predecessor to the Cleveland Foundation) under Dolph Norton (formerly a Case Western Reserve University professor) in supporting a study of housing problems in greater Cleveland. Released in March 1967, the study pointed to the need to provide open access for blacks to housing throughout the metropolitan area.

This study was soon followed by the creation of PATH. Between its creation in 1967 and its demise in 1974, PATH received a total of $450,165 from the Cleveland Foundation.

The Cleveland and Gund Foundations have provided critical support for virtually every major fair housing organization that has existed in Cleveland since the 1960s, for example, Fair Housing, Inc.; Operation Equality; the Heights Community Congress; the Cuyahoga Plan; Euclid Community Concerns; Hillcrest Neighbors; ESCOC; and Open Door West. The two foundations have provided seed money to launch fair housing organizations, operating support during their lives, and funding for special projects and programs. From 1965 to 1990, the Cleveland Foundation cumulatively spent at least $2.5 million on fair housing activities. In 1990, of $3,933,930 distributed for "civic affairs" (and $30.5 million distributed overall), the Cleveland Foundation distributed $174,329 for fair housing to support four fair housing organizations: the Cuyahoga Plan, the Metropolitan Strategy Group, the Heights Community Congress, and Open Door West (Cleveland Foundation, 1990). The George Gund Foundation has regularly joined the Cleveland Foundation in supporting fair housing in metropolitan Cleveland; from 1965–1990 it cumulatively distributed at least $1,432,342 for fair housing. In 1990, out of total charitable distributions of $12 million, it distributed $88,000 to support three fair housing organizations: the Cuyahoga Plan, the Heights Community Congress, and the Heights Fund (George Gund Foundation, 1990). Thus, over about a quarter- century, these two philanthropic foundations have spent about $4 million to support fair housing organizations in metropolitan Cleveland.

A growing concern has been a proliferation of fair housing organizations seeking funding and the need to better coordinate these efforts in the face of the limited availability of funding and the lack of adequate governmental support. This led to the convening of several fair housing "summits" in greater Cleveland during 1990–1991, in an attempt to resolve the problem. So far the only coordinating body remains the Metropolitan Strategy Group, which provides a monthly forum for informational meetings. The idea of some sort of countywide federation of fair housing agencies has not received support.

Success and Failure in Suburban Racial Transition

Measuring the success of these sustained fair housing activities is difficult. On the one hand, spatial and demographic data show little overall change. The neighborhoods of the city of Cleveland and most of the surrounding suburbs of Cuyahoga County remain highly segregated by race, with only a few notable exceptions. Most suburban governments have taken few or no affirmative steps to promote greater racial diversity in housing and neighborhoods. On the other hand, fair housing proponents can point to some positive changes. Public attitudes, if not the actual choices made by people moving within the metropolitan area have become more tolerant of racial diversity. The cities of Cleveland Heights and Shaker Heights have managed to maintain racial diversity for two to three decades, a remarkable accomplishment compared to most suburbs of their kind in the United States.

What has blocked greater progress has been the absence of state or federal mandates for metropolitan strategies that would apply to all suburbs, not just to those few that voluntarily have tried to deal with racial issues in housing. The lack of a viable metropolitan fair housing strategy or, in the alternative, countywide incentives for pro-integrative policies has resulted in piecemeal progress at best. The need for a metropolitan strategy and its viability are discussed in Chapter 13.

Warrensville Heights: Suburban Resegregation

Meanwhile, resegregation has occurred. The case of East Cleveland is recounted in detail in Chapter 5. A comparable example is that of Warrensville Heights, which lies to the east of Shaker Heights and the neighboring black, middle-class Cleveland area of Lee–Harvard.

Warrensville Heights in 1960 was all white. By 1970, 21 percent of its population was black. Warrensville Heights became one of the magnets for black suburbanization because of its lower-priced "starter" homes and affordable rentals. In 1990 the median price of a single-family house in Warrensville Heights was $56,900, compared to $82,500 for suburban Cuyahoga County overall.

The first "pioneer" black family moved into Warrensville Heights in 1963. Support for a peaceful and successful racial integration came from the clergy, which has been in the forefront of the fair housing movement throughout metropolitan Cleveland. In the 1950s the Aldersgate Methodist Church, under the direction of the Reverend Robert Raines, sought to promote interracial harmony (e.g., through an annual exchange of ministers and choirs with a black church, beginning in 1957). Raines's policy was continued by his successor Alan Davis, who is now co-pastor of an inner-city black church in Cleveland and has been the longtime president of the prestigious Cleveland City Club (Davis, 1990). A Davis sermon on racial integration contributed to the formation of the Warrensville Heights Neighborhood Forum in 1963.

This forum worked with the Brentwood and Shakerwood neighborhood associations to try to prevent the racial "blockbusting" that began to occur in East Cleveland and the white flight that was occurring in the adjoining Lee–Harvard neighborhood of Cleveland. Its efforts failed, however, and it eventually disbanded. By 1980 the population of Warrensville Heights was 75 percent black. In 1990, 89 percent of Warrensville Heights's population of 15,745 was black. In neighboring Lee–Harvard, virtually all of the residents were black by 1980.

Unlike East Cleveland, which experienced a tremendous decline since racial transition led to the resegregation of most of the city, Warrensville Heights has maintained itself as a desirable suburb, providing good public services and public education and maintaining its housing stock. Ironically, Raymond Grabow, a white lawyer, remains its mayor. First elected in 1967, he has defeated several challenges by black candidates; the latest of these was in 1991, when Grabow won by 65 percent of the vote.

Warrensville Heights stands as a prime example of the likelihood of resegregation in the path of concentrated black suburbanization in metropolitan Cleveland. Unless pro-integrative policies are pursued on a metropolitan basis, especially with the support of those municipalities undergoing significant racial transition, such resegregation seems probable.

Maple Heights: A Suburb in Racial Transition

Maple Heights, which borders Warrensville Heights and Cleveland's Lee–Harvard neighborhood to the south, typifies the continu-

ing process of racial transition in many of Cleveland's eastern
suburbs, which threatens to result in eventual resegregation. Maple
Heights has long had a small black population, which has been
concentrated in an area called Presidential Streets. In the early 1980s,
however, black in-migration began to increase significantly. By 1990,
16 percent of the city's population of 27,089 was black, compared to
only 3 percent in 1980.

In 1985, Maple Community United was formed to try to prevent white flight (Brown, 1987a). It successfully lobbied for passage
of a municipal fair housing ordinance in 1987. Originally introduced in 1983, the ordinance regulates real estate solicitation
(Brown, 1987b). A fair housing committee was established to oversee
its implementation. Racial discrimination testing by the Cuyahoga
Plan through the use of white and black "checkers" led to an
unsuccessful lawsuit in 1990 against a real estate agent accused of
racial "steering" in Maple Heights. Further controversy was occasioned by a city official in 1990 who publicly questioned whether a
black city staffer should be appointed as the city's fair housing
coordinator. In the wake of this controversy, the position was
eliminated.

In the 1991 mayoral election, the incumbent mayor Dennis
Love accused his challenger, city council president Santo Incorvaia (a lawyer and real estate agent), of promoting pro-integrative
loans to prospective black homebuyers. Incorvaia responded that
he favored only subsidies for white homebuyers in neighborhoods threatened by resegregation (Segall, 1991). Incorvaia defeated Love in a close runoff election. Currently, the Maple Heights
schools must continue to deal with the issue of racial imbalance
in the public schools, due to a concentration of black elementary school children that is related to housing patterns. In 1990,
25 percent of the Maple Heights school district's students were
black.

A major voice for policies to promote stable racial transition in
Maple Heights is Christian Neighbors, which represents many
churches in Maple Heights and neighboring communities. Whether
Maple Heights will eventually follow in the footsteps of Warrensville Heights, however, is an open question.

Five Cleveland Suburbs

Case studies of five specific Cleveland suburbs follow in Chapters 5 through 9: the suburbs are East Cleveland, Shaker Heights, Cleveland Heights, Parma, and Euclid. The striking differences among these suburbs is illustrated by their fair housing expenditures in 1992 (Table 5).

East Cleveland and Parma illustrate respectively, the resegregation of a formerly all-white suburb into a predominantly black suburb and the resistance of an almost all-white suburb to minorities. The rapid racial transition in the 1960s that led to the resegregation of East Cleveland has served as the most striking example of what can happen if a community fails to deal effectively with racial transition. Although there has been some change in Parma since a 1980 remedial federal court order requiring it affirmatively to promote greater racial diversity, its population a decade later remained more than 99 percent white. Euclid was also the subject of lawsuits that claimed the suburb excluded minorities. Like Parma, it has only gradually adopted measures to prevent discrimination. However, unlike Parma, which is located on Cleveland's west side, Euclid has a much more sizable minority population. Since 1980 Euclid has also had an interracial community organization (Euclid Community Concerns) that has supported racial diversity. Whether Euclid manages integration successfully in the future remains to be seen.

In contrast, Shaker Heights and Cleveland Heights represent two of the most successful examples in the United States of suburbs

Table 5. Fair Housing Expenditures in Five Cleveland Suburbs, 1992

City	Fair Housing Budget	Per Capita Fair Housing Spending
Shaker Heights	$440,800	$14.30
Cleveland Heights	$290,000	$5.37
East Cleveland	$20,000	$.60
Euclid	$20,784	$.38
Parma	$10,000	$.11

Source: MSG, *Metro Eye*, March 1993

undergoing racial transition that have voluntarily adopted pro-integrative policies and have maintained them. Though these two suburbs cannot be said to have overcome all racial conflicts and problems, they have nevertheless served as beacons of hope that long-term, stable residential racial diversity is possible in metropolitan Cleveland and elsewhere in the United States.

5

East Cleveland: Black Suburbanization, White Flight, and Rapid Resegregation

East Cleveland was the destination of the initial wave of black suburbanization in metropolitan Cleveland. One of the first and once one of the most prestigious of Cleveland's suburbs, its non-white population was less than 1 percent in 1950 and was still only 2 percent in 1960. In the decade spanning 1960 to 1970, however, East Cleveland and the composition of its population changed dramatically. A rapid period of racial transition fueled by real estate blockbusting resulted in a proportional increase of the black population to 67 percent by 1970. During the 1970s, East Cleveland resegregated into a predominantly black suburb. In 1990 the proportional black population was 94 percent. By that time East Cleveland had a much poorer population, and its reputation had suffered from political and fiscal scandals.

East Cleveland is a textbook example of the type of "invasion and succession" scenario, described in the study of human ecology, in which racial transition can result in racial resegregation (Frey, 1979). The suburb's failure to sustain racial diversity stands in contrast to the successful efforts, beginning in the 1960s, of the city of Shaker Heights to prevent black suburbanization from turning into resegregation. East Cleveland's rapid resegregation served as a warning to adjacent Cleveland Heights and to fair housing activists who promoted racial diversity in other Cleveland suburbs.

Origin and Evolution of East Cleveland

East Cleveland is located on the city of Cleveland's northeastern border and is bordered by Cleveland Heights to the east and south. The city of South Euclid lies to its east and the city of Euclid to its northeast.

First settled in 1895, East Cleveland grew as a residential and industrial suburb in the early twentieth century, following the tremendous growth of the city of Cleveland in the late nineteenth century. A major industry was General Electric's Nela Park facility, which opened in 1911 as the first suburban industrial park in the United States.

East Cleveland was primarily a residential community but also had strong commercial and industrial sectors. Its housing stock and neighborhoods were bifurcated: the city had modestly priced housing in working-class areas, and it also had very expensive and prestigious housing in exclusive residential areas. Its best-known resident was industrialist John D. Rockefeller, who built a magnificent estate called "Forest Hill." Like Rockefeller, the city's wealthier residents lived in the southern "up-the-hill" section. Originally a mansion district, much of this section was subdivided and developed, both before and after World War II. These elite neighborhoods were separated from the neighborhoods occupied by low- and moderate-income residents, who lived "down the hill" to the north, adjacent to the city of Cleveland.

The housing stock consisted largely of single and double homes and small apartment buildings. The greatest growth took place in the 1920s; most of the housing stock was built by 1940. In 1960, East Cleveland was the most densely populated suburb of Cleveland, even though in the decade spanning 1950 to 1960 the population declined by 5 percent (similar to the city of Cleveland). Over the same decade its newer suburban neighbors continued to grow in population, following the national trend.

East Cleveland enjoyed an excellent reputation as it developed.

It prided itself on good government, low taxation, and a high level of municipal services (e.g., thrice-weekly garbage collection). Its public schools also had a very good academic reputation (Price, 1970).

Neighborhoods and Population

East Cleveland consists of five neighborhoods: Rozelle–Superior, Chambers–Mayfair, Prospect, Superior Hill, and Forest Hill. The two "up-the-hill" neighborhoods—Superior Hill and Forest Hill, which are both adjacent to Cleveland Heights—contain the most luxurious housing in East Cleveland. Chambers–Mayfair is the largest of the three "down-the-hill" neighborhoods. The Rozelle–Superior neighborhood is adjacent to the Glenville neighborhood of the city of Cleveland. The Prospect district straddles the Euclid Avenue commercial strip.

Prior to the 1960s, East Cleveland's population was a mix of ethnic and income groups. The population included many former residents of the city of Cleveland. In 1960, East Cleveland's population reached 37,991.

Governance

East Cleveland was a reform city, governed by a city manager and city commission. For four decades (1922–1962), Charles Carran ran East Cleveland as its city manager. Carran gained renown for his honest and efficient administration, which prided itself on the high quality of city services and the low property-tax rate. He influenced the selection of the members of the city commission through a system of appointments to replace retiring members, under which the temporary appointees then ran unopposed as incumbents. The nonpartisan city commission generally deferred to the judgment of its longtime city manager. Carran's administration was unchallenged, and he was the city's dominant public figure.

There was a tradition of civic involvement by East Cleveland's elite ("up-the-hill" residents). Other than the churches, however, there were no community organizations, and there was no other active citizen involvement in governance. The major civic event was the city's annual community picnic.

The Beginning of Racial Transition

The Glenville district of the city of Cleveland abuts East Cleveland. Historically, Glenville had been one of the main areas of Jewish settlement in Cleveland (Vincent and Rubinstein, 1975). In the 1950s the Jewish population began to migrate to the suburbs, primarily to Cleveland Heights. The Glenville census tracts adjacent to East Cleveland were predominantly white in 1950, with the exception of Census Tract 2, which was two-thirds black. By 1960, none of the seven Glenville census tracts had a black population of less than 32 percent, and Census Tracts 2 and 3 were almost entirely resegregated (Table 6).

The resegregation of so much of Glenville into a predominantly black urban neighborhood between 1950 and 1960 was a precursor of what would occur in the following decade in neighboring East Cleveland, which lay next in the path of black migration. Although a small number of more affluent blacks had migrated to the suburbs of Cleveland Heights and Shaker Heights, East Cleveland's aging and less expensive housing stock, especially its rental housing (60 percent of the stock in 1960), was more accessible to blacks than was the stock in the other suburbs. In 1960 the median value of owner-occupied housing in East Cleveland was $15,100; this is only 8 percent higher than in the city of Cleveland but 20 to 30 percent less than the median values in the neighboring cities of Euclid and Cleveland Heights. Rents in East Cleveland were only 12 percent higher than in the city of Cleveland; however, they were 23 percent lower than in Cleveland Heights and 50 percent lower than in

Table 6. Black Population in East Cleveland by Census Tracts, 1950–1960

Census Tract	1950 (%)	1960 (%)
r2	66	96
r3	14	95
r4	0.3	91
r5	7	88
r6	5	90
r7	1	32
p6	5	64

Source: U.S. Census, 1950 and 1960

Shaker Heights. Hence better-off blacks in Cleveland could afford to buy and rent housing in the East Cleveland market.

In addition to the "pull" of East Cleveland, there was a "push" factor in the extensive relocation of blacks in Cleveland. Many blacks were displaced by the city's massive urban renewal–slum clearance program, which resulted in the greatly increased black population in the Hough and Glenville neighborhoods in the early 1960s. Finally, unlike the Heights communities, there was no clear physical demarcation line between Cleveland and East Cleveland.

In 1960 only 2 percent of East Cleveland's population was nonwhite. The median income for nonwhites was $5,412, below the median income of $6,846 for whites but about 30 percent higher than that of the black population of Cleveland. Eighty-three percent of blacks in East Cleveland were renters. Only forty-seven nonwhites owned their homes, principally those living in the Rozelle–Superior district, where the black renter population was also concentrated.

Black pioneers in East Cleveland were attracted to Rozelle–Superior. As had previously happened in east-side Cleveland neighborhoods, the more the black population increased, the more the white demand for housing in the neighborhood decreased. The withdrawal of white demand was reinforced by real estate brokers, who steered black homebuyers to neighborhoods, like Rozelle–Superior, that had black residents while steering white buyers to white neighborhoods. The brokers' unscrupulous practices enabled them to reap windfall gains at a time when such practices were not illegal and not condemned by the real estate industry. In contrast, the exclusive Forest Hill neighborhood remained white through restrictive policies, such as the screening of prospective homebuyers by the homeowners association.

Rapid racial transition can be tracked by the number and timing of real estate transactions. For example, according to the Cuyahoga County Recorder's Office, in the Hayden–Phillips–Superior–Lockwood section of the Rozelle–Superior district—the section that borders the Cleveland city line—159 of 172 parcels changed ownership in the first half of the decade, mostly between 1961 and 1963. This phenomenon is an exaggerated version of the "filtering" process, in which older, less-expensive housing is occupied successively by lower-income residents.

The Response to Black Suburbanization and Neighborhood Transition

In general, East Cleveland's white population was wary about the prospect of racial transition (Grossman, 1966). There was an undercurrent of concern in reaction to the rapid racial resegregation occurring across the border in Cleveland. With power concentrated in the city manager's office, there was not another likely public forum for a response. Independent, neighborhood-based community organizations did not exist, and the weekly newspaper did not publicly address the issues raised by racial transition until its later stages.

Schools

The black migration to East Cleveland was reflected in enrollment in the suburb's public schools, which enjoyed an excellent reputation. The growing black enrollment in the Rozelle elementary school became a noticeable indicator of racial transition.

The East Cleveland schools made no attempt to establish special or remedial programs for incoming black students who needed assistance. One parents group argued that such programs would lower overall educational standards. Another parents group, representing incoming black students, countered that the schools had an obligation to provide necessary assistance to meet the needs of new students (e.g., technical training in addition to college preparatory course work). The school board was criticized for its failure to plan for racial integration of the schools.

City Government

In 1962, at the beginning of the turbulent civil rights era, Grant Apthorp, Carran's longtime assistant, succeeded Carran as city manager. With indicators of the beginning of "white flight" from those neighborhoods experiencing racial transition, the city initiated contacts with real estate brokers to persuade them not to contribute to this process. Apthorp believed that any attempt by the city to block black entry would be morally wrong. However, the effort to convince the brokers proved fruitless.

In 1962 the city manager convened a citizens group to discuss the racial transition in East Cleveland. This resulted in the following proposals (Little, 1967):

1. open access to the city manager's office as a forum for the discussion of race and community issues;
2. initiation of a study to show that housing prices increase following black home purchases and communicating this information to white homeowners;
3. strengthening municipal services; and
4. strict enforcement of housing codes.

However, Apthorp made no public pronouncements concerning these proposals, racial transition in neighborhoods, or white fears. He also made no further attempt to deal forcefully with the real estate industry, which felt no pressure to discontinue practices that resulted in white flight and racial resegregation. Apthorp believed that any problems arising from racial transition would be overcome simply by maintaining East Cleveland's reputation for good government. He met with groups of concerned white residents, but this did not quell the fears of many about racial transition.

To his credit, Apthorp did nothing to prevent black migration to East Cleveland. However, instead of an orderly transition to racial diversity, what eventually resulted was resegregation.

Civic Leaders and Community Groups

In general, civic leaders did not address the issue of racial transition. East Cleveland did not have a history of active community organizations. Management of civic affairs was left to the paternalistic city manager system.

The churches were the most important community institutions in East Cleveland, but the clergy did not take the lead in responding to the serious social problem of racial transition and white flight. An exception was the liberal minister of the Congregational Church, who ran a coffee house called The Well, where interracial groups could meet and discuss issues.

Media

The local newspaper was the East Cleveland *Leader*, and its reporting was confined to local "news" and social events. Black residents did not appear in its pages until 1965. For example, when the city commission rejected the application of the Freewill Baptist Church to open a storefront church early in the 1960s, the *Leader* never mentioned that the application was made by a black congregation.

White fears about the black influx and efforts to calm these fears also went unreported in the press in this early stage of the transition. Thus the "news" about the city's racial transition was passed on orally, including rumors as well as facts.

Stages of White Flight

The resegregation of East Cleveland occurred in three stages. During the first stage, in the early 1960s, those whites who were uncomfortable with the increasing black presence and who were able to move left the area. During the second stage, in the mid-1960s, those whites who were fearful of economic loss from depreciation of property values fled, spurred by blockbusting and steering practices of some real estate brokers. During the last stage, continuing into the 1970s, those whites who were supportive of racial integration grew discouraged and many left, leaving behind a shrinking white population, except for the largely white Forest Hill enclave.

In 1963 more concerted efforts were made to stem the tide of white flight. Neighborhood associations were formed, with the assistance of the city, in Rozelle–Superior and Chambers–Mayfair. These associations organized interracial neighborhood meetings to try to build trust and allay fears. To promote better interracial understanding, they sponsored social events.

The city manager appointed an East Cleveland Citizens' Advisory Committee (CAC), an interracial group that was asked to study integration problems. Chaired by a minister, the committee conducted a survey on civil rights issues and petitioned the U.S. Congress for civil rights legislation to open up all residential areas for blacks. The CAC was critical of school policies, but a defensive school board refused to take any special action to deal with race-related issues in the public schools. Neighborhood–sponsored efforts to persuade the city manager and commission to ban "for sale" signs, discourage solicitation of homeowners, and regulate real estate agents were rejected.

The year 1964 can be seen as the beginning of the second stage of racial transition. While black–white conflict was noticeably absent, white flight accelerated. During the period from 1963 to 1966, there was massive turnover of the housing market in the Rozelle–Superior and Chambers–Mayfair areas. This paralleled previous patterns of white flight from east-side neighborhoods in the city of Cleveland. Though many initial black suburbanites could be considered middle-class, those who followed, both renters and homeowners, were more and more working-class in background and income.

As real estate brokers continued to warn prospective white homesellers of declining property values, older white residents began to resist increased property taxes to maintain municipal services. In a *Leader* editorial supporting a tax increase (1964), Apthorp referred to East Cleveland as "the changing community or the city with one leg in the grave and the other on a banana peel." Public participation, including voting, declined. In the fall of 1964, when a "for sale" sign ban was debated before the commission, only representatives of the real estate industry (including black realtors, known as "realtists," opposed to any restriction on their sales activities) appeared. The opposition of the real estate representatives won a delay.

As the pace of racial transition increased, the image of East Cleveland presented publicly was that of "a city actively striving to create and maintain a climate for successful racial integration" (*Cleveland Plain Dealer*, Nov. 7, 1964). Despite the city's code enforcement efforts, however, incipient signs of the decline of the housing stock appeared. As much as 25 percent of the housing stock was changing hands in some areas at the peak of the second phase of while flight. In addition to the housing market, the commercial strips began to change as many businesses closed or relocated. The decline of the commercial strips resulted in reduced city revenues and, in turn, a further decline in municipal services.

By 1966 racial transition was so pervasive that the Rozelle

elementary school reported a 33 percent annual student turnover rate. Open public debate began about how to deal with the problems caused by this transition. Attempts were made to improve the public schools with more teachers and lower student–teacher classroom ratios.

The year 1966 was a turning point in the failure of East Cleveland to stabilize during racial transition. In February 1966, the Rozelle–Superior Civic Association, led by prominent black leader and early residential pioneer Dr. Jonathan Booker, attempted to persuade the city commission to establish a community relations position within city hall. The attempt failed. However, in the spring of 1966, with the support of the city manager, the commission finally enacted a "for sale" sign ban, despite continued real estate broker opposition.

That same spring, the Foundation for Action by Citizens Together (FACT) was sponsored by the YMCA and YWCA to stabilize the community and prevent resegregation. Led by several prominent citizens—ministers, academics, and businessmen—FACT conducted a community survey and attempted to raise funds. Although the city government endorsed FACT and its aims, it provided no direct support. FACT's efforts failed when only a handful of citizens turned out for a general meeting that fall after organizational meetings were held during the summer. An indicator of the problems faced by FACT was the cancellation of the community picnic in June 1966, the first cancellation in thirty-six years. The reason cited was lack of interest.

Further, the city manager's attempt to persuade the commission to enact an ordinance to require pre-sale inspection of homes failed in August 1966, again in the face of strong real estate broker opposition (however, the ordinance was finally adopted in December 1966). It had been hoped that requiring the repair of code violations would slow the rate of home sales.

In the spring of 1966, a *Leader* editorial titled "The Hour of Our Discontent" begged its readers to understand what was happening to the city and to work together to maintain stability: "Whispers spread the dogma of fear and disillusionment. [They] chronicle the flight of whites. Buildings still look as good but the only thing changed is people's minds." While supporting the city manager's actions, by the fall the *Leader* had despaired of FACT achieving its goals, and it declared East Cleveland a "political wasteland." The rapid racial change of these years appeared to have discouraged most whites who supported racial integration. The Hough race riots of July 1966 in the city of Cleveland further disheartened many whites who had not initially been inclined to leave.

The 1967 Development Plan and Increased Efforts by Address Resegregation

In 1967 the city of East Cleveland attempted to stem the tide of deterioration by using federal programs. HUD funding was obtained for a neighborhood code-enforcement workshop. In 1968, in addition to promoting housing improvements, the workshop's three coordinators became involved in efforts to restrain real estate brokers (who were mostly black, at this point) from harassing homeowners.

The city's leadership decided that a development plan was needed for future guidance on the issue of racial transition and hired the consulting firm of A. D. Little to prepare an economic development report. The report was to answer these questions: Who would move to East Cleveland? Can a racial balance be maintained? What will be the impacts on housing and human services? How will new leadership be developed?

By this time, the city's leaders apparently had decided that East Cleveland was likely to resegregate. Apthorp reportedly believed that, if resegregation was inevitable, it was necessary to prepare black leadership to pave the way for the best possible governance of a black East Cleveland by black leaders. He appointed the first black—John Turner—to the city commission in 1967. Turner, a faculty member at the School of Applied Social Sciences at Case Western Reserve University, and fellow commission member Mark Chamberlain, Case Western Reserve's provost, enjoyed national academic reputations.

The perception that resegregation was likely was not misconceived. By 1967, it was estimated that East Cleveland's black population was approximately 45 percent of the overall population (Little, 1967: 27). Four of five black suburbanites in metropolitan Cleveland lived in three suburbs: East Cleveland, Shaker Heights, and War-rensville Heights. Of this total, half of the black suburbanites lived in East Cleveland (Little, 1967: 3). Black in-migration was three times that of whites (Little, 1967: 45), while large numbers of whites continued to leave.

Typical of many communities that have undergone racial transition on this scale, there was sentiment in East Cleveland for "integration." Blacks surveyed in 1967 overwhelmingly (91 percent) preferred living in a racially integrated community. In contrast, only 47 percent of whites surveyed in 1967 preferred living in an integrated community. By comparison, in 1968, in a national survey, a majority (56 percent) of whites agreed that "white people have a right to keep blacks out of their neighborhood." Only 19 percent disagreed strongly with this statement (Schuman, Steeh, and Bobo, 1985: table 3.1, 74–75). More disturbing was the prevailing white view that too many blacks and poor people were moving into East Cleveland (Little, 1967: 66). When asked whether it was important to bring new white residents into East Cleveland to preserve the city's racial balance, 58 percent of whites agreed, as did 55 percent of blacks (Little, 1967: 16). The Little report concluded: "Racial fear and prejudice led to wholesale panic and flight in areas of the city, creating the impression that an almost overnight transition had occurred in the city." (Little, 1967: 7).

In March 1968 the *Leader* reported that only one of three white residents planned to stay in East Cleveland, based upon a survey conducted by FACT (*East Cleveland Leader*, March 27, 1968). It later retracted this story, claiming that a miscalculation had reversed the finding that 70 percent of white residents surveyed actually planned to stay (*East Cleveland Leader*, March 28, 1968).

The last serious efforts to promote racial integration were made in 1968. Cleveland State University professor Leon Soule organized an East Cleveland house tour to attract prospective white buyers through a citizen-operated housing office. However, the city refused to officially support such a housing office, and an influential black realtist led the opposition. East Cleveland maintained its race- neutral policies. An East Cleveland Community Theatre was inaugurated to promote interracial culture (Garvin, 1987). But these efforts proved to be "too little, too late" to stem the tide of white flight.

In 1968 blacks began to appear in the *Leader*. There was more open debate on such issues as regulating real estate brokers to prevent racial blockbusting and steering. A fair housing law was proposed and finally passed in the fall of 1968 (several months after passage of the federal fair housing law in April 1968). However, these efforts also proved to be too late. The data in Table 7 indicate the extent of housing turnover in the period from 1965 to 1968 in some areas of East Cleveland.

The Pressures of Cleveland's Racial Tensions

Yet another blow to any hope of maintaining racial integration in East Cleveland was the Glenville riot in the city of Cleveland in July 1968. On July 23, armed black nationalists and Cleveland police clashed, and a gun battle ensued. Violence in the Glenville neighborhood continued over the next five days, with sniping and firebombing. Initially, Cleveland's new black mayor, Carl Stokes, ordered that only black police officers and civic leaders patrol and enter Glenville. This caused controversy and a backlash by many white police officers and citizens. After trying this strategy, Stokes changed his policy and the mostly white National Guard entered Glenville to restore order (Masotti and Corsi, 1969; Zannes, 1972).

This racially based battle at the doorstep of East Cleveland undoubtedly had an impact on the suburb's remaining white residents, as the police and National Guard were sent to guard the border between East Cleveland and Glenville. If looting had spilled over the city line, Apthorp had apparently decided to let

Table 7. Property Turnover in East Cleveland, 1965–1968

Area	Number of Parcels	Number of Transfers
Hayden/Eddy	300	236
Manhattan/Shaw	197	146
Hayden/Fourth	203	164

Source: Cuyahoga County Auditor's Office

the rioters pass rather than order the police and military to fire upon them.

The 1969 Little Report

The Little report was not issued until 1969. During the two-year period of its preparation, the city had undertaken no major pro-integrative initiatives. Little recommended a series of urban redevelopment projects, which included a focus on developing prime commercial sites and a gateway beautification project near the city's border with Cleveland. The report proposed the creation of an East Cleveland Development Corporation to buy properties in those areas threatened with panic selling. It recommended home ownership assistance and "prospecting" for new residents by race and income to restore a racial and socioeconomic balance. Finally, Little called for the promotion of new commercial development and the improvement of the city's public schools (Little, 1967: 283).

Little saw three choices facing the city. First, it could ignore the report and simply allow the city's racial, social, and economic transformation to continue unabated. Second, it could initiate only some of the recommended policies and proceed piecemeal, as best as it could, thus probably delaying the city's negative transition but not altering it in the long run. Third, it could try to implement all of these programs as soon as possible, slow the transition down, and then reverse the transition. However, the Little report did not explain how East Cleveland could finance its recommendations. Having raised expectations, the report proved to be anticlimactic, and it had no positive impact on the city's future.

By the time the Little report was issued, the national tide of liberalism and federally supported domestic reform was turning. The Nixon administration had been elected and promised to end the domestic reforms of President Lyndon Johnson's "Great Society." The model cities program was in disarray and doomed to failure, the urban renewal program was in its final phase before being replaced by the Community Development Block Grant Program, and President Richard Nixon's HUD was focused on new housing production, not the enforcement of fair housing (Hays, 1985).

The End of the Old Regime: 1969–1979

In March 1969, Grant Apthorp retired. Carran's longtime assistant and successor had served seven years, which he called the most difficult of his four decades of public service (East Cleveland *Leader*, March 30, 1969). He was succeeded by William Gaskill, his assistant, who served only one year and was the last white city manager of East Cleveland. Gaskill appointed two black assistant city managers, Gladstone "Mickey" Chandler and Curtis Hall. They replaced him successively after Gaskill resigned in 1970 to become director of public utilities of the city of Cleveland, under Mayor Carl Stokes.

In 1970 the East Cleveland *Leader* closed. In part this resulted from the refusal of advertisers (e.g., property owners in nearby Collinwood and Euclid, who did not want to advertise rentals that might attract black applicants) to continue to operate in an increasingly black market. An attempt, sponsored by FACT, to publish a community newspaper (the *East Cleveland Citizen*) in its place eventually failed. Thus there was no longer a local publication to serve as a public forum for discussion of the changes affecting East Cleveland. Also, federal funding for the neighborhood workshops ceased (except for the Hayden Avenue project), undercutting the viability of fledgling neighborhood organizations.

The year 1970 marked the beginning of the third phase of East Cleveland's racial transition. The city now had a black majority population of 67 percent. Its economic profile more closely resembled the city of Cleveland than its suburban neighbors. East Cleveland's 1970 median income of $9,819 was actually lower by 7 percent than the median income in the city of Cleveland and much lower than that of the cities of Euclid (17 percent higher) and Cleveland Heights (27 percent higher). Eleven percent of East Cleveland's population was below the poverty line, compared to only 3 percent in Euclid and Cleveland Heights. Median housing values in East Cleveland ($16,500) were still higher than in the city of Cleveland, in part due to the Forest Hill district maintaining its prestigious status.

As East Cleveland came to resemble closely its urban neighbor Glenville, its problems multiplied. City services declined as its revenues plummeted. From 1967 to 1970, East Cleveland's tax base declined by 20 percent (*Cleveland Plain Dealer*, April 1, 1973). A federally funded commercial neighborhood development project was completed in the Hayden area, but it did not lead to commercial revitalization.

Resegregation

By 1980, 86 percent of the population of East Cleveland was black. Among major suburbs in the United States, this concentration of a black population was second only to that of impoverished East St. Louis, Illinois. East Cleveland's socioeconomic profile revealed further decline. Its median income was now 33 and 43 percent lower, respectively, than those of nearby Euclid and Cleveland Heights. The unemployment rate was 12 percent, and the poverty rate was 22 percent. In 1971, City Manager Chandler declared: "We are an inner-city suburb with all the problems of the central city" (Delaney, 1971).

Only 30 percent of the households in East Cleveland owned their homes. Most homeowners were white, and the median value of their homes was almost twice that of homes owned by blacks. Only 14 percent of the city's white residents had moved into East Cleveland since 1970. In 1973 the city's second black city manager declared that he was not concerned about whites leaving East Cleveland and that he would do nothing to attract whites to promote racial diversity (*Cleveland Plain Dealer*, April 1, 1973).

The Decline of East Cleveland: Municipal Mismanagement and Political Corruption

Coincidental with the ascendancy of black politicians in East Cleveland, the city's tax base declined and increased its troubles. Known for its conservative fiscal policies and prudent management under Carran and Apthorp, East Cleveland gained a reputation in the 1980s for fiscal mismanagement and corruption. Bickering broke out among city commissioners and there was a regular turnover of city managers. In the mid-1980s, major scandals erupted as the embezzlement of city funds came to light, and several prominent city officials were jailed (O'Connor, 1986).

As operating deficits were uncovered by state audits of the city's finances, East Cleveland's credit rating was suspended, and in 1988 a financial emergency was declared. The city's financial woes led to even more political bickering, including charges of racism by the last white members of the city council. In 1985 East Cleveland's charter was revised, and the city government adopted the mayor–city council form of government.

The rapid decline in East Cleveland's finances and the low level of available municipal services in part reflects the increased poverty of the city's population, especially as the poor black population increased. However, increased poverty does not explain the emergence of widespread corruption in a black-dominated city government, under which the city went bankrupt. The responsible black leadership that Apthorp, in the mid 1960s, had envisioned would arise, as racial transition grew rapidly and as large numbers of whites withdrew from civic affairs and left the city, simply did not develop. Instead, opportunism characterized much of black politics in East Cleveland in the two decades following Gaskill's resignation and the eventual black domination of East Cleveland's government.

Conclusion

The 1990 U.S. Census indicated a black population in East Cleveland of 94 percent. East Cleveland had almost completely resegregated. It had the highest poverty rate by far of any suburb of Cuyahoga County (43 percent, almost the same as the rate for the city of Cleveland). According to the Cuyahoga County Auditor's Office, the median sales price of a house in East Cleveland, $39,900, was the lowest of all of the Cuyahoga County suburbs in 1990 and almost exactly that of the city of Cleveland, which was $40,000. A poor and mismanaged community, East Cleveland's image was tarnished by political corruption and scandal and by the takeover of its finances in the late 1980s by the state of Ohio. In a 1993 survey of residents of the thirty-five largest suburbs in Cuyahoga County, residents were asked to rate their government: East Cleveland received the worst rating (O'Malley, 1993).

There are several explanations for East Cleveland's rapid decline from one of the best-managed older suburbs in the United States to this sorry state of affairs. First, East Cleveland faced the earliest major black migration in suburban Cleveland, even greater than the migration to Shaker Heights. This occurred because of East Cleveland's lower-priced housing stock, which made housing in this suburb more affordable to blacks moving from the city of Cleveland. The suburb might have handled this except for the unscrupulous activities of real estate brokers, first white and then black, who engaged in massive racial blockbusting and steering. Unlike Shaker Heights, East Cleveland failed to address this problem through regulatory legislation until it was far too late. Unfortunately, its racial transition occurred just as the civil rights movement was underway and before federal fair housing legislation was enacted in 1968.

East Cleveland's failure to successfully confront housing turnover on this scale and white flight can be attributed to the decisions of its two longtime political leaders—city managers Carran and Apthorp—to reject the race-conscious approaches later adopted first in Shaker Heights and then in Cleveland Heights. By continuing race-neutral policies, the city and the schools actually contributed to racial resegregation.

Second, there was no significant independent, active civic leadership or body of community organizations that emerged to offer alternative leadership. Except for a few ministers and college professors, there was a leadership vacuum. The organization of block clubs to resist resegregation came too late to be effective. The same is true of the city's belated adoption of fair housing legislation and the urban redevelopment plan presented by A. D. Little in 1969.

Third, East Cleveland's problems after its resegregation can be attributed in part to its increasingly poor population. Unlike Shaker Heights, East Cleveland did not enjoy a continued succession of black middle-class families to replace its former white population. Instead it attracted working-class and poor black residents with limited resources. Black political leadership all too often placed self-interest first. Corruption and incompetence in city government hastened the decline of East Cleveland as an attractive suburb.

Under different circumstances and perhaps with different timing, East Cleveland could have sustained racial diversity and prevented racial resegregation. Unfortunately, it did not, and its fate served as a dire warning of the debilitating effects of allowing black suburbanization to result in the creation of what amounts to a suburban black ghetto next to an urban black ghetto.

6

Shaker Heights: Integration Maintenance in a Once Exclusionary, Planned Suburb

Shaker Heights is a leading example of a suburb that has successfully maintained stable racial diversity over a long time period. Its pro-integrative housing policies and programs have served as a model for other communities in metropolitan Cleveland and elsewhere in the United States (DeMarco and Galster, 1993). This model status in the area of racial diversity represents a dramatic change from Shaker Heights's beginnings as an exclusive, planned suburb, which deliberately excluded members of minority racial, ethnic, and religious groups.

Origin and Evolution of Shaker Heights

Shaker Heights is adjacent to the city of Cleveland on the latter's southeast border. The area was first settled in 1822 by the religious colony of North Union Shakers. The colony was disbanded in 1889.

In 1905 the Van Sweringen brothers (Oris P. and Mantis J.) began to buy land for what they envisioned as a planned garden suburb. In 1911 Shaker Heights incorporated as a village, separate from the adjacent suburb of Cleveland Heights to the north. The population of the new village was 1,250. The Van Sweringens bought a railroad right-of-way in 1920 for development as a rapid transit line, enabling future residents of the community to commute to their professional and corporate offices in downtown Cleveland. The brothers later built the Terminal Tower in downtown Cleveland as the terminus of this suburban commuter rail line. In 1929 they developed Shaker Square (located just across the border in the city of Cleveland), one of the earliest American shopping centers. Although bankruptcy in the Great Depression ended their other plans, by the time of their deaths in 1935 and 1936 the success of the Van Sweringens's suburb was assured.

The Van Sweringens's city was intended as an exclusive suburb whose housing and development would be strictly controlled (Condon, 1967). To assure this, restrictive covenants to Shaker Heights deeds were created to exclude members of "undesirable" racial, ethnic, and religious minorities. Despite this exclusionary policy, a black physician did move into Shaker Heights in 1925. Although he received considerable harassment by whites and lived under police protection, this pioneer black resident remained; but he was a notable exception in an otherwise all-white suburb (Kusmer, 1976: 168).

Physically, Shaker Heights's residential neighborhoods were carefully planned around community schools. A variety of houses for both ownership and rental were built. Commercial development was concentrated in Shaker Square and in the Van Aken–Chagrin corridor. At the chartering of Shaker Heights as a city in 1931, its population had grown to 17,783 and it had already gained renown as a planned suburb (Jackson, 1985: 169). Property values steadily increased, and the city's public school system earned a national reputation for academic excellence.

Racial Transition

Racial change came to Shaker Heights in the 1950s. This change was presaged by the 1948 U.S. Supreme Court decision (*Shelly v. Kraemer*) that made restrictive racial covenants unenforceable. In 1950 the nonwhite population of Shaker Heights was only about five hundred people (less than 1 percent), and of this small number only three were homeowners and only seven were renters. The remainder were presumably black live-in domestic servants, whose presence was a feature of Shaker Heights from its inception (Molyneaux and Sackman, 1987).

The first dramatic incident in the racial transformation of Shaker Heights occurred in the Ludlow neighborhood. Ludlow bordered on Cleveland and was the focus of the first influx of black Clevelanders. In 1954 the home of black attorney John Pegg was bombed as it was being built near the Ludlow school. In the wake of this bombing, white residents came to the support of their prospective black neighbors. The uniting of these residents eventually led to creation of the Ludlow Community Association (LCA) in 1957. The LCA was formed to counteract racial steering by realtors and to prevent white flight (Blank, 1968; Saltman, 1990: 300). It actively sought to attract white buyers and provided financial assistance where possible. The LCA received broad support, including funding from David Lincoln, the principal owner of the Shaker Square shopping center.

The LCA became the model for the formation of the Moreland Community Association in 1962 and the Lomond Association in 1963 (Alfred and Marcoux, 1970). Both the Moreland and Lomond neighborhoods are adjacent to the Cleveland–Shaker Heights border, and they too sought to prevent white flight and to attract whites in order to maintain a stable real estate market and racial diversity. These neighborhoods, along with Ludlow, contained the least expensive housing (ownership and rental) available to black residents of Cleveland who were interested in moving into Shaker Heights.

The commitment of black pioneers in Shaker Heights was extraordinary. For some, this initial integrative experience led to a lifelong involvement in fair housing. Prominent among the black pioneer residents were Winston Richie and Joseph Battle. Richie, a dentist, moved into Ludlow in 1956, but only after he canvassed his prospective neighbors and obtained their approval, as required under the Van Sweringen Compact. In 1971, Richie was the first black elected to the Shaker Heights City Council (and he returned to the city council in 1991). He became a prominent advocate of housing integration and later directed the East Suburban Council for Open Communities (ESCOC) during its life (1985–1990). Battle, who became the first black member of the Cleveland Area Board of Realtors (CABOR) in 1963 and was a founder of National Neighbors, moved into Ludlow in 1960 (one of ten black Shaker Heights homeowners listed in the 1960 census, all residing in the Ludlow district). He later directed Operation Equality, a foundation- funded fair housing program sponsored by the Urban League of Cleveland.

Among the factors that made Shaker Heights a focus for black suburbanization was the 1950s migration to this suburb of the Jewish population of the Kinsman and Woodland neighborhoods of Cleveland. Jews, themselves previously prevented from living in Shaker Heights, were more receptive to living with black neighbors than were many other whites (Vincent and Rubinstein, 1975: 23). The racial changes that occurred were quite similar to those in Lee–Harvard. In 1950, Lee–Harvard's population was predominantly white. However, in the decade spanning 1960 to 1970, Lee–Harvard changed from a predominantly white urban neighborhood to a predominantly black neighborhood—96.8 percent black in 1970, compared to only 2.6 percent white. (In 1990, Lee–Harvard, still one of Cleveland's best neighborhoods and with a high percentage of home ownership, remained a virtually all-black neighborhood.)

The LCA's policy of actively attracting white residents to prevent neighborhood resegregation has characterized Shaker Heights's pro-integrative, affirmative housing policy for more than three decades, occasionally leading to controversy. A prominent voice in the implementation of this policy was corporate attorney Stephen Alfred. A resident of the Lomond neighborhood who became active in its pro-integrative activities, Alfred was elected to the Shaker Heights City Council in 1971 and became mayor in 1983 (Whelan, 1985), serving until 1991.

The Development of Pro-integrative Housing Policies in Shaker Heights

The LCA, the Moreland Community Association, and the Lomond Association all received financial assistance from philanthropic foundations and individual donors in the early 1960s. This funding enabled them to hire staff, which supplemented the efforts of their volunteers, and to provide modest financial assistance to white "prospects" to purchase homes. The three neighborhood-based organizations also lobbied the city of Shaker Heights to support pro-integrative efforts to promote racial diversity and neighborhood stabilization. They tried to persuade realtors to show their neighborhoods to white buyers and to end discriminatory racial practices.

In 1964 the mayor, city council, and the board of education joined to form the Shaker Citizens Advisory Commission to address community issues, including housing problems. This resulted in the passage in the same year of a ban on "for sale" signs, designed to prevent the "blockbusting" that had contributed to resegregation elsewhere (e.g., in East Cleveland). This ban was controversial; real estate brokers, especially black realtists who were denied membership on the real estate board and access to its multiple listings, opposed this restriction on the normal process of advertising available real estate but failed to prevent its enactment and implementation. In 1966 sixteen real estate brokers signed an agreement with the commission and the community associations, under which they agreed to show whites racially diverse Shaker Heights neighborhoods (Alfred and Marcoux, 1970). Although this agreement expired after a year, it did establish the basis for future cooperation between the city of Shaker Heights and the real estate industry.

Also in 1966, the Lomond Association hired a housing coordinator with funding from the Cleveland Foundation (Alfred and Marcoux, 1970). This hiring marked the beginning of the systematic effort by the associations to attract white prospects to Shaker Heights. The following year the community associations (numbering four, with the addition of Sussex's neighborhood association) successfully lobbied the city council and the board of education to establish the Shaker Heights Housing Office (Jordan, 1990; Milgram, 1977; Saltman, 1990). The housing office took over the role of the community associations—at their behest—in trying to attract whites to their neighborhoods.

Black "prospects" initially were not the focus of the housing office, leading to concern among blacks. In 1969 the housing office modified its practices:

With very little publicity to disrupt the negotiations [an agreement was reached so] the Housing Office not only made arrangements to show homes to blacks throughout Shaker Heights, but also encouraged them to move into unintegrated sections. In addition, they were told that if they wanted a home in an integrated area, they were free to use black brokers with full access to such areas, while white brokers would assist them in the unintegrated areas. (Milgram, 1977: 97–98)

However, this change did not end the perception that the Shaker Heights Housing Office's services favored white prospects; tension continued. In 1978 two black and three white staff members of the housing office quit in protest, charging that the agency did not provide sufficient assistance to prospective black residents (Husock, 1989; Jordan, 1990: 78). This issue erupted again in 1992. Shaker Heights was sued by a black woman who sought housing information and claimed that she was treated in a discriminatory manner because of her race (Hoke, 1992a). This lawsuit triggered a crisis that led to the firing of the entire staff of the Cuyahoga Plan because of its director's refusal to pursue the discrimination complaint against Shaker Heights, a funder of the Cuyahoga Plan (Hoke, 1992b).

Finally, the opportunity for blacks to buy homes in the more expensive areas of Shaker Heights remained dependent on their incomes. This limited the access of many black home seekers to much of the city's higher-priced housing and explained, at least partially, the concentration of black residents in the least expensive housing.

Stable Racial Diversity: Schools and Housing

By 1970 the black population of Shaker Heights had grown to 14.5 percent, compared to a nonwhite population in 1960 of only 1 percent (an average annual increase of almost 1.5 percent). The black population was concentrated in the four neighborhoods that had organized to promote stable racial diversity, particularly the Ludlow and Moreland neighborhoods. Meanwhile, across the border in the city of Cleveland, racial transition continued. Of the nineteen census tracts in Cleveland that were nearest Shaker Heights, only three (nonadjacent) remained predominantly white by 1970.

In 1967 and 1968, the Shaker Heights Board of Education addressed racial imbalance in the school system by voluntarily instituting busing and magnet schools. This strategy evolved into the Shaker Schools Plan, which took effect in 1970. The continued excellence of the city's public school system was a major factor in attracting "prospects" to Shaker Heights.

While the incipient efforts to promote racial diversity in those neighborhoods of Shaker Heights initially settled by blacks (e.g., Ludlow and Moreland) did stabilize the housing market, it was recognized that other areas in the eastern suburbs that were predominantly white must also be opened up to blacks. Otherwise, Shaker Heights ran the risk of becoming one of the few magnets for black suburbanization, which would make it more difficult to maintain racial diversity. In 1967, therefore, the Lomond Association formed Suburban Citizens for Open Housing (SCOH), to assist blacks seeking to move into all-white areas to find housing in other eastern Cleveland suburbs that would be in the same price range as was available in Shaker Heights. This organization provided an escort service to show blacks homes in other suburban cities, participated in housing audits to document racial discrimination, and operated a rental service. This effort was the forerunner of the East Suburban Council for Open Communities (ESCOC), created in 1984.

Conflict and Cooperation with the Real Estate Industry

During the 1970s, the Shaker Heights Housing Office won national acclaim for its success, including favorable articles in the *New York Times* in 1972 and 1975. Investigation of housing discrimination problems was left first to Operation Equality (1966–1973), directed by Shaker Heights realtor Joseph Battle, and to SCOH. Later such investigations were left to the Cuyahoga Plan (which was created in 1974 with the active support of Shaker Heights).

Although Shaker Heights sought the cooperation of realtors, CABOR filed a complaint in 1974 with the state of Ohio's Real Estate Commission, charging that the Shaker Heights Housing Office was practicing real estate without a license. The state commission upheld CABOR's claim; the board then filed suit in 1977. However, the courts rejected the realtors' challenge in 1980. (During the same period,

CABOR was itself under federal investigation for the discriminatory impact of its exclusion of black real estate brokers from access to its multiple listing service [MLS].)

The Department of Community Services and Pro-integrative Programs

Since 1980, relations between the city's housing office (located within the Shaker Heights Department of Community Services from 1982 to 1992) and the real estate industry have greatly improved. Shaker Heights continues its tour and escort services to other suburbs for black prospects, in cooperation with private real estate firms and rental property managers.

Under the direction of Don DeMarco, hired as community services director in 1982 (from Park Forest, Illinois, where he had worked on its integration maintenance programs), Shaker Heights continued a wide range of programs aimed at sustaining and enhancing the city as an attractive suburban community with a diverse racial mix. These programs include public relations and advertising; education; promotion of sales and rental housing, including the use of financial incentives; liaison with the real estate industry and affirmative marketing; maintenance of the housing stock through zoning, point-of-sale inspections, and code enforcement; fair housing monitoring; commercial development and revitalization; and school desegregation.

Shaker Heights adopted a comprehensive fair housing ordinance in 1985, established a human relations commission, and contracted in 1986 with the Cuyahoga Plan to investigate any complaints of fair housing violations. In 1979 and 1987 the city hosted the annual Oak Park Exchange of cities and organizations involved in integration maintenance. In 1988 the Ford Foundation and Harvard University's John F. Kennedy School of Government recognized Shaker Heights and its partner cities, granting it $100,000 through its "Innovations in State and Local Government" award program.

Shaker Heights's pro-integrative housing programs are based on the premise that race-conscious programs are necessary to prevent resegregation. Their goal of housing market integration "means that all the people in a given area, both minority and non-minority, actually compete for housing in numbers generally reflective of their purchasing power and proportion of the region's population. All Department programs to promote 'integrated and balanced living patterns' (a prime purpose of fair housing legislation) shall be option expanding" (DeMarco, 1989).

In 1990 the Shaker Heights Department of Community Services had a budget of $574,100 ($33,000 from the board of education and the rest from the city of Shaker Heights) and a staff of seventeen persons, six of whom were full-time employees. In 1992, after the election of a new major, Patricia Mearns, and in the wake of the controversy over the discrimination complaint and lawsuit against the city, DeMarco resigned as the department's director, and the city decided to merge its community services and public affairs departments into a new department of community affairs. The new department was charged with continuing to implement the city's integration maintenance policies and programs (Hoke, 1992c).

ESCOC: Revival of the Areawide Strategy of Housing Integration

Even with Shaker Heights's success in maintaining racial diversity, concern continued about the suburb's ability to prevent resegregation if it remained one of the few Cleveland suburbs to which blacks were moving. Therefore, Shaker Heights (both the city and the board of education) joined with the cities and school boards of neighboring Cleveland Heights and University Heights in 1984 to form the East Suburban Council for Open Communities (ESCOC). The council's director was former Shaker Heights City Council member Winston Richie.

With governmental and foundation support, ESCOC opened its office in the Hillcrest area in 1985. The council offered assistance, including financial incentives, to prospective black homeowners and help to black renters. The council's work may be viewed as a continuation of the concept of promoting broader suburban integration, initiated in 1967 by the Lomond Association and its SCOH.

Due to internal disagreements over the scope of its future operations, ESCOC was dissolved in 1991, although its Hillcrest Housing Service was continued. Director Winston Richie, once Shaker Heights's first black councilman, then ran again for city council and was reelected in November 1991.

Fund for the Future of Shaker Heights

In 1985, Shaker Heights established the Fund for the Future of Shaker Heights (FFSH). Funded by the Cleveland and George Gund foundations and by matching contributions from private donors, FFSH provides secondary mortgage financing for pro-integrative home purchases. Loans to white homebuyers are targeted for the Lomond, Ludlow, and Moreland neighborhoods and for small parts of four other neighborhoods. Loans to black homebuyers are targeted for the Fernway, Mercer, and Malvern neighborhoods. The FFSH is a recent version of the pro-integrative mortgage assistance programs pioneered by the Ludlow and Lomond community associations prior to the creation of the Shaker Heights Housing Office.

Secondary loans at interest levels below the market rate (i.e., at 6 percent) for down payments or interest-rate buy-down and mortgage supplements are available from the fund in amounts varying from $3,000 to $6,000. Repayment is deferred for three or four years and is then payable over the next three years. Loan eligibility does not depend on either the buyer's income or first-time home ownership. Since the fund's implementation through 1990, seventy-five homebuyers received these pro-integrative mortgage incentives. Of these incentives, seventy-one went to whites, sixty-six of whom bought houses in the Lomond neighborhood, and only four went to black homebuyers (Cromwell, 1990). By 1992 the FFSH had made 150 such loans.

A study by a Federal Reserve Bank economist analyzed the impact of the FFSH in the Lomond neighborhood (Cromwell, 1990). Concern over racial transition first arose in Lomond in 1963, when home sales to blacks were only 15 percent; these sales grew to 51 percent by 1966. The result of the efforts of the Lomond Association and the newly created Shaker Heights Housing Office was to increase the percentage of white home purchases in Lomond to 61 percent in 1968 (Alfred and Marcoux, 1970: 98).

The city again became concerned about Lomond as housing sales to whites declined from 81 percent of sales in 1981 to 47 percent in 1985, and housing prices did not appreciate. Between 1986 and 1989 the percentage of sales to whites again rose, fluctuating between 56 and 70 percent (Table 8).

Table 8. Racial Composition of Lomond (Shaker Heights) Housing Sales, 1980–1989

Year	To Whites (%)	To Blacks (%)
1980	65	35
1981	81	19
1982	NA	NA
1983	70	30
1984	50	50
1985	47	53
1986	56	44
1987	58	42
1988	70	30
1989	59	41
Decanal Average Percentage	60	40

Source: Cromwell, 1990: table 2

Cromwell estimated the impact of the FFSH mortgage incentives on the racial composition of homebuyers in Lomond, using econometric analysis, and on appreciation of housing prices in the neighborhood, using a hedonic price equation. He found that the program had a positive influence in both respects. He concluded that the probability of white homebuyers purchasing in integrated areas (streets with a nonwhite population of 30 to 70 percent) had increased by 20 percent and that housing prices appreciated by 5.8 percent annually.

In 1992, Shaker Heights announced a new program to provide low-interest loans for exterior home repairs in the western part of the Lomond and Moreland neighborhoods, to help maintain housing quality in now predominantly black neighborhoods.

The Friends of Shaker Square Controversy

Founded in 1976, the Friends of Shaker Square (FOSS) is a nonprofit development corporation created to preserve the greater Shaker Square area (both commercial and residential). The population of the Cleveland neighborhoods bordering Shaker Square has become increasingly black. The nonwhite proportion of the Buckeye–Shaker area population increased from a minority of 46 percent in 1976 to a majority of 76 percent a decade later.

In 1982, FOSS became involved in promoting residential stability when it created the Rental Connection. Originally a race-neutral service for landlords and tenants, the Rental Connection adopted a pro-integrative policy in 1988 after FOSS became aware of the resegregation trend in the residential neighborhoods of the Shaker Square area. FOSS's Rental Connection offered its free services only to whites seeking rental housing in areas in which they were under-represented. Black tenants seeking assistance were referred to pro-integrative agencies that served areas in which blacks were under-represented.

In July 1989, a black tenant who was denied assistance from the Rental Connection filed a discrimination complaint against FOSS with the Ohio Civil Rights Commission (OCRC). This complaint was settled through conciliation, but it reopened the debate over the pro-integrative housing marketing policies that had been used in Shaker Heights for three decades. FOSS continued its race-conscious rental referral service (on a seasonal basis) but agreed to show its rental list to blacks as well as to whites, while also referring black prospects to fair housing agencies that concentrated on integrating predominantly white areas.

In the face of criticism of the Shaker Heights pro-integrative policy (most notably from black realtists), DeMarco stated: "We are an integration service, not a housing service. We are not an exclusive agent for any [property]. People are able and regularly do find housing which results in further resegregation. But, we would not think of using taxpayer dollars to help people pursue segregative options" (*Cleveland Plain Dealer*, August 27, 1989).

The majority of the black and white residents of Shaker Heights have consistently supported the pro-integrative housing policies enunciated by DeMarco. These policies have never occasioned political controversy in municipal elections. Surveys of new homebuyers, a majority of whom used the services of the Shaker Heights Housing Office, have indicated overwhelming support for the city's policies (Keating, Pammer, and Smith, 1987). Nevertheless, the legality of Shaker Heights's race-conscious housing policies continues to be questioned.

The Cuyahoga Plan Controversy

The Cuyahoga Plan crisis of 1992 was occasioned by a black home seeker, who claimed that she was denied assistance by the Shaker Heights Department of Community Services in October 1991. She sought apartment listings but, because she was black and to prevent resegregation, was not given all available listings. She filed a complaint with the Cuyahoga Plan's discrimination complaint service, which found probable cause; this resulted in the filing of a complaint with HUD in November 1991.

The HUD complaint led to the March 1992 firing of the director of the Cuyahoga Plan's discrimination complaint service and to the layoff of the service's entire staff in April 1992 following a protest. In May 1992, the complainant, represented by the black former president of the Cleveland City Council, sued Shaker Heights (Drexler, 1992). The case was settled out of court without any major change in the city's housing policies (Hoke, 1992d).

Racial Controversies

Despite Shaker Heights's success in maintaining stable racial diversity for more than three decades, racial tension and racially related controversies are not unknown in the city today. These can always threaten the confidence, nurtured over more than three decades, in continued racial diversity and neighborhood stabilization (Whelan, 1985).

The Shaker Heights public schools have always been one of the city's strongest assets. However, in the face of a declining school-age population, the board of education was forced to close several schools. This generated considerable controversy during the period from 1984 to 1987, when school reorganization was debated. Those most vocal about the changes expressed concern about the need for neighborhood-based schools and the racial balance in these schools. In 1989–1990, the racial balance of the Shaker Heights public schools was 50 percent white and 46 percent black in elementary schools and 47 percent white and 51 percent black in secondary schools (the enrollment of black students from the city of Cleveland in some Shaker Heights schools skews the percentages for blacks upward).

Another emotional controversy arose from a claim by some elected black officials in the city of Cleveland, most notably the powerful president of the city council, George Forbes, that traffic barricades Shaker Heights had erected in the 1980s to prevent traffic congestion in residential neighborhoods bordering Cleveland's Lee–Harvard neighborhood were intended as racial barriers to deter black migration into the suburb. Shaker Heights denied this charge and claimed that the black residents of the protected neighborhoods supported the traffic diversion. Cleveland sued Shaker Heights to force removal of these barricades, but the Ohio Supreme Court ruled in favor of Shaker Heights (*City of Cleveland v. City of Shaker Heights*, 30 Ohio St. 3d 49 [1987]). Nevertheless, critics kept the controversy alive. In 1990 they erected a large banner over a main street leading into Shaker Heights, proclaiming that Shaker Heights was pro-apartheid.

In the same vein, opponents of a commercial renewal project (Shaker Town Centre) in an area near the city of Cleveland claimed that a covert goal was to eliminate small black businesses, a charge denied by the city of Shaker Heights. In a 1989 referendum, Shaker Heights voters overwhelmingly approved the renewal project and rejected amendments proposed by its opponents.

Although the claims of covert racism by black critics of Shaker Heights have not gained much credence, the negative publicity associated with these controversies was not welcome in a community trying to maintain its image as a stable and attractive racially diverse suburb. Maintaining a positive image is especially important in attracting those people whom the city hopes to have as future residents, both black and white prospects and especially middle- and upper-income homeowners. Yet some uneasiness among black residents remains about the city in effect rewarding white homebuyers who would be willing to live in racially integrated neighborhoods (Wilkerson, 1991).

Profile of Shaker Heights

In 1990 the black population of Shaker Heights was 30 percent of a total population of just over thirty thousand. This compared to 24 percent of the total population in 1980, with the black proportional population continuing to increase but at a rate of 0.5 percent annually during the decade spanning 1980 to 1990. This annual rate is about half of the annual rate of increase during the decade spanning 1970 to 1980.

The black population continues to be concentrated in the Lomond, Ludlow, and Moreland neighborhoods (Table 9 and Map 2), where the least expensive housing in Shaker Heights is to be found (Wilkerson, 1991). In contrast, there is much less of a black presence in those Shaker Heights neighborhoods with the highest incomes and housing prices (Wilkerson, 1991). In 1980 the mean income for households in Cuyahoga County was $21,387. In two of Shaker Heights's seven census tracts, the mean household incomes were $84,444 and $69,215, respectively, and the black proportion of the population was 3 and 4 percent, respectively. In contrast, in the two census tracts with the highest proportion of blacks (69 percent in each), the mean incomes were the lowest and second lowest in the city— $24,068 and $32,475, respectively. In 1990, the mean household income in Shaker Heights was $80,153. However, the mean white household income ($95,373) was more than double the mean black household income ($44,184).

The spatial distribution of the black population in Shaker Heights has remained uneven, reflecting income differentials and

Table 9. Black Population in Three Shaker Heights Neighborhoods, 1980, 1990

	1980 (%)	1990 (%)
Lomond		
Census Tract 1836.01	69	–
Census Tract 1836.04	–	68
Ludlow		
Census Tract 1834	40	–
Census Tract 1834.02	–	77
Moreland		
Census Tract 1836.01	69	–
Census Tract 1836.03	–	95

Source: Northern Ohio Data and Information Service, College of Urban Affairs, Cleveland State University; Cuyahoga Plan

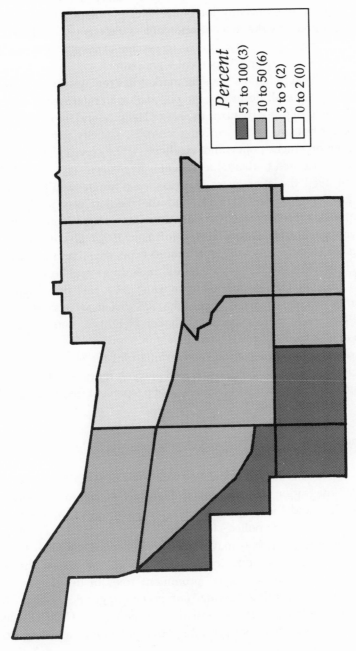

Map 2. Black Population of Shaker Heights, Ohio, by 1990 Census Tracts

Percent

■ 51 to 100 (3)
▨ 10 to 50 (6)
▢ 3 to 9 (2)
□ 0 to 2 (0)

price disparities in the housing market. Black entry into Shaker Heights and the concentration of the black population are facilitated and reinforced by the concentration of less-expensive rental housing in certain parts of the city. In 1990, 65 percent of the city's households were homeowners and 35 percent were renters.

The Shaker Heights housing market has remained strong in the face of the overall decline of the population in metropolitan Cleveland, the high property taxes in Shaker Heights, and the competition of newer housing in the outlying suburbs. The city's strict housing code enforcement policy and excellent public services and schools have contributed to this achievement.

In 1989 the average sales price for a single-family home in Shaker Heights was $179,581 and the median was $140,000. In comparison, the 1989 median sales price for a single-family home in Cuyahoga County was $79,000 (Hoffman, 1990). Shaker Heights's housing stock is generally much more expensive than that of most other suburbs in Cuyahoga County, including neighboring Cleveland Heights. However, housing in some other east-side Cuyahoga County suburbs, such as Pepper Pike ($253,500 median sales price in 1989), is even more expensive. Shaker Heights's owner-occupied housing stock has appreciated in value. During 1984 to 1989, the overall rate of appreciation (above inflation) for Shaker Heights's single-family housing stock was 19.8 percent, more than three times higher than the countywide average of 5.6 percent (Hoffman, 1990).

Conclusion

Shaker Heights is one of the few examples of sustained suburban racial integration in the United States. The city, the board of education, and the civic leadership have strongly supported pro-integrative housing policies for more than a quarter-century. Shaker Heights officials such as mayors Walter Kelley and Stephen Alfred, community services director Don DeMarco, and ESCOC director Winston Richie have played prominent roles in developing and financially supporting regional fair housing agencies such as the Cuyahoga Plan and ESCOC and in persuading the Ohio Housing Finance Agency to adopt pro-integrative policies for assisting first-time homebuyers. Shaker Heights has adopted innovative policies, such as pro-integrative mortgage programs, voluntary school busing, magnet schools, and redistricting, to prevent resegregation. In these efforts it has received continuing support from civic and foundation leaders prominent in Cleveland, especially the Cleveland Foundation's current director, Steve Minter, a resident of Shaker Heights, and the George Gund Foundation's present and former executive directors, David Bergholz and James Lipscomb, who also chose Shaker Heights as their home.

Shaker Heights's greatest success has been maintaining racial diversity in those neighborhoods that otherwise most likely would have completely resegregated (e.g., Ludlow, Lomond, and Sussex). Its greatest problems have been its inability to prevent the apparent resegregation of the Moreland neighborhood and the recurrent controversy over the city's race-conscious policy of concentrating its efforts and financial assistance primarily on attracting whites to the city. Finally, as in most American communities, there has not been economic integration in a majority of Shaker Heights neighborhoods, a reflection of its origin as an upper-class suburb; and three neighborhoods—Fernway, Malvern, and Mercer—have a very small (about 5 percent) black population.

7

Cleveland Heights: The Struggle for Long-term Stable Racial Diversity

Cleveland Heights is one of the oldest of Cleveland's suburbs. Originally part of East Cleveland, it first became an independent village in 1902 and then a city in 1922. Cleveland Heights's greatest growth took place in the 1920s, when its population more than tripled from 15,396 in 1920 to 50,945 in 1930 (Harris and Robinson, 1963). Once the city was mostly developed, its population remained stable, peaking at 59,988 in 1950. Since then, its population declined gradually to 54,052 in 1990, little more than it had been six decades earlier.

Cleveland Heights has been primarily a residential suburb. Its housing stock is varied, from large mansions to modest homes, with a variety of rental housing. Located on the eastern border of Cleveland and adjacent to University Circle (which features Case Western Reserve University, hospitals, and museums and cultural institutions such as the Cleveland Orchestra), it has proven to be a popular home for many Cleveland commuters. Many of its employed residents work in the professions, music, and the arts.

The city has provided excellent public services, including schools, libraries, and parks. It has also developed cultural attractions, such as the outdoor summer theater and arts activities in Cain Park (named after Cleveland Heights's longtime mayor Frank Cain [1914–1946]). The major commercial area is Severance Center, the first major suburban enclosed shopping mall in greater Cleveland, which opened in 1963.

Cleveland Heights Prior to Racial Transition

In its early development phase as a twentieth-century suburb, many residential developments in Cleveland Heights were subject to restrictive covenants, which barred blacks and other minorities. The racial transition of Cleveland Heights began in the 1960s and escalated in the early 1970s. In the early 1960s, Cleveland Heights had a negligible black population (less than 1 percent in 1960). The city was then still a traditional suburb, almost entirely white and predominantly Protestant and Republican.

Cleveland Heights became a major focus of the Jewish exodus from Cleveland neighborhoods, especially the Glenville and Hough districts, in the 1950s. By 1961, 35 percent of the Jewish population of Cuyahoga County lived in Cleveland Heights, doubling the percentage of the late 1930s. By the 1960s, many Jewish institutions (e.g., temples and synagogues, the Jewish Community Center, the Hebrew Academy, and the College of Jewish Studies) were concentrated in the Taylor Road area of Cleveland Heights (Vincent and Rubinstein, 1975).

The Beginning of Racial Transition and the Initial Response

The black influx into Cleveland Heights began in the early 1960s, particularly in those neighborhoods in the northeastern part of the city that borders the city of East Cleveland. The black in-migration showed in the public schools as much as in residential neighborhoods. For example, black enrollment in the Millikin School, located in an entry area for black newcomers, reached 17 percent in 1971, more than doubled to 36 percent in 1972, and reached 43 percent in 1974 (according to the Cleveland Heights–University Heights School District's *1968–1974 Minority School Enrollment* report).

As the rapid racial transition occurring in adjacent East Cleveland became known through word of mouth, some Cleveland

Heights residents became concerned. Then residents were shocked in October 1965 when the home of the director of Karamu House, Cleveland's black theater and arts center, was firebombed. The city council reacted by issuing a proclamation denouncing the incident, and the Heights Citizens for Human Rights (HCHR) staged a candle-light protest march.

The HCHR was an interracial (but mostly white) citywide citizens group, which formed in 1964 to support civil rights and racial integration and to prevent resegregation in Cleveland Heights. Its membership included many who became prominent in fair housing and civil rights affairs in the city. For example, its first president was Barbara Roderick, who later became head of the city's real estate program; and HCHR activists Phil Hart and Ken Montlack served on the city council.

HCHR members also became active in Cleveland civic and political affairs. Many Cleveland Heights residents concerned about racial discrimination first became involved in protests by demon-strating against racial segregation in the city of Cleveland's public schools (these protests that had resulted in the tragic death of the Reverend Bruce Klunder in 1964). Some became active in the unsuccessful 1965 mayoral campaign of liberal Democratic state representative Carl Stokes and again in his successful 1967 cam-paign, which made him the first black mayor of a major American city. HCHR organized house meetings, interracial social events called "soirees," and block clubs to persuade whites to welcome blacks and encourage them to move into Cleveland Heights. It distributed a list of minority services and urged its members to "buy black," that is, to purchase goods and services from blacks. Its real estate committee escorted prospective black homebuyers, urged sellers to show their homes to minority homebuyers, and lobbied lenders not to discrimi-nate racially.

The first major conflict with the real estate industry in Cleve-land Heights occurred in 1967. That year the city became aware of heavy solicitation of homeowners by real estate brokers in certain areas east of Taylor Road. In contrast to the city of East Cleve-land's belated response to the appearance of blockbusting tech-niques, the city of Cleveland Heights passed an emergency ordi-nance banning "for sale" signs. The legality of this approach was strengthened by the passage of the federal Fair Housing Act in the spring of 1968.

The end of the 1960s was a time of change in Cleveland Heights. In 1969 the city saw the creation of the Heights Area Project by Jewish organizations, community organizing in Coventry Village (the focal point of Cleveland's "counterculture"), and the first attempt by liberal Democrats to gain control of the Cleveland Heights City Council. The Democratic slate, representing "Citizens for Effective Heights Government," lost, although one of the party's candidates, lawyer Arthur Brooks (later a state representative), lost only by the narrowest of margins. In 1970 the St. Ann's Social Concerns Committee began to investigate racial discrimination in housing in Cleveland Heights; at that time, only 2 percent of the city's population was black.

The St. Ann's Housing Audit

St. Ann's Catholic Church, located in the Roxboro district, was founded in 1915 (Bellamy, 1990). Like all Roman Catholic parishes, it was affected by the changes in the late 1960s emanating from the reforms of the Second Vatican Council (Powers, 1980). For this parish, these changes eventually led to the formation in 1970 of the St. Ann's Social Concerns Committee, headed by Tom Reim.

Five female members of the committee—Sue Nigro, Lana Cowell, Jeanne Martin, Linda Johnston, and Nancy Capelletti—became interested in housing as a social issue after undergoing training in 1970 at the Commission on Catholic Community Action. They decided to investigate racial discrimination in housing, steering, and blockbusting. After contacting Operation Equality, a foundation-funded fair housing agency that assisted blacks seeking housing and investigated complaints of racial discrimination in housing, and learning about housing audits conducted to document racial discrimination in housing, the committee decided to do an audit of major real estate firms that operated in Cleveland's eastern suburbs, including Cleveland Heights. This audit involved the use of "checkers" (black and white volunteers posing as prospective homebuyers and renters for housing that had been advertised for sale and rental) to detect racially discriminatory practices.

The results of the committee's audit were released in September 1972. It found discrimination in the practices of ten prominent suburban realty firms. After presenting their data to the realty firms that had been studied, the committee members met with the city manager and city council of Cleveland Heights, as well as the Cleveland Area Board of Realtors.

The Cleveland Heights city government was very concerned about the impact on the city's image of the study and the attendant publicity. That spring there had been a bombing of a black family's house in the Oxford district, and the city had passed a temporary six-month ban on telephone solicitation of homeowners by realtors (to be enforced voluntarily). Also, Mayor Oliver Schroeder had convened a meeting of eastern suburban mayors to discuss the problems of racial segregation and blockbusting (with no immediate results). In the face of denials of racial discrimination by leading realty firms and with a reluctance by the city council to regulate the real estate industry, fair housing activists pressured the city government to act. Community activists acted independently of the city and began to organize in neighborhoods to prevent white flight and resegregation from occurring in Cleveland Heights. The city also undertook efforts to encourage the organization of block clubs and neighborhood organizations.

The Heights Area Project

The Heights Area Project (HAP) was initiated by the Jewish Community Federation (JCF) in 1969. It grew out of a concern that black in-migration to the Taylor Road area might trigger an exodus of Jewish residents and institutions from Cleveland Heights similar to the previous movement out of Cleveland's Glenville neighborhood, which had resulted in a concentration of these same residents and institutions in Cleveland Heights. The cost of relocating these institutions was estimated to be $100 million. The Temple on the Heights (which had originally moved to Cleveland Heights in 1922) had already announced that it was relocating further east (Vincent and Rubinstein, 1975: 20); it moved to Pepper Pike in 1980. A major concern was the possible relocation of the Jewish Community Center; if this institution had left, it would have been a major blow to the efforts of the HAP. Instead, the community center stayed in Cleveland Heights, even though a second Jewish Community Center was built in Beachwood in 1986. The other Jewish institutions declared their intention to remain and most have done so.

To stabilize the area, the JCF hired and assigned an organizer—David Sarnat, who had previously worked in the antipoverty program in St. Louis—to the HAP. He recruited Irene Shapiro, whose first task was to revive a dormant homeowners association. They were later joined by Rabbi Marvin Spiegelman, HAP's first full-time staffer. The HAP organized block clubs and involved key religious leaders in their efforts.

The HAP represented a combination of political ideology (fair housing), religious sentiment (Jewish support for—or toleration of—racial diversity), and pragmatism (Jewish institutional concern about the cost of relocation and Jewish homeowners' concerns about protection of their property values). It initially focused its efforts on the Taylor Road area of Cleveland Heights, where the Orthodox Jewish community is concentrated. A significant innovation by the organization was the creation of a program of mortgage incentives to Jewish homebuyers who would be willing to buy in Cleveland Heights and neighboring communities like Shaker Heights and University Heights. Since the program's inception, more than four hundred such loans have been made. This was similar to the mortgage incentive program developed earlier in Shaker Heights for pro-integrative home purchases by whites in racially transitional neighborhoods like Ludlow and Lomond.

The HAP succeeded in preventing any major and immediate movement of the Jewish population out of Cleveland Heights. In 1970, 65 percent of greater Cleveland's Jewish population was concentrated in what the JCF designated as the "Core I" area, comprised of Cleveland Heights, Shaker Heights, South Euclid, and University Heights. By 1980 this number had declined, but only to 54 percent, with most of the population that had been lost apparently moving to the neighboring "Core II" area, composed of Beachwood, Lyndhurst, Mayfield Heights, and Pepper Pike (whose Jewish population increased from 18 to 26 percent of the total during this period) (JCF, 1982: chart 1).

By the time of Sarnat's departure from the HAP in 1976, the project's work was considered successful:

> Panic selling had been avoided, and change was taking place at a viable pace, in contrast to the situation in neighboring East Cleveland, but the reasons, including a recession that slowed down home purchases, were complex. Nevertheless, enough had been accomplished to encourage many homeowners and institutions to remain rooted, it they wished to do so. The Cleveland Heights Project became a model to communities throughout the country eager to retain Jewish neighborhoods in inner-ring suburbs, while avoiding any suggestion of organizing to keep out other groups, particularly blacks, also seeking to enter the neighborhood. (Vincent and Rubinstein, 1975: 22)

Sarnat's other important legacy was his important role in the formation of the Heights Community Congress.

The Heights Community Congress

Critical to pro-integration efforts in Cleveland Heights was the formation of the Heights Community Congress (HCC) in 1972. The HCC grew out of meetings held in the basement of the Carmelite monastery by Catholic and Jewish (and later Protestant) leaders concerned about problems of discrimination and racial transition. The Heights Interfaith Council was formed to promote interdenominational social action, including support for pro-integrative policies. The findings of the St. Ann's housing audit spurred them to form a community organization to deal with these issues. Participants included David Sarnat of the HAP, Howard Berger of the JCF, Harry Fagan of the Commission on Catholic Community Action, and several other Cleveland Heights clergy.

With its formal creation in January 1973, the HCC replaced the HCHR as the constituent organization supporting racial integration of housing and neighborhoods in Cleveland Heights. Unlike the all-volunteer HCHR, the HCC was to have a paid staff. Its objective was "promoting and maintaining an open and integrated community." To achieve this primary objective, the congress established three related goals: (1) an open, citywide housing market, (2) a high-quality physical environment, and (3) resident involvement in neighborhood and city affairs.

The emphasis of the HCC was community organizing and citizen empowerment (Gray, 1989). It represented a marriage of religious conviction and "liberal" political reform to pursue a civil rights agenda as applied to the neighborhoods and schools of Cleveland Heights. The clergy and liberal Democratic activists were key participants in the organization.

A key structural decision was to form a large organization made up of other organizations. Membership was divided according to classes of organizations: civic organizations and citizen groups, neighborhood organizations, black citizens groups, Jewish organizations, Catholic organizations, Protestant organizations, independent religious groups, youth organizations, city government, school board and library, school-related organizations, and business organizations. In 1974 womens' rights organizations were added as a class. Thus each Cleveland Heights neighborhood, represented through its own association, had a voice through the HCC representative of neighborhood organizations.

The congress also formed fourteen task forces. Key task forces related to racial transition in housing were those dealing with housing and open housing (chaired by Sue Nigro of the St. Ann's audit group), real estate practices, lending institutions, rental practices, and code enforcement. Other task forces were concerned with such issues as education, community relations, and public safety.

After receiving an initial one-year grant of $48,500 from the Cleveland Foundation, the HCC hired Harry Fagan as its director in November 1973. He assembled a staff, which numbered six by 1974. The organization's first president was the Reverend Charles Mayer of Hope Lutheran Church. The representative of black citizens was Bernice Lott, a leader of the black Committee to Improve Community Relations, who later became president of the school board and who gave her strong support to the goals of the HCC. The congress was governed by a board of trustees, consisting of representatives of each class. Annual meetings were to determine the HCC's overall policy and to energize its member groups and supporters.

The HCC set about its work with energy and enthusiasm. The Open Housing Task Force conducted a housing audit in the summer of 1973. The audit confirmed the findings of the 1972 St. Ann's housing audit, that racial steering continued. The task force recommended the creation of a housing office, to be operated by the HCC, in order to promote Cleveland Heights and thus attract prospective residents. While similar in concept to the housing office operated by the neighboring city of Shaker Heights, the HCC Housing Service rejected the Shaker Heights Housing Office policy of using its escort service to promote only those neighborhoods with a significant black population and only to white prospects. Instead, the policy of the HCC Housing Service and its volunteer escorts would be to promote the entire city and all of its neighborhoods to all prospective home purchasers and renters, white and black. The housing service was to be the focal point of publicizing Cleveland Heights as a racially integrated community.

The housing service began operation in June 1974, with Sue Nigro as its director and a staff of five. It was funded by the city but operated independently out of the HCC office, a very unusual arrangement for Cleveland Heights. The semi-autonomous status of the housing service reflected some tension between the HCC and the city government: despite the financial support, some in the HCC did not fully trust the extent of the city's support for its activities, particularly community organizing and real estate audits, which might result in serious controversies and publicity that could reflect negatively on Cleveland Heights. The HCC wanted to retain its independence to the fullest extent possible. In turn, some city officials believed that the congress's leadership was too politically liberal and that the organization might operate beyond the city's control.

As it turned out, however, the city government and HCC Housing Service worked cooperatively. In Shaker Heights, the neighborhood organizations that had initiated pro-integrative programs asked the city of Shaker Heights assume responsibility for operation of their programs. In Cleveland Heights, the HCC and the city eventually worked out an effective partnership arrangement.

The HCC's Real Estate Practices Task Force monitored real estate advertisements and surveyed new homebuyers about their experience with realtors and lenders. This information was then reported to the Cleveland Heights Real Estate Advisory Committee (REAC).

The REAC had been formed in early 1973 to monitor the antisolicitation ordinance and consisted of three representatives each from the city government, the Cleveland Area Board of Realtors (CABOR), and the Cleveland Area Real Estate Board (CAREB), an organization of black realtists. Due to resistance by black realty firms to voluntary compliance, it had been necessary to pass a city ordinance regulating solicitation in order to ensure compliance with fair housing laws. In response, an unsuccessful lawsuit was filed by a black realty firm, challenging the city's regulation of realtors.

The city of Cleveland Heights initiated a preferred realtor program in 1976. If realtors were found to have engaged in such practices as racial steering, the REAC could then investigate and recommend action against them. In 1974 the HCC sued the Rosenblatt realty firm to enjoin its racial steering practices. The case was eventually settled and the HCC was awarded a judgment of $15,000. In turn, realtors sued both the city and the HCC, alleging that the housing service constituted an illegal real estate operation. However, their suit was unsuccessful.

Housing Code Enforcement and FHC Housing

In order to prove wrong the myth that racial integration leads to a decline in the quality and value of housing, Cleveland Heights has actively worked to maintain housing quality. The HCC Code Enforcement Task Force also has worked on improving housing code compliance, to assist in demonstrating that the quality of housing need not decline because of racial transition.

To assist homeowners who are unable to obtain conventional financing for home repairs and improvements, the Forest Hill Church (FHC) Housing Corporation was organized in 1971 to provide long-term, low-interest financing. The organization was created as a result of this Presbyterian church's credo supporting social action, including support for racial integration. The FHC Housing Corporation's first and only director, Diana Woodbridge, a Shaker Heights High School graduate, had encountered racial steering when seeking a home in Cleveland Heights in 1963.

With the support of the church, this nonprofit community development corporation began a home repair loan program. A challenge fund to provide favorable financing has been supported by businesses, religious institutions, and philanthropic foundations. A primary aim of the fund, when formed, was to show that property values would not decline because of racial transition.

FHC Housing Corporation coordinates its efforts with the Cleveland Heights Office of Housing Preservation. During its first twenty-one years, the corporation provided $3.5 million in home repair assistance, making 432 loans with only thirteen defaults (FHC Housing Corporation, 1992). It also provides housing counseling and operates home repair training and "tool loan" programs.

Changes in Municipal Fair Housing Policy

The same year that saw the creation of the HCC (1973) also saw the election of liberal Democrat Jack Boyle as mayor of Cleveland Heights. In 1971, Boyle had been the first Democrat ever elected to the city council. Boyle was much more supportive of the HCC than some of his colleagues at city hall, although his predecessor, liberal Republican Oliver Schroeder, had worked cooperatively with the HCC. Boyle headed a four-to-three majority on the city council, which had become much more partisan in the early 1970s than previously.

However, Boyle was defeated for reelection in 1975, and Republican Marjorie Wright became mayor. The same year saw renewed tension between the HCC and the new administration over the location of the housing service. Wright, her political allies, and then city manager Layman wanted the housing service moved into city hall, where it would be subject to more direct oversight by the city manager. The HCC resisted this, preferring to maintain its independence, including the right to criticize city policies. The transfer occurred nonetheless in 1976 under a new city manager, Robert Edwards, when the housing service became part of the city's community relations department. Sue Nigro did not continue as its director, but eight HCC Housing Service staffers transferred to the city. Former HCC staffer Susanna Niermann supervised the service's operation. The new overall supervisor of the program was Barbara Roderick, the city's former housing coordinator, who had assumed direction of the city's Community Development Block Grant (CDBG) program after its creation by the federal government in 1974. She later became commissioner of the city's real estate programs.

The basic operation of the housing service was not affected by its shift to city hall, despite the misgivings of some in the HCC. During the start-up and transitional period (1974–1977), approximately 90 percent of the prospects served by the city-managed Heights Housing Service were white (City of Cleveland Heights, 1978), continuing the service's efforts to prevent resegregation.

A potentially more serious conflict than control of the housing service was the HCC's position that the city should adopt a comprehensive fair housing policy, based on the HCC's research on real estate and lending practices that violated fair housing law. Real estate interests were still resistant, objecting to the underlying premise for such a policy, that is, violations of fair housing laws by realtors. Nevertheless, in March 1976 the city council unanimously adopted a nine-point plan, introduced by Council member Oliver Schroeder, "to promote the city as a well-maintained, full service residential community and to prevent racial segregation." The plan was introduced only after behind-the-scenes negotiations between city hall and the HCC. The HCC had threatened continued public attacks on the practices of realty firms and lenders.

The key city policies and programs articulated in the nine-point plan included:

- establishment of the preferred real estate agent program to qualify agents based on fair housing compliance;
- continuation of the Heights Housing Service;
- passage of a fair housing law, to be enforced by a housing board that would replace the REAC;
- establishment of a Financial Institution Advisory Committee to review the mortgage lending practices of financial institutions;
- cooperation with the Cuyahoga Plan, which was established in 1974 to promote fair housing for the entire metropolitan Cleveland area; and
- establishment of an Evaluation Committee to monitor the city's progress toward meeting these goals.

With the passage of this legislation, political debate over the city's fair housing policies virtually ended, and a consensus on goals and the implementation structure was reached. The resolution was amended in December 1979 by adding the following language regarding the Heights Housing Service:

> The policy of the Heights Housing Service is to assist in maintaining the rich cultural and racial diversity that Cleveland Heights has now proudly achieved. Since efforts to achieve diversity are nullified by the potential resegregation of neighborhoods within the community, it is essential to continue to attract white homeseekers of all ages, but particularly young families with children who wish to explore the advantages of living in Cleveland Heights. It is equally essential that Cleveland Heights continue its commitment to area-wide open housing to assure that minority prospects be offered opportunities to explore a wide range of locational choices through the efforts of the City in cooperation with County-wide fair housing programs.

With this statement, Cleveland Heights essentially maintained the practice of its housing service while overtly acknowledging that it was primarily seeking young, white homeowners to maintain racial balance. Unlike the policy of the Shaker Heights Housing Office, however, the Heights Housing Service showed black prospects the entire city.

With David Sarnat's departure from the HAP and Harry Fagan's from the HCC, 1976 proved to be a watershed year. Fagan was succeeded as HCC director by former Cleveland State University history professor and HCC staffer Kermit Lind. At about the same time, Ned Edwards, pastor of Forest Hill Presbyterian Church, became the second president of the HCC Board of Trustees.

Lind faced an immediate budget problem, due to the loss of the housing service to the city. In 1977 he succeeded in obtaining alternative CDBG funding from the city. At the suggestion of a volunteer, he also organized the first Heights Heritage Tour, a citywide house tour with special themes designed to promote Cleveland Heights as a residential community and to serve as an HCC fund-raiser. The first tour raised about $5,000. The HCC also conducted a neighborhood phone-a-thon, which raised about

$6,500. Since 1977, the Heights Heritage Tour and the phone-a-thon have raised funds annually for the HCC. In 1991 the tour earned $46,000 and the phone-a-thon, $27,000 (HCC, 1992).

Only a year after he succeeded Fagan, Lind resigned to become director of the Cuyahoga Plan. He was succeeded by Lana Cowell, one of the members of the St. Ann's Social Concerns Committee and an HCC staff member since 1975. She remained director for twelve years, during which the HCC matured into a fixture in Cleveland Heights.

The Hilltop Realty Lawsuit and Its Aftermath

In 1978 the HCC again conducted a major housing audit of real estate firms operating in Cleveland Heights, using checkers to uncover evidence of racial steering and discrimination. This audit was funded by the city and designed by Juliet Saltman, a Kent State University sociologist long involved in fair housing and racial discrimination research.

The audit results led the HCC to its second fair housing lawsuit. In March 1979 it sued Hilltop Realty (later renamed Realty One), one of the largest real estate firms in the region. The HCC suit alleged that the firm and several of its agents engaged in racial steering and violated the city's antisolicitation ordinance. The lawsuit sought damages amounting to $500,000 and agreement to an affirmative marketing program, which would give priority to minority homebuyers by showing them nearby communities with predominantly white populations. The city government of Cleveland Heights joined the lawsuit as a plaintiff.

After a lengthy trial, the federal judge hearing the case arrived at a split decision in November 1983 (*Heights Community Congress v. Hilltop Realty*, 629 F. Supp. 1232 [N.D. Ohio 1983]). He found the agency and some of its agents guilty of violations of the federal Fair Housing Act by engaging in racial steering and in blockbusting through mail solicitation. However, he denied the plaintiffs injunctive relief on the grounds that the agency closed its Cleveland Heights office in 1980 and the accused agents were no longer employed with the firm. Based upon these facts, the judge awarded the plaintiffs nominal damages in the amount of only one dollar and attorney's fees. This ruling was upheld on appeal, with the exception of the finding of blockbusting (*Heights Community Congress v. Hilltop Realty*, 774 F.2d 135 [6th Cir. 1985]).

Although the HCC did not win judicial relief in the form of serious damages and a remedial affirmative marketing program, the decision was a still considered a significant victory by fair housing advocates. Once again the HCC housing audits had led to recognition of fair housing violations by realtors. The city's fair housing policies were, in effect, upheld, and other real estate firms were put on notice of the city's intent to enforce those policies.

In 1980 the HCC and the city of Cleveland Heights found themselves the object of a fair housing lawsuit. William H. Smith, a black attorney and resident, claimed that the city's comprehensive fair housing policies and programs (including the housing service and the preferred realtor program) denied blacks their civil rights (e.g., by steering them away from Cleveland Heights through referrals to the Cuyahoga Plan) and stigmatized them (*Smith v. City of Cleveland Heights*, 760 F.2d 720, *cert. denied*, 474 U.S. 1056 [1986]). A federal district court judge dismissed the case in 1983 because the plaintiff failed to prove any actual personal injury and thus lacked legal "standing" to bring the suit. This dismissal was overruled by the U.S. Court of Appeals for the Sixth Circuit in 1985; however, the plaintiff withdrew from the lawsuit in 1986.

What made this case intriguing was that Smith's legal expenses were paid by the Ohio Association of Realtors, with support from CABOR and the National Association of Realtors. In June 1984 the HCC countersued these three realtor organizations, claiming that the Smith lawsuit was contrived to retaliate against the filing of the lawsuit against Hilltop Realty. Although the HCC was, without support from the city and special fund-raising, financially unable to engage in this type of expensive litigation, it felt that its purpose and future were at stake and therefore filed the countersuit.

When the final rulings in *Smith* and the HCC's countersuit came down in 1986, those realty firms willing to accept the city's fair housing policies cooperated with the city. Smythe–Cramer, one of the region's largest firms, instituted its own internal fair housing training program, as did Realty One. Many realtors from these and other realty firms that accepted the city's policies took fair housing law educational courses from the Cuyahoga Plan.

Schools

The reputation of the public schools and community support for educational excellence are critical to the maintenance of racial integration. If a majority of the white population abandons its public schools due to racial imbalance, then maintaining racial diversity in residential neighborhoods becomes difficult, if not impossible.

At the onset of racial change in the early 1970s, the Cleveland Heights–University Heights school district enjoyed an excellent academic reputation. Its graduates generally went on to attend college, a positive reflection on its college preparatory programs; it regularly had National Merit scholars; and it enjoyed broad community support. In 1970 the voters approved a major program for physical improvements to the school system.

Racial transition brought various changes to the school district, among which was a shrinking school-age population. In 1970 only 4 percent of the student body was black. The district had eleven elementary schools, ten of which were located in Cleveland Heights, and a central high school. With a concentration of new black residents, some elementary schools (e.g., Millikin and Oxford) developed a racial imbalance by the mid-1970s. In 1974 the Committee to Improve Community Relations, led by Bernice Lott, demanded the hiring of more black teachers, mandatory black studies courses, and more recognition of black culture in the curriculum (*Cleveland Plain Dealer*, July 16, 1974). The committee's complaint to the U.S. Justice Department contributed to the increasing hiring of black teachers.

In 1976 the school board appointed a Citizens Committee to Integrate Education to study the reduction of racial "isolation" in the public schools, in accordance with state requirements. At that point, 32 percent of the students enrolled in the elementary schools were minority (mostly black), compared to only 12 percent of the population. The committee's 1977 report recommended among other options, school closings, pupil reassignments, and the creation of magnet schools. In 1979, Millikin Elementary School was closed (and converted to another use) and two magnet schools were created. Despite parent opposition, two other schools (including the only school located in neighboring University Heights) were closed in 1984, reflecting a continued decline in enrollment.

In 1985, a forty-member task force was created by the school district, the HCC, and the Heights Interfaith Council to develop a "schools consensus" on critical issues. The task force's 1987 report identified certain race-related problems in the schools concerning academic assignment (grouping students by level) and performance and discipline (*Sun Press,* July 30, 1987).

In 1987 the Taylor Elementary School, closed in 1984, reopened as Taylor Academy. Its aim was to provide special education for ninth- and tenth-grade potential dropouts. Because most of the new academy's student body was black, some residents, many of them black, opposed it on the ground that this special school constituted a form of racial segregation. Despite these protests, Taylor Academy continued and was deemed a success in a February 1990 report issued by the Heights Commission on Excellence and Equity in Education (*Cleveland Plain Dealer,* May 12, 1991).

The Heights Commission on Excellence and Equity in Education had been established in February 1990 in the wake of parent and student protests against alleged racism at Heights High School. These protests had been followed by the gang shooting death of a young black student in March 1990. The commission's recommendations on curriculum reform led to foundation funding in October 1990 of a program of expanded multicultural education.

Over two decades of racial transition, the public schools have had to deal with serious problems related to racial tension amid integration. In addition, declining enrollment and increased costs have led to budgetary problems, resulting in teachers' strikes and several voter rejections of local school levies. The disproportionate black enrollment (62 percent) in the public schools compared to the city's black population (37 percent) in 1990 reflects the decision of some white parents to enroll their children in private schools, several of which enjoy outstanding academic reputations. This is a long-standing pattern. The public schools have generally maintained a good academic reputation, which has been critical in

attracting new residents with school-age children. However, controversy has continued about the schools' commitment to academic
excellence, centering on the ability grouping of students.

While the city government and the school board both have had
to deal with racial transition, they have not always worked together
and have used different strategies. However, both have supported
pro-integrative marketing efforts.

HCC Continuity and Impact

In its second decade, the HCC continued and expanded its activities
of its first decade. It claimed credit for an important role in the
creation of numerous city-sponsored agencies and programs, including the Landlord–Tenant Commission, the Heights Child Care
Association, and the Community Improvement Awards Program.
The organization initiated a home weatherization and energy con-
servation program and it participated in numerous community
improvement projects, primarily through its member neighborhood
associations. The HCC's contributions to the city were included in
1976 in the city's first All American City Award designation by the
National Municipal League.

On the fair housing front, the HCC continued its housing audits
(Galster, 1990a) and worked with such broader-based organizations
as the Cuyahoga Plan, the County-Wide Financial Institutions Advisory Committee, and the Metropolitan Strategy Group. It worked
with and initially staffed Hillcrest Neighbors. It maintained its
constituent organizational support and in 1982 created individual
memberships. However, as with any community organization, it has
proven difficult to sustain the level of resident participation in the
HCC. In its early years, the organization's annual meetings were
attended by hundreds of citizens. In more recent times, a much
smaller number of representatives of organizations has attended.
Thus the direction of the organization is determined more by its staff
and board of trustees, working with the city, than through widespread citizen participation.

The HCC has maintained funding support, primarily from philanthropic foundations, government grants (including grants from the

city government of Cleveland Heights), and fund-raising activities. From the beginning and especially in its formative years, foundation support has been critical for the HCC: through 1990 the organization received a cumulative total of $976,474 from this source.

In 1989, Lana Cowell left the HCC and was succeeded as its director in May 1990 by Martha Goble, the director of the Shaker Heights/Beachwood Meals-on-Wheels program. In 1991 the HCC had a paid staff of six and revenue of $269,000. Of this budget, only $13,750 came from contracts with the city of Cleveland Heights and only $66,000 from foundations (HCC, 1992).

The HCC has continued its role as a catalyst for community support for the city's policies and as a citywide umbrella group for neighborhood-based organizing. Over its life, it has achieved national recognition as a model community organization and especially as one of the leading affiliates of National Neighbors.

City Government

In promoting itself as a racially integrated suburb, the city of Cleveland Heights has emphasized its racial and religious diversity, its municipal services and facilities, and the quality of the housing stock and the schools. Its services and facilities are considered to be very good, and the voters have continued to support capital improvement bonds to maintain and upgrade them.

Through a combination of housing code enforcement (including mandatory point-of-sales inspections), zoning, and low-interest rehabilitation loans for homeowners and landlords in need of financial assistance (through the Cleveland Heights Housing Preservation Office and the FHC Housing Corporation), the city has generally succeeded in maintaining an attractive housing stock. However, problems associated with an aging housing stock, particularly the lower-priced units, still remain. For example, the city's 1987 citizen survey revealed that 16 percent of the population overall felt that the quality of housing in their neighborhood was a problem (City of Cleveland Heights, 1987).

Compounding these problems is the increase in the poverty rate in the city's population, which reached 11 percent in 1990, compared to 8 percent in 1980 and 5 percent in 1970 (*Cleveland Plain Dealer*, June 28, 1991). If most of these poor people are elderly, the city must devise means to assist elderly homeowners in maintaining their homes adequately. Assistance must also be provided to the nonelderly (e.g., single female-headed households), although college students may account for a significant proportion of this percentage.

Between 1980–1981 and 1989–1990, the median price of a single-family house in Cleveland Heights increased by 30.8 percent (unadjusted for inflation), compared to 34.3 percent for all other Cuyahoga County suburbs (Hoffman, 1990). In 1990 the median sales price for a single-family house in Cleveland Heights was $69,500, compared to the countywide suburban median price of $82,500. In the future, Cleveland Heights, like other older, inner-ring suburbs of Cleveland, must compete with newer, outer-edge suburbs for younger, middle-class residents (Levin College, 1990). With little vacant land for new development, a small commercial and no industrial tax base resulting in higher tax rates for residential property, and an aging housing stock, Cleveland Heights must maintain its reputation as a highly desirable community, especially for homebuyers.

The city's housing service continued its promotional activities, including the escort service for housing prospects. In 1990 it had a paid staff of eight (only one of whom worked full time) and a budget of $135,000, and it served 1,071 renters (83 percent white and 11 percent black) and 362 homebuyers (75 percent white and 23 percent black). Of these, 141 renters and 30 homeowners already lived in Cleveland Heights. Of all the housing service's prospects, 257 renters (90 percent white and 6 percent black), ultimately rented in Cleveland Heights and 120 home purchasers (93 percent white and 6 percent black) bought homes in Cleveland Heights (City of Cleveland Heights, 1990). Thus the preponderance of prospects and actual homebuyers and renters served were white, but the housing service continued to serve blacks as well.

In 1987 the city, in cooperation with the neighboring city of University Heights, established the Heights Fund to provide pro-integrative mortgage incentives, which would supplement the existing incentives offered to first-time homebuyers through the Ohio Housing Finance Agency's set-aside program and to Jewish homebuyers through the HAP. The Heights Fund offered incentives in the form of a maximum $5,000, four-year deferred loan at 5 percent interest and a graduated second mortgage up to $3,600. During its first three years (1988–1990), sixty-three homebuyers (sixty-one whites and two blacks) received these mortgage incentives: forty-five were formerly renters, and twenty-four were Cleveland Heights residents. They bought homes in all Cleveland Heights neighborhoods, as well as in University Heights (Heights Fund, 1991). In 1992 the Heights Fund provided fifteen mortgage incentives (fourteen in Cleveland Heights and one in University Heights), with fourteen going to white homebuyers and one to a black homebuyer (City of Cleveland Heights, 1992).

The city's pro-integrative housing policies have the support of the citizenry. Citizen surveys were conducted by the city government in 1983, 1984, 1986, and 1987. In 1983, when asked whether they agreed that it was essential to continue to attract white home seekers in order to maintain an integrated community, 84 percent of the 530 households who were surveyed agreed. Eighty-three percent agreed that race relations were not a problem, and 78 percent also agreed that the city's changing racial makeup was not a problem (City of Cleveland Heights, 1983).

In the last and most recent citizen survey (1987), 93 percent of the 855 residents who were surveyed thought that it was important for the city to remain integrated, 88 percent agreed with the city's policy of attracting whites, and 54 percent would vote for tax increases or bond issues to finance pro-integrative housing programs (City of Cleveland Heights, 1987). More than three-fourths of the respondents did not consider race relations to be a problem in the city, and about one-half thought that race relations were better in Cleveland Heights than in other suburban Cleveland communities. Most residents were satisfied with their neighborhoods and with the quality of housing. There were variations by neighborhood and race, but they were not significant with respect to the overall pattern.

The Cleveland Heights Housing Service has regularly surveyed new homeowners and has found that overall they have been satisfied with their choice of community. In a 1986 metropolitan Cleveland survey of suburban homebuyers who purchased in 1985, 76 of the 422 who were surveyed had purchased in Cleveland Heights. Of the sample covering seven suburban areas, the white

Cleveland Heights homebuyers (totaling fifty-two) had a high rate of awareness of the city's pro-integrative housing policies and had the highest rates of support for pro-integrative housing among the suburban white homebuyers who were surveyed: for example, 98 percent favored pro-integrative neighborhood efforts, 98 percent were favorable toward blacks living in their neighborhood, and 96 percent were favorable toward blacks living next door to them. When asked their preferred neighborhood racial composition, 44 percent favored an even racial balance (50 percent white, 50 percent black) in their neighborhood (Keating, Pammer, and Smith, 1987).

Profile of Cleveland Heights

In 1980, 25 percent of Cleveland Heights's population was black. This was a tremendous increase from only 2 percent in 1970, but the racial transition was orderly, conforming to the city's stated desire to be a racially diverse and open community. It is possible that more white homeowners might have moved out but were unable to afford another house because of the dramatic rise of mortgage interest rates and housing prices in the late 1970s. By 1990 the city's black population had increased to 37 percent. During the 1980s, the city's overall population decreased by 4 percent and its white population by 21 percent, while the black population increased 42 percent.

Within the city's fifteen census tracts, there is great variation in the racial mix. The highest concentrations of blacks are in those six census tracts where their proportional numbers between 1980 and 1990 reached or exceeded 50 percent (Table 10 and Map 3).

At the other extreme, two census tracts in 1990 had a black population of 10 percent or less: tracts 1414 (10 percent) and 1413 (8 percent). In only two census tracts did the black population in 1990 proportionally approximate the citywide average of 37 percent: tracts 1404 (35 percent) and 1416 (39 percent). The aim of the Heights Fund has been to assist white and black homebuyers interested in buying homes in those neighborhoods where their race is underrepresented.

On the one hand, the rate of growth of the black population slowed in the 1980s compared to the 1970s. Between 1970 and 1980, the black population's average annual increase as part of the city's

Table 10. Black Population in Six Cleveland
Heights Census Tracts, 1980–1990

Census Tract	1980 (%)	1990 (%)
1410	34	74
1403	54	71
1407	43	61
1401	29	60
1409	42	57
1406	38	51

Source: U.S. Census, 1980 and 1990

population was 2.2 percent; between 1980 and 1990, this annual rate of increase fell to 1.2 percent. On the other hand, there was a racial imbalance in several neighborhoods. But there were no signs of white flight in those neighborhoods with the highest concentration of blacks, and there is still at least some white demand for housing in all areas of the city.

The disparity in neighborhood racial compositions can be explained in part by income differentials between whites and blacks and price variations in the housing market. Because whites generally have higher incomes than blacks, they can afford to pay for higher-priced housing, which is clustered in several Cleveland Heights neighborhoods. In 1990, the mean household income in Cleveland Heights was $46,407. Mean white household income was $49,778, compared to $40,370 for black households. During the period from 1981 to 1989, white homebuyers consistently paid more for houses than did black homebuyers: in 1981, for example, the average price paid by white homebuyers was $72,000, compared to $51,500 paid by black homebuyers, and in 1989 the respective figures were $94,900 for white homebuyers (a 32 percent increase) and $62,900 for black homebuyers (a 22 percent increase) in Cleveland Heights (City of Cleveland Heights, 1990).

Conclusion

Without a doubt, Cleveland Heights has taken the most progressive pro-integration position of any Cleveland suburb. This is explained

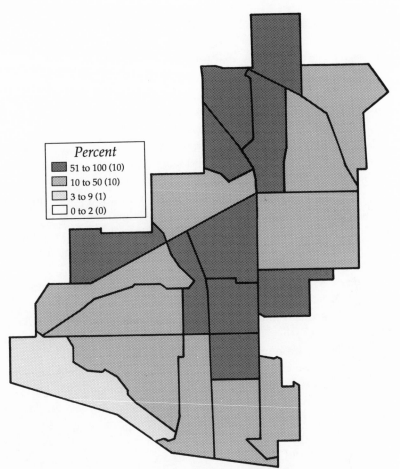

Map 3. Black Population of Cleveland Heights, Ohio, by 1990 Census Tracts

in part by the organization and survival of the HCC (as well as its predecessor, the Heights Citizens for Human Rights [HCHR]) as a major force in civic affairs and politics. The HCC's advocacy of pro-integrative community empowerment and its early efforts in 1970s influenced the city to adopt the nine-point comprehensive fair housing policy in 1976. The programs and goals outlined in that policy became accepted community policies. Since the mid-1970s, the city, in partnership with the HCC, has forged a long, enduring community consensus in which racially integrated housing, neighborhoods, and public schools are accepted and supported by the city's residents. The city and the HCC seem to have achieved the necessary change in how real estate brokers and lenders deal with the city as a racially diverse community.

Despite the absence of a major industrial or commercial tax base and vacant developable land, the city has been able to maintain a high level of services. It has persisted in its efforts to promote pro-integrative housing throughout metropolitan Cleveland, for example, through its financial and staff support for the Cuyahoga Plan, ESCOC, and the Metropolitan Strategy Group. Maintaining racial diversity over a long period of time without a wider housing choice for blacks in a largely segregated regional housing market is difficult. Cleveland Heights, because of its pro-integrative housing policies and other attractions, remains a major magnet for black suburbanization in the eastern suburbs.

Negative publicity resulting from racially focused events can jeopardize a city's ability to maintain interracial community cooperation and harmony and to continue to attract newcomers. Cleveland Heights has weathered many such storms so far. In the 1960s and early 1970s, the firebombings of homes of black residents and a black realty office and attempted real estate blockbusting and steering posed the threat to the city's stability and image. From 1970 through 1992, controversies have included disputes over the racial impact of educational policies in the public schools, especially at the experimental Taylor Academy and Heights High School; racial imbalance in the schools; and school funding, as well as a gang slaying. And through the mid-1980s the city was attacked and even sued by some white and black real estate representatives for its fair housing policies.

Despite racial imbalances in several of its neighborhoods, reorganization of the public schools, and occasional racial incidents and controversies, Cleveland Heights has surmounted many difficulties and successfully adhered to its pro-integrative policies. This is a tribute to the community organizations and organizers who have led the fight over these many years—the HCHR, the HAP, FHC Housing, and the HCC. They have been critical for the city's successful adaptation to racial change and support for racially diverse neighborhoods. Clergy and religious congregations also have played significant roles. In the wake of the racial conflicts in the South Central area of Los Angeles in the spring of 1992, Cleveland Heights churches, the HCC, and city participated in an interracial march to promote racial harmony (Theiss, 1992). The city has been a leader, along with Shaker Heights, in support for fair housing, both within its borders and throughout the metropolitan area.

8

Parma:

Court-ordered Racial Integration

Parma is the city of Cleveland's largest suburb. In 1990 it had a population of 87,876. Its population peaked in 1970 at 100,210. Parma's major growth period was the post–World War II era, when suburban development boomed as the central-city population began its long decline. In 1950, Parma's population was only 28,897. By 1960 it had grown to 82,845, a phenomenal increase of 186 percent, followed by a much more modest increase of 20 percent in the 1960–1970 decade.

The suburb became home to many eastern European nationality groups. Many of these were made up of former Cleveland residents who left their ethnic central-city neighborhoods. Along with the people, several Catholic parish churches relocated from Cleveland to Parma. Parma not only offered the attractions of a well-located, residential suburb with good city services but also had a strong employment base, featuring such industrial opportunities as the Chevrolet plant (Kubasek, 1976).

Parma gained a reputation as a white, ethnic, suburban enclave on the southwestern side of Cleveland. In 1970 there were only forty-one black residents (or only about 0.04 percent of its total population). By 1980, Parma's black population had increased to 364, representing only about 0.40 percent of its total population. In 1990, a decade after a remedial federal housing integration order took effect, the black population had increased by 75 percent over the 1980 census count but was still minuscule, only about 0.75 percent of the total population. In the 1980–1990 decade, Parma gained a net total of 275 black residents. In 1990 the suburb's combined black and Hispanic population comprised only 1.6 percent of the total.

Parma is not alone among southwestern Cuyahoga County suburbs in having this population pattern. Its immediate suburban neighbors in 1990 had similar racial patterns (Table 11). However, in the case of Parma the tiny number of black residents, combined with the statements and actions of high-ranking city officials and complaints of harassment of blacks, led to a federal suit against the suburb for repeated violations of the Fair Housing Act.

The 1973 Federal Lawsuit

In 1973 the U.S. Justice Department sued Parma, alleging that the city had violated the 1968 federal Fair Housing Act. The city's actions that became critical in the lawsuit included:

- the defeat in the city council of a fair housing resolution in 1968, following Martin Luther King, Jr.'s assassination;
- rejection of a proposed subsidized housing project, based on stringent zoning requirements;

Table 11. Racial Population Patterns in Seven West-Side Cleveland Suburbs, 1990

City	Population	White (%)	Black (%)	Hispanic (%)
Broadview Heights	12,219	96.6	1.15	0.75
Brooklyn	11,706	97.25	0.9	2.0
Brookpark	22,865	97.2	1.4	1.6
Middleburg Heights	14,702	97.2	0.7	0.7
North Royalton	23,197	97.7	0.4	0.6
Parma Heights	21,448	98.3	0.7	0.9
Strongsville	35,308	96.6	0.8	0.95

Note: Total racial percentages may not add up to 100 due to rounding.
Source: U.S. Census, 1990

- refusal to accept the racial integration of future subsidized housing as a condition for receiving a Community Development Block Grant (CDBG) from HUD (after this entitlement program was created in 1974).

Statements by city officials were used at the trial to prove the city's discriminatory intent and actions. Most notable was a statement by then city council president Kenneth Kuczma that he did not want Negroes in the city of Parma.

The city's defense rested largely on the theory that its almost exclusively white population was due to migration patterns from the city of Cleveland. The city and its expert claimed that many white ethnic groups migrated from west of the Cuyahoga River in Cleveland's west-side neighborhoods to near western suburbs, thereby recreating the almost entirely white composition of those neighborhoods. In contrast, Parma pointed to the mostly eastern migration patterns of blacks, who left east-side Cleveland neighborhoods to move to suburbs such as East Cleveland, Warrensville Heights, Euclid, Shaker Heights, and Cleveland Heights.

Based on the testimony of the government's experts (including Professor John Kain of Harvard University) which disputed this theory, and on the evidence, Judge Frank J. Battisti (the same judge who had ordered the racial desegregation of the city of Cleveland's public schools in 1977) found Parma guilty of patterns and practices of intentional racial discrimination (*U.S. v. Parma*, 494 F. Supp. 1049 [N.D. Ohio, 1980]) (Cooper, 1988). The judge then issued a detailed remedial order designed to promote residential racial integration in Parma (*U.S. v. Parma*, 504 F. Supp. 913 [N.D. Ohio, 1980]). The order required the city of Parma:

- not to engage in conduct that promotes racial segregation in housing;
- to enact a fair housing resolution;
- to establish a fair housing committee to ensure implementation of the order and to work to develop low-income housing in Parma;
- to develop an educational program to ensure that Parma

officials understand federal fair housing law and to inform
minorities that they are welcome in Parma;

- to apply for CDBG funds from HUD and to use such funding to
  provide equal housing opportunities and cover the city's
  expenses in implementing the remedy to current segregation
  problems;
- to develop new public housing, either through the Cleveland
  Metropolitan Housing Authority (CMHA) or by creation of
  Parma's own housing authority;
- not to use its planning and zoning powers to exclude low- and
  moderate-income rental housing development.

Implementation of the Federal Court Order

The Old Guard: The Petruska Era (1980–1987)

Parma's old guard, led by longtime mayor John Petruska (first
elected in 1967) and some members of city council and the law
department, initially resisted implementation of the remedial order.
The city appealed the order. Battisti had appointed a special master
to oversee implementation. Although the rest of the order was
sustained, the appellate court disallowed the appointment of the
special master (*U.S. v. Parma*, 661 F.2d 562 [6th Cir. 1981]). Instead, a
citizen evaluation committee was appointed to review proposals of
the Parma Fair Housing Committee and to report its views to
Battisti. In addition, Battisti appointed fair housing attorney Avery
Friedman as a "friend of the court" to assist in evaluating progress
in the implementation of the remedial order. Friedman is nationally
known for his successful fair housing litigation and training activities.

With the appointment of a fair housing committee by the city of
Parma in 1983, the implementation of the court order began. Since
then, the city has taken the following steps:

- enacted a fair housing resolution in 1983 and a fair housing
  ordinance in 1988;

- applied for and received CDBG funding from HUD, some of which has been used by the city's community development department to implement the order;
- established its own public housing agency (rather than relying on CHMA) and built the city's first public housing project, as well as using HUD's other subsidized housing programs;
- conducted outreach programs for minority real estate brokers and, beginning in 1988, for potential homebuyers and renters, advertising Parma as an open community.

Perhaps the most unusual aspect of the remedial order was a course on fair housing presented by the director of the Cuyahoga Plan, which city officials were required to attend (Beard, 1984).

Since 1982, Parma has received considerable CDBG funding, which has been instrumental in funding the city's compliance efforts. In 1987, Parma's first public housing project, the sixty-unit Chevybrook Estates, opened. As of November 1991, 94 of its 178 residents were white, 81 were black, and 3 were Hispanic. A second HUD-subsidized rental project for the low-income elderly and handicapped is planned. In addition to public housing, Parma's Public Housing Agency has used HUD's Section 8 Housing Assistance and Housing Voucher programs to attract low-income tenants. A total of 297 persons had been housed in the suburb through the Section 8 Housing Assistance Program as of November 1991, of whom 96 (33 percent) were black and 19 (6 percent) were Hispanic. By the same time, a total of 382 persons had been housed in Parma through the Section 8 Housing Vouchers, of whom 158 (41 percent) were black and 29 (8 percent) were Hispanic. Virtually all of the black and Hispanic recipients of housing assistance certificates and housing vouchers were not previously residents of Parma.

The three federal subsidized housing programs being utilized in 1991 by Parma housed a total of 286 minority residents, who most likely otherwise would not be living in Parma (Table 12).

The pace of the court order's implementation proved to be controversial. The first major disagreement between the Parma Fair Housing Committee and the Parma Evaluation Committee arose over the city's proposed advertising campaign. The Evaluation Committee objected to the content of the city's proposed advertise-

Table 12. Minority Beneficiaries, Parma
Subsidized Housing, 1991

Program	Black Beneficiaries	Hispanic Beneficiaries
Public Housing	81	3
Housing Assistance	96	19
Housing Vouchers	158	29
TOTAL	235	51

Source: Eighty-seventh monthly report of defendant, city of Parma, to U.S. District Court (N.D. Ohio), November 27, 1991

ment and the city's plan to publish it in Cleveland's black newspaper (the *Call and Post*) but not in the city's major newspaper (the *Plain Dealer*) (Cooper, 1988: 75). This controversy was not resolved until 1987, and a professionally prepared advertisement began running in these newspapers (and in the suburban *Sun Press*) only in the spring of 1988. Parma attributed this long delay to Battisti, whereas Friedman publicly blamed the city for not preparing a proper advertisement that sufficiently emphasized fair housing.

In 1985, Friedman submitted a list of suggested actions that he believed would provide for a more active and comprehensive approach to fair housing by the city:

1. a professional marketing campaign to correct the Parma image;
2. meetings with minority groups and others who would be likely to actually convey the message to minority groups in greater Cleveland;
3. development of a housing information office in Parma;
4. enactment of a Parma fair housing ordinance;
5. efforts to make builders and financial institutions more aware of Parma's new policies to encourage those minorities who had previously been discouraged by their encounters with the city;
6. community meetings to educate Parma citizens on the benefits of open housing;
7. development of construction incentives to encourage developers to consider building in Parma; and

8. provision of staff for the Evaluation Committee so that it could make a greater contribution to implementation.

Friedman saw the implementation process from the perspective of a fair housing lawyer who perceived an opportunity for a major change in the housing picture of the greater Cleveland area (Cooper, 1988: 79).

The city's attorneys viewed Friedman's criticism as unwarranted and repeatedly objected to his participation in the implementation process (Gabe, 1985). The antagonism culminated in a statement by Battisti in 1985 that "Parma's repeated, unwarranted and unprofessional attacks on Mr. Friedman before this court are intolerable" (Cooper, 1988: 78–79). But the conflict continued into the spring of 1992, as Friedman continued publicly to criticize Parma for the inadequacy of its efforts and the city's attorneys continued to respond that Friedman's comments were unfounded (O'Malley, 1992).

There was also delay in Parma's application for funding for public housing and in beginning public housing construction, due to the city's choice not to work with CMHA but rather to create its own public housing agency. This choice affected the city's ability to obtain HUD subsidies during a period in which the Reagan administration was trying to eliminate funding altogether for new federally subsidized low- and moderate-income housing. The city's first public housing project was not completed and occupied until December 1987, after public controversy over its location.

In September 1987, as Petruska faced a serious political challenge in his reelection campaign, Battisti publicly criticized the city for moving at a "snail's pace" toward racial integration. He also criticized the U.S. Justice Department under President Ronald Reagan for not pursuing implementation of the remedy to Parma's fair housing problems more vigorously (DeLater, 1987).

A New Mayor: A New Era?

In November 1987 longtime mayor John Petruska was defeated by Michael Ries. The Ries regime, while it relied on the same legal and housing staff that had belonged to the old guard under Petruska, seemed more inclined than its predecessor to proceed affirmatively to comply with the court order.

In June 1988 the city enacted a fair housing ordinance (McBride, 1988). At a November 1988 meeting commemorating Parma's adoption of a fair housing resolution in 1983, Cleveland's black congressman Louis Stokes praised the efforts of Parma's new leadership for trying to erase the city's past racist image (Kahoun, 1989).

Nevertheless, the new ordinance did not indicate that there had been much discernable progress in trying to attract new minority residents to Parma, at least as reflected in the numbers of newly attracted minority residents. The city's efforts, working with the Cuyahoga Plan and minority realtors, had not resulted in significant gains. In 1988, after the initial six months of effort to attract blacks to Parma through outreach programs, only fifty-seven blacks had responded to the city's advertising, of whom only three actually decided to move into Parma (Wilkerson, 1988). In February 1989, Parma decided not to renew its contract with the Cuyahoga Plan for pro-integrative marketing and educational services (Perry, 1989). Instead the city decided to hire its own part-time coordinator, which it did in December 1990.

Obtaining the interest of minority real estate professionals has continued to prove very difficult for Parma (Kahoun, 1989). This reflects the persistence of Parma's past racist image among black residents of Cleveland, some of whom moved into predominantly white west-side Cleveland neighborhoods in the 1980s. Blacks seeking fair housing information from the Cuyahoga Plan who expressed an interest in Parma "are usually fearful for their safety and [that of] their children" (Wilkerson, 1988, quoting a Cuyahoga Plan staff member).

The perceived attitudes of Parma's mostly white residents may affect the decision of minority homebuyers considering Parma. A 1986 survey of homebuyers who purchased in 1985, prior to Parma's 1988 minority outreach advertising campaign, found no blacks among purchasers. In comparison to homebuyers—black and white—in selected eastern suburbs, the Parma homebuyers were more likely to prefer to live in all-white neighborhoods (chosen by 40 percent of those surveyed in Parma) and fewer preferred racial parity in their neighborhood (chosen only by 15.5 percent of those surveyed in Parma) (Keating, Pammer, and Smith, 1987).

The lack of black representation in the city's work force has not helped to overcome Parma's negative image in the eyes of blacks, despite the city's advertising in the *Call and Post*. In 1989 there was only one black in the city's full-time municipal work force of approximately five hundred (Kahoun, 1989). Parma has a residency requirement for city employees, which it relaxed by allowing newly hired employees eighteen months to locate within the suburb. Its residency rule led to a lawsuit filed by the NAACP, claiming that the city's hiring practices discriminate against minorities. In April 1993, Parma hired its first black police recruit, denying that it was a response to the NAACP lawsuit (O'Malley, 1993b).

While the city did sponsor subsidized housing, including the Chevybrook Estates public housing project, it has not yet agreed to institute a pro-integrative mortgage incentive program similar to the East Suburban Council for Open Communities (ESCOC) program established in the Hillcrest area of the eastern suburbs. (The Hillcrest program was proposed by the Innovations Program, which represented the three cities that created the ESCOC, but was not approved by Parma). Presumably, financial incentives such as subsidized second mortgages could attract more black homebuyers. In 1990 the average price of a single-family house in Parma was $80,235, compared to the Cuyahoga County suburban average of $100,979. Parma led the county in sales with 1,010 (about 10 percent of all 1990 single-family homes sales).

In the November 1991 mayoral election, former mayor John Petruska attempted a comeback against his successor, Michael Ries. However, Petruska finished third behind a Republican newcomer in heavily Democratic Parma and Ries won reelection, although he garnered only about 44 percent of the vote. The federal court order and racial integration in the city's housing were not election issues.

Conclusion

What lessons can be learned from Parma a decade after issuance of the federal remedial court order? At least two conflicting conclusions are possible.

On the one hand, it could be argued that Parma has made some measurable progress, which is primarily, if not exclusively, attributable to the court order and its implementation. Parma has enacted a fair housing ordinance, applied for and received federal low-income housing subsidies and used this funding to attract minority tenants, built a public housing project, and conducted a minority outreach program in an effort to attract minority homebuyers and renters. Compared to its surrounding predominantly white suburban neighbors, Parma has affirmatively attempted to attract minority residents. Although this process took many years and the cumulative net increase of minority residents by 1990 was very small, the city of Parma has argued that it has complied with the court order and its intent.

On the other hand, from a critical perspective, not only has progress been extremely slow in the implementation of the court order but Parma has not done enough to overcome its past image. Delays have been occasioned by the city's appeal of the court order, the dispute over the advertising campaign, the formation of the public housing agency, and nonrenewal of the city's contract with the Cuyahoga Plan. In light of Avery Friedman's 1985 recommendations, Parma has done nothing to date to educate its own citizenry about the value of living in racially diverse neighborhoods. The city has neither approved the proposal to establish a privately funded, pro-integrative mortgage incentive program, in order to try to attract more minority homebuyers, nor hired more than a few minority employees.

However positive the city's past compliance efforts may have been, the 1990 census data indicates that the results have been meager. The black population of Parma only increased to 0.75 percent during the decade spanning 1980 to 1990.

Whichever viewpoint is taken, the Parma case underscores the limitations on the ability of courts to impose massive social change on communities. The mere existence of the remedial order and the city's compliance actions cannot necessarily change the attitudes of many white residents of Parma toward racial diversity and the negative image that most minority residents of Cuyahoga County have toward Parma.

Parma certainly pales in comparison to Yonkers, the New York City suburb that provides a more recent example of a federal, court-ordered remedy to correct past violations of fair housing law. In the case of Yonkers, in addition to numerous appeals of the trial judge's decision, the city engaged in protracted resistance to compliance, leading to an unusually harsh enforcement order by the judge, which in turn became a central issue in the city's electoral politics (*JPER*, 1989). Progress toward meeting the requirements of new subsidized housing sited to promote racial diversity remains far behind schedule in Yonkers (Stern, 1991), and public outcry over the outcome of the lawsuit and attempted resistance by at least some city officials has been much more pronounced than in Parma.

Even if Parma had moved much more vigorously in the early 1980s affirmatively to promote racial diversity, it is not clear just how great an increase of interest among blacks to move to the suburb there would have been. Probably more blacks would have chosen to move to Parma sooner if the city had provided financial incentives to homebuyers and increased the city's number of minority employees. Any increases beyond those arising from such measures cannot be determined. In 1990, if 10 percent of all homes sold in Parma had been purchased by minorities, 101 minority households would have been added to the population. (The rate of turnover in rental housing units in Parma is unknown.)

This raises the question left unanswered by the courts: what is the standard for successful implementation of a fair housing judicial remedy affecting a suburban municipality? One possible alternative to a good-faith effort is numerical goals, either for new minority residents or for newly built housing units sited and occupied on an interracial basis. While usually only the decennial U.S. Census can measure the former goal, it is possible for cities to monitor real estate sales and determine the number and ratio of new minority homebuyers. The latter goal can easily be monitored. This then raises the question of whether numerical goals are seen as "goals" or as minimum targets, which some would characterize as racial quotas. Whereas the federal courts have sought to achieve numerical racial balance in public school desegregation orders, this cannot be so easily achieved in housing, where turnover and rental and home purchase decisions are almost entirely private. To rely solely or primarily on subsidized housing to achieve greater racial diversity is to assume two risks: first, an inadequacy of funds; and second, the possible stigmatization of minority occupants of publicly subsidized housing, particularly if they are low-income residents.

Over approximately seven years, the city's use of HUD-subsidized housing programs added only approximately four hundred minority residents to the city's population. While this is no small achievement when one considers that Parma had no subsidized housing at all prior to implementation of the court order, if this standard continues the city's tiny minority population will increase annually only at an infinitesimal rate. The best hope for greatly increased racial diversity in Parma, as in most other suburbs, lies in the private, unsubsidized housing market, which requires the cooperation of realtors, lenders, homesellers, and landlords.

The Parma case, after nineteen years of litigation and continuing implementation of the remedial court order, suggests that it may take another generation for attitudes toward racial integration in housing to change. One small but hopeful sign may have been the appearance by presidential candidate Jesse Jackson at Parma Senior High School in 1988, without racial incident (Kahoun, 1989). Perhaps this indicates a more tolerant attitude among the next generation of Parma's citizens. While more tolerance among the students may not necessarily mean increased racial diversity in the city, it does indicate a positive change in racial attitudes among the city's younger generation.

9

Euclid: A Suburban City
in the Path of White Flight

Incorporated in 1903, Euclid is one of Cleveland's oldest suburbs. It grew from a rural area on the eastern urban fringe of Cleveland to a mixed residential, industrial, and commercial community. Euclid gained renown when its adoption of zoning, in anticipation of future growth, was upheld as constitutional by the U.S. Supreme Court in 1926 (*Euclid v. Ambler*, 272 U.S. 365). Its population in 1990 was 54,875.

Euclid grew rapidly after World War II, as did most of Cleveland's suburbs. Collinwood, a Cleveland neighborhood that borders Euclid, and St. Clair–Superior, another east-side Cleveland lakefront neighborhood, originally had large numbers of Irish, Italian, and Slovenian residents. During World War I, blacks moved into Collinwood near the rail yards. In the 1950s, Collinwood began having racial problems. Such racial conflicts were one of the major reasons that many whites began leaving Collinwood to resettle in Euclid. Homeowners' fears that their property values would decline when the neighborhood was racially mixed fueled the flight.

By the 1960s and 1970s, blacks were moving into formerly all-white areas, mostly in South Collinwood (the pattern of black in-migration is shown in Table 13). The black population of South Collinwood increased between 1960 and 1980 by 6,846 percent. In the decade spanning 1980 to 1990, the black population of North Collin-

Table 13. Black Population in Collinwood Neighborhood (Cleveland), 1960–1990

	1960 (%)	1970 (%)	1980 (%)	1990 (%)
North Collinwood	1.95	2.34	9.10	29.60
South Collinwood	.59	17.77	37.01	40.98

Source: U.S. Census, 1960–1990

wood tripled. The racial divide in Collinwood along the commercial strip of Five Corners is still called the "Mason–Dixon" line.

Racial incidents have continued to occur in Collinwood into this decade. A November 1991 article on the problems faced by black migrants to previously all-white Cleveland neighborhoods featured the experience of a black social worker who moved onto a previously all-white block in South Collinwood. In her complaint to the Cleveland Community Relations Board, she cited the following incidents: a brick thrown through her front window the day after her arrival in the summer of 1990, slashed car tires, a threatened assault on her daughter-in-law at a school bus stop, and racial ephithets against her three grandchildren (Bernstein, 1991).

Some real estate agents played to people's fears of declining property values and blockbusting hastened the departure of whites. Many of the people who left Collinwood to go to Euclid were victims of these unscrupulous tactics and often lost money on the sale of their property. Euclid offered security as a nearby suburb that would maintain its homogeneity and where property values would remain stable.

In 1950, Euclid's population was 41,396, with a black population of only 79. In 1960 the population was 62,998, with an even smaller black population of only 44. In the 1970s, however, blacks began moving into Euclid as the black influx into neighboring Collinwood continued. The blacks moved into formerly white neighborhoods, mostly into apartments along Euclid Avenue. In 1970 the total population of Euclid peaked at 71,552 and the black population had increased, but only to 299 (0.4 percent).

In the 1980s racial conflict continued in Collinwood, reinforcing Euclid residents' concerns about racial transition. The 1980 U.S. census showed that the total population of Euclid had declined by 16 percent to 59,999, while the black population had climbed to 4,548, an 1,800 percent increase.

Euclid's political leaders of the 1970s and 1980s were keenly aware of the fears of their constituents and did not want to bring any undue attention to the increasing black population. Their policy was to maintain public silence about the issue of racial transition as much as possible.

Euclid in 1970 was a virtually all-white, working-class community. The 1970 U.S. census showed that the median income in Euclid was $11,830, whereas the median incomes in Cleveland Heights and Shaker Heights were $13,368 and $19,928, respectively. The 1980 U.S. Census showed that Euclid still had a lower median income than Cleveland Heights and Shaker Heights, with Euclid's at $17,997, Cleveland Heights's at $20,762, and Shaker Heights's at $28,331. The 1980 census data also showed that only 58.23 percent of Euclid's employed population held white-collar jobs, whereas 71.41 percent of Cleveland Heights's employed population and 83.53 percent of Shaker Heights's employed population were white-collar workers.

There are also differences in the median owner-occupied housing values in the three communities (Table 14). The median value of owner-occupied housing in Euclid is lower than the median values of such housing in Cleveland Heights and Shaker Heights. Thus housing has been generally more affordable in Euclid for black homebuyers than in these two more racially mixed suburbs.

Fair Housing in Euclid

Fair housing has not been a priority of Euclid's government. This is in part because many of its white residents had negative experiences

Table 14. Median Values of Owner-occupied
Housing in Three East-Side Suburbs, 1970–1980

	1970	1980
Euclid	$23,450	$52,122
Cleveland Heights	$28,269	$56,119
Shaker Heights	$43,875	$100,603

Source: U.S. Census, 1970 and 1980

with racial transition in their former Cleveland neighborhoods, including a loss of money on the sale of their homes as a result of blockbusting. Fear of a repetition of this experience has influenced Euclid's policies. Politicians used these fears to explain their failure to promote fair housing in Euclid, presumably in an attempt to prevent yet another cycle of white flight (Jordan, 1984).

In 1973, Euclid was found to be racially discriminatory by a federal district court in a lawsuit brought by the Plan of Action for Tomorrow's Housing against five suburbs of Cleveland. All five were found to be racially discriminatory on the basis of low percentage of black residents, the need for low-cost housing, and their refusal to cooperate with the Cuyahoga Metropolitan Housing Authority (CMHA) to provide public housing. The court then instructed these suburbs to negotiate agreements with CHMA for the location of subsidized housing within their boundaries. However, the decision was overturned in 1974 by the U.S. Court of Appeals for the Sixth District (*Mahaley v. CMHA*).

There was some subsidized housing in Euclid at the time of the lawsuit, which had been built as temporary homes for war workers during World War II. Two public housing complexes had been built: Briardale and Euclid Homes. These units were occupied by white, working-class families. In the 1960s, Briardale was considered "blighted" for purposes of urban renewal and was torn down; today it is the site of a golf course. Euclid Homes, transferred from the federal government to the city in 1956, was sold to a private developer in 1978 and rehabilitated and then was converted into owner-occupied housing (O'Donnell, 1992).

The CDBG Complaint to HUD

In February 1977, the Citizens Coalition for Block Grant Compliance filed a complaint with HUD against both the city of Euclid and HUD. The complaint stated that Euclid had failed to "undertake any action affirmatively to promote fair housing." It further charged HUD with violating the Civil Rights Act of 1968 and the Housing and Development Act of 1974 by giving Euclid Community Development Block Grant (CDBG) funding in the face of its refusal to promote fair housing.

In 1978 the citizen's group filed a lawsuit, asking the U.S. district court to stop federal housing funds to Euclid and charging Euclid with maintaining itself as a majority white community. The suit sought to prevent Euclid from spending the $764,000 it had received from HUD.

In the spring of 1978, HUD and Euclid had agreed to a fair housing program that established a discrimination complaint service, promoted housing subsidies for persons working in Euclid, and initiated a marketing program for the then city-owned Euclid Homes. The lawsuit claimed that this program was not adequate. After three years, the case was settled out of court. The agreement that was reached required Euclid and HUD to cooperate with the Citizens Coalition for Block Grant Compliance, which would monitor fair housing practices (Siemon, 1981). However, the coalition soon ceased to exist.

Opposition to a Fair Housing Ordinance

Since the inception of Euclid Community Concerns, a fair housing organization, in 1980, continuing attempts were made by various fair housing groups to pass a fair housing ordinance. However, the administration of Mayor Anthony Guinta and the Euclid City Council could see no purpose in such an ordinance.

Even after the defeat of Guinta in 1987, adoption of a fair housing ordinance was still opposed. The city council questioned the need for such an ordinance when the city had already signed an agreement with the state to assure fair housing.

Fair Housing Organizations

The main organization in Euclid that has been involved in promoting fair housing has been Euclid Community Concerns (ECC). This group has been a positive force in the city, even though it did not receive support from the city until 1993. A spin-off of ECC is the Euclid Black Caucus, which was formed to take a more proactive role in promoting racial equality in Euclid.

Euclid Community Concerns

In 1979 a group of Euclid clergy and other community leaders began to meet informally to discuss problems related to racial transition. Some clergy had previously been sympathetic to the PATH attempt to force Euclid to accept more public housing. A major concern facing the group was the concentration of blacks living in the apartments and duplexes off Euclid Avenue.

The group formed a committee to explore the idea of establishing a fair housing organization in Euclid. This committee produced a constitution for the new organization, Euclid Community Concerns (ECC). The constitution states the goal of ECC as "dedicated to maintain Euclid as a City with stable and attractive neighborhoods with an openness to racial and cultural diversity among its residents, by working with citizens and civic and cultural organizations, including schools and churches for the general benefit of the community."

In 1981, ECC received funding from the Cleveland and George Gund foundations for a three-year period. It then was able to hire a full-time staff member, James Miller, who attempted to promote ECC to the citizens of Euclid. ECC also charged dues and took contributions (totaling approximately $500 per year). The objectives of the group included promoting fair housing in an attempt to mitigate fear and panic selling and promoting intercultural and racial understanding through education and cooperation (Siemon, 1982). As part of the latter objective, for example, ECC started a program in 1983 called the Martin Luther King Poster, Poem and Essay Contest, which was conducted annually in cooperation with the public school system and other community organizations.

Politically, ECC received no support from longtime Euclid Mayor Anthony Guinta. He did not officially recognize the group and would not give them space in the civic center with other nonprofit organizations. When ECC originally approached the philanthropic foundations for money, the Guinta administration told the foundations that such a group was not necessary for Euclid.

Miller left ECC in June 1985 when the funding ended. His "Saul Alinsky style" of organizing around conflict had clashed with ECC's nonconfrontational approach. The Reverend Erv Block became the next head of the group. The early board of ECC had several clergy members, but over time the ministerial leadership has changed and today they are no longer represented on the board. However, Euclid clergy continue to take the lead in promoting racial diversity. For example, in February 1991 the congregation of Euclid's Master's United Methodist Church voted to become racially diverse and hired a black co-pastor. The church, located in southeastern Euclid, is in a racially transitional area where most of the city's black population resides (Holland, 1992).

In 1990–1991, ECC had modest funding of $4,800 and relied on volunteers; the group did not have paid staff. It has a small number of individual members. ECC continues to monitor housing trends in Euclid. The city is still largely racially segregated, and in some areas along Euclid Avenue it has become resegregated. This is due in part to the large number of rental units.

Today the Euclid neighborhood of Indian Hills is becoming integrated. When blacks first started moving in, there was some panic selling and some racial steering. ECC's Ed Dickson, a black homeowner in Indian Hills, heads a neighborhood organization that works at preventing resegregation of the area. The organization distributes newsletters to every Indian Hills homeowner in an effort to prevent panic selling.

ECC has worked quietly to promote racial harmony and integration in a nonconfrontational style. Between 1960 and 1990, the black population of Euclid has increased almost 2,000 percent (from 44 to 8,765).

Euclid Black Caucus

While ECC believes that the quiet, behind-the-scenes method of promoting integration has worked, the Euclid Black Caucus (EBC), an outgrowth of ECC, is more politically active. The EBC is supportive of ECC and its long-standing effort to pass a fair housing ordinance but would also like the city to promote itself to black families.

Meanwhile, most of the black population still lives in rental housing, although, as noted, there are some black homeowners in Indian Hills. The more expensive residential areas along Lake Erie remain mostly white.

The EBC would like to see Euclid promote a more positive image directed toward blacks. It would also like to see pro-integrative policies adopted by Euclid. The caucus worked for passage of the fair housing law, and it has been vocal in its criticism of the minority hiring record of the Euclid public schools.

Schools

The early concerns of ECC regarding the concentration of blacks in the apartments along Euclid Avenue proved to be well founded, and the result of this concentration was seen in Thomas Jefferson School, where in 1980, 80 percent of the students were black. In the 1980s, Euclid was a racially divided city, with distinct white and black sections, and the school board was forced to face the issue of racial balance.

A formula provided by the state has been used to determine whether or not Euclid schools are racially isolated. The state says that schools that are less than 9 percent black or more than 39 percent black are isolated. The 1987 data for the Euclid elementary schools (Table 15) clearly show that all of Euclid's elementary schools were thus racially isolated. According to Euclid School Superintendent James Wilkens, this isolation was the result of de facto segregation or a separation of races caused by housing patterns (McMillian, 1986).

In early 1987 the state intervened and required the Euclid School Board to submit a comprehensive plan to improve racial balance in its elementary schools. The plan consisted of establishing magnet schools, closing schools, and pairing schools so that one school

Table 15. Black Enrollment in Euclid Elementary Schools, 1987

School	Black Students (%)
Thomas Jefferson	84.0
Indian Hills	40.7
Roosevelt	7.5
Upson	2.0
Lincoln	1.4

Source: Euclid School District

would house kindergarten through the third grade and another would house the fourth through the sixth grades. Three elementary schools were closed in Euclid in the 1980s: Indian Hills, Memorial Park, and Noble.

According to 1990 enrollment figures (Table 16), two of the schools—Thomas Jefferson and Glenbrook—would be considered racially isolated under the state formula. When the three elementary schools were closed in the 1980s, the schools were redistricted. The improved racial balance is a result of this redistricting.

Politics

Anthony J. Guinta was the major of Euclid from 1979 to 1987. Prior to becoming major, he was the service director of the city. He was quite a success story. Guinta was a common laborer who worked his way up the ladder and eventually became mayor of Euclid. He was well liked by his constituents because he was similar to many of them—a blue-collar worker. Guinta could relate to those residents of Euclid who had left Cleveland to escape declining housing values and problems associated with racial transition.

In Euclid's general election in 1979, William Mabel, Fourth Ward Councilman, was running for reelection, and Joe Farrell was running for mayor. Mabel and Farrell had been working to help establish a fair housing group (ECC) in the city. The week before the election,

Table 16. Black Enrollment in Euclid Public Schools, 1990

School	Black Students (%)
Thomas Jefferson Magnet	56.2
Upson	36.5
Roosevelt	26.3
Lincoln	13.5
Glenbrook	45.0
Forest Park	37.9
Euclid Central Middle School	35.0
Euclid High School	28.5

Source: Euclid School District

campaign literature was distributed throughout the city linking Farrell and Mabel with slum housing, public housing, and school busing. The literature stated that Guinta wanted to keep Euclid's neighborhoods decent. While Guinta claimed he had no knowledge of the fliers, his campaign manager's name was on the literature. Mabel lost his council seat and Farrell lost his bid for mayor. This effectively ended open support by elected city officials for fair housing until after Guinta's defeat in 1987.

Guinta's administration was never supportive of ECC and claimed that the group was antagonistic toward the city because the city would not provide funding for the group's projects. Guinta thought that the community services department of Euclid was already addressing the concerns that ECC had.

As a former public service director, Guinta focused heavily on providing services to residents of Euclid. But with the loss of businesses and the declining tax base, the city found itself in a financial crisis. It was this crisis that led to Guinta's defeat by David Lynch in 1987. Lynch accused Guinta of cronyism, and he promised to reform government.

Under the Lynch administration, the city has been more cooperative with ECC and now has open communications with the group. While Lynch has been more supportive of fair housing issues than Guinta was, the city did not pass a fair housing ordinance until 1992, following his reelection. There is continued political concern about support of policies that are seen as promoting "affirmative action." This political conservatism reflects the experience of many of Euclid's older residents, who fled Cleveland in the face of racial transition in their former city neighborhoods.

In 1989, Lynch created a community relations department to focus on the problems of discrimination and housing in the city. Chuck Cominsky was named special projects coordinator for the city of Euclid, and his responsibilities include handling issues of fair housing and antisolicitation. In 1989 a fair housing law was introduced in city council, but it was not adopted until June 1992. In November 1992, Euclid adopted a partial ban on real estate "for sale" signs, prohibiting their display on lawns. Although the justification for the regulation was not directly related to blockbusting and white flight, the ban has remained controversial and was only narrowly approved, by a five-to-four city council vote (Heider, 1992a). The Cleveland Area Board of Realtors sued, claiming that the regulation was unconstitutional (Heider, 1992b). The realtors claimed that fear of white flight was behind the regulation (Heider, 1993).

Under Lynch the city has encouraged neighborhood organizations to be watchdogs for illegal real estate practices. Euclid contracted with the Cuyahoga Plan to help train volunteers from ECC to investigate problems of racial steering and blockbusting and to help ECC better educate the public about open housing. In 1993 the city directly funded ECC.

The Lynch administration is pro-business and considers the tax base as the strength of the city. Through increasing the tax base, more services can be provided to the residents and will also add value to the housing stock, thus attracting upper-income, white-collar workers to the city. In 1991, Guinta again entered the mayoral race in an attempt to defeat Lynch, but his comeback attempt was unsuccessful. Fair housing was not an issue in the campaign.

Minority Hiring in Euclid

Due to the fiscal crisis that Lynch inherited from Guinta, the mayor was forced to lay off city employees. In particular, Lynch found that it was cheaper to privatize garbage collection. This resulted in the layoff of twenty-eight city garbage collectors, all but two of whom were black. As of 1991, Euclid employed seven fewer full-time minority workers than when Lynch took office. Only 33 of 243 new employees hired were black. Only 4 percent of the city's employees are minority members, compared to a black population of 16 percent in the city according to the 1990 U.S. Census (Heider, 1991a, 1991b).

The school system also has problems with its minority hiring record. At the start of the 1991–1992 school year, one-third of the students in Euclid schools were from minorities, while only 3.5 percent of the seven hundred full-time school employees were from minorities. In 1980 minority enrollment in the schools was 13.6 percent, compared to 33 percent in 1990. The percentage of minority faculty and administrators in 1980 was 2.2 percent, increasing only to 4.3 percent in 1990. While minority student enrollment increased 143 percent in ten years, minority faculty and administrators increased only 95 percent (Heider, 1991c).

Conclusion

Euclid has experienced a significant racial transition over the past two decades. While the city has refused to promote racial integration, racial transition continues and has led to changes in the public schools and criticism of the hiring policies of the city and the public schools. Like other community-based fair housing organizations, ECC has tried to influence city policy but without much success, at least until the election of Mayor David Lynch and the 1992 enactment of a municipal fair housing ordinance.

With its black population both concentrated in certain areas and rising, Euclid must eventually address racial transition, probably in the near future. The outcome to the city's racial change remains uncertain. If Euclid had responded positively to earlier criticism (e.g., from PATH and the Citizens Coalition for Block Grant Compliance in the 1970s) and had supported the activities of Euclid Community Concerns from its inception, its chances of success in the 1990s would be much better.

10

Six Cleveland Fair Housing Organizations

Fair housing organizations are critical to the promotion and success of pro-integrative housing policies and programs. In the preceding suburban case studies, several community-based organizations were featured, including Euclid Community Concerns, neighborhood-based associations in Shaker Heights, and the Heights Community Congress. All of these organizations continue to exist today.

In this chapter, four important Cleveland fair housing organizations that no longer exist are profiled, as well as two that exist today. Fair Housing, Inc. (an interracial real estate firm), Operation Equality, and Plan of Action for Tomorrow's Housing (PATH)) were all formed in the 1960s to promote interracial housing and greater racial diversity in Cleveland suburbs. At about the time that they lost support and ceased to operate, the Cuyahoga Plan, a countywide fair housing agency, emerged in 1974 to assume at least some of their functions. The Cuyahoga Plan continues to exist, although it has encountered many major crises throughout its existence, the most recent of which, in 1992, threatened its very survival.

The East Suburban Council for Open Communities (ESCOC), formed in 1984 with support from the suburbs, (and school boards) of Cleveland Heights, Shaker Heights, and University Heights and from Hillcrest Neighbors, resumed the challenge of Suburban Citizens for Open Housing (which also expired in the early 1970s) to promote greater racial diversity in six eastern suburbs known as the Hillcrest area. The ESCOC enjoyed only a five-year life (1985–1990), but pro-integrative efforts continue in Hillcrest despite its demise.

Finally, this chapter also includes the Metropolitan Strategy Group, a regional fair housing monitoring, informational, and advocacy group affiliated with the Cuyahoga Plan and national fair housing organizations. The successes and failures of all of these organizations, some of which have died and others of which survive, are chronicled below.

Interracial Housing Trailblazers

Fair Housing, Inc.

In 1963, Stuart Wallace arrived in Cleveland to direct a newly formed nonprofit real estate firm named Fair Housing, Inc. (FHI). Wallace had previously worked with Morris Milgram, a nationally known advocate of interracial housing. FHI was formed by individuals who supported interracial housing and subscribed to stock to capitalize the firm. Its purpose was to find houses for black homebuyers in suburban white neighborhoods and houses for white homebuyers interested in living in racially mixed suburban neighborhoods.

FHI's efforts met with resistance, and it was only with support from the U.S. Department of Justice that the Cleveland Area Board of Realtors (CABOR) finally admitted Wallace as a member after his fifth application. Just as most of his buyers were "pioneers" on the racial frontiers of white suburbia, so too was Wallace as a pro-integrative realtor. Many who worked with him became prominent in efforts to promote racial diversity in Cleveland's east-side suburbs.

FHI ended its operations in 1971, having placed about 350 homebuyers (approximately 200 blacks and 150 whites) in Cleveland's suburbs. Wallace then started his own realty firm and became a fair housing advocate within CABOR. In 1991 he was appointed director of the Cuyahoga Plan, only to resign in 1992 after the controversy over a racial discrimination complaint filed against

Shaker Heights (where Wallace lived), which led to the firing of the Cuyahoga Plan's entire staff.

Operation Equality

Operation Equality was the Cleveland version of a national fair housing program that had been initiated by the National urban League in 1966, with funding from the Ford Foundation. With the help of the Greater Cleveland Associated Foundation (predecessor to the Cleveland Foundation), Cleveland was selected as one of eight sites for this program (Milgram, 1977; Tittle, 1992).

Operation Equality began trying to promote fair housing in 1967. After the enactment of the federal Fair Housing Act in April 1968, the program actively sought to encourage black home seekers to consider housing outside the traditional "Negro" neighborhoods on Cleveland's east side. Joseph Battle, its director, was one of the first blacks to move into the Ludlow neighborhood of Shaker Heights. In 1963 he became the first black member of the previously all-white, segregated CABOR. Much of Operation Equality's efforts went into attempts to persuade real estate firms to comply with federal and state fair housing law.

With assistance from the Cleveland Bar Association's Committee for Law in Urban Affairs, Operation Equality began to encourage clients who experienced racial discrimination in housing to sue. In a major case involving the U.S. Department of Justice, Operation Equality successfully sued the Associated Estates Corporation, a major Cleveland real estate development and management firm. The lawsuit resulted in that firm instituting affirmative marketing policies and hiring a fair housing officer, Susie Rivers (Milgram, 1977). Rivers was later Stuart Wallace's predecessor as director of the Cuyahoga Plan.

With its formation in 1974, the Cuyahoga Plan assumed the functions of Operation Equality, whose foundation support expired in 1973. The program had been a pioneer, along with Fair Housing, Inc., PATH, and Suburban Citizens for Open Housing, in promoting racially mixed housing in the suburbs of metropolitan Cleveland. Its director, Battle, gained national prominence in 1970 when he was elected as the first president of National Neighbors (Milgram, 1977: 140; Saltman, 1990: 321).

PATH: The Failed Attempt at a Regional Fair-Share Plan

Cleveland was one of the first metropolitan areas to try to develop a regional fair-share plan. Attempted in the 1970s (e.g., in Dayton, Ohio) and supported by HUD, such plans were aimed at providing racially integrated, low-income rental housing, including public housing, throughout metropolitan areas, even in those predominantly white suburbs that had no such housing or had excluded federally subsidized low-income housing.

Plan of Action for Tomorrow's Housing (PATH) was the brainchild of the Greater Cleveland Associated Foundation, its director Dolph Norton, and its housing and program advisory committees. Following the issuance in March 1967 of a consultant's report on housing, funded by the foundation, that focused on the need for black access to Cleveland's suburbs and for improved and racially integrated housing in the city of Cleveland, the PATH Association was formed (as were Operation Equality and the Fair Housing Council) to promote the dispersal of subsidized housing in Cleveland and its suburbs (Tittle, 1992). Irving Kriegsfeld was named PATH's first director but then became director of the Cuyahoga Metropolitan Housing Authority (CMHA) in May 1968, at the behest of the administration of Carl Stokes, Cleveland's newly elected and first black mayor.

In addition to unsuccessful attempts to place public housing in Cleveland's white wards, Kriegsfeld sought to persuade the suburbs to sign cooperation agreements with CMHA in order to provide scatter-site low-income housing throughout Cuyahoga County (Krumholz and Forester, 1990). When this attempt failed, the PATH Association sued five suburbs—Euclid, Garfield Heights, Parma, Solon, and Westlake—in March 1971 for their refusal to enter into cooperation agreements with CMHA. The lawsuit went through despite Kriegsfeld's firing in January 1971. In early 1972, PATH filed a second suit, challenging the constitutionality of the requirement for cooperation agreements between CMHA and the suburbs before public housing could be built in suburban municipalities (*Mahaley v. CMHA* [1975]). Both lawsuits were dismissed, ensuring that predominantly white Cleveland suburbs could not be forced to accept public housing (and its minority tenants).

In the face of its unsuccessful efforts to work cooperatively with Cleveland's suburbs, its legal defeats, and its lack of a vocal or influential constituency, the PATH Association was unable to secure further foundation support. Consequently, its life ended in 1974, just as the Cuyahoga Plan was being born.

The Cuyahoga Plan: Countywide Fair Housing

The Cuyahoga Plan's creation was initiated primarily by officials in suburban communities, such as Cleveland Heights and Shaker Heights, that were pursuing pro-integrative policies, including challenging practices of the real estate industry that either violated the federal fair housing law or did not contribute to increased integration. Politicians such as Mayor Oliver Schroeder of Cleveland Heights and Mayor Walter Kelley of Shaker Heights were convinced of the need for broader fair housing efforts, lest their cities became the only major magnets for black suburbanization. The migration of blacks only to magnet suburban cities could eventually lead to the resegregation of those cities, much like what was then occurring in the nearby suburbs of East Cleveland and Warrensville Heights.

Overtures to other suburbs in Cuyahoga County made by Schroeder and Kelley did not meet with a positive response. Nevertheless, the hope of the Cuyahoga Plan founders was that a private, nonprofit, countywide organization could have a regional impact, even if most suburban governments did not choose to join and fund the Cuyahoga Plan.

Obvious omens indicated the tremendous suburban resistance to racial integration in housing that the Cuyahoga Plan would have to overcome. For example, in 1974, PATH became defunct, confirming the powerful opposition to the construction of racially integrated low-income housing throughout the metropolitan area. In 1975 PATH's lawsuit (*Mahaley v. CMHA*), aimed to force the five Cleveland suburbs to accept public housing by challenging the constitutionality of required cooperative agreements between the suburbs and Cleveland's public housing authority, was dismissed. Earlier, in 1973, the U.S. Department of Justice had sued the city of Parma, Cleveland's largest suburb, for alleged patterns and practices that violated the federal fair housing law, a charge which Parma vehemently denied. Suburban Citizens for Open Housing, which had tried to promote racial integration in the east-side suburban Hillcrest communities, also ended its operation in the early 1970s, having made few inroads in convincing blacks to move into these predominantly white suburbs. And in 1973, Operation Equality had ended. Its functions were assumed by the Cuyahoga Plan, which emerged as the primary countywide fair housing organization.

A positive development, however, was the enactment of the Community Development Block Grant (CDBG) program by the U.S. Congress in August 1974. The CDBG program would provide entitlement funding to the city of Cleveland, Cuyahoga County, and several suburban cities (e.g., Cleveland Heights, Euclid, Lakewood, and Parma). Because the CDBG legislation had as one of its goals "the reduction of the isolation of income groups within communities and geographical areas and the promotion of an increase in the diversity and vitality of neighborhoods through the spacial deconcentration of housing opportunities for persons of lower incomes" (U.S. Code Annotated, vol. 42, sec. 5301[c]), it was seen as an important source of public funding for fair housing activities throughout Cuyahoga County.

Organization of the Cuyahoga Plan

Organizational meetings for the Cuyahoga Plan were held in 1972–1973. Key figures in its formation included Harry Fagan of the Heights Community Congress; Barbara Roderick, then housing coordinator for the city of Cleveland Heights; prominant corporate attorney Jim Houston; and Bob Cavano. After a year of planning, the Cuyahoga Plan was launched in 1974. It was one of many regional fair housing organizations that were formed during this period. Others included the Toledo Fair Housing Center (1974); Chicago's Leadership Council for Open Metropolitan Communities (1966); the

Milwaukee Fair Housing Council (1977); and and the Detroit Fair Housing Center (1977) (U.S. Commission on Civil Rights, 1986). The Cuyahoga Plan's first director was Jim Campbell. Financial support was provided by the Cleveland and George Gund foundations in the amount of $134,754 for 1974–1975, with assurances of continuing support in the future. Dolph Norton, director of the Cleveland Foundation, was instrumental in providing this funding for the Cuyahoga Plan.

The organization's stated goals were:

1. to stop and prevent racial discrimination in the rental and sale of housing;
2. to reduce the pattern of racial segregation in housing;
3. to encourage patterns of permanent integration.

To achieve these goals, the Cuyahoga Plan was organized into three separate components:

1. Housing Information Service, which attempts to expand housing choices for renters and homebuyers;
2. Discrimination and Complaint Service, which investigates complaints of housing discrimination and periodically conducts housing audits, using testers;
3. Research and Education, which conducts housing research and training programs to educate public and private actors about fair housing law and policy and patterns of housing discrimination.

In assessing the Cuyahoga Plan's success over its first eighteen years, its performance must be judged by both tangible indicators and intangible indicators. Tangible indicators include complaints about racial discrimination in housing filed and settled; the time required for the resolution of discrimination complaints; information on discrimination in housing generated and used to address the problem; the passage and implementation of fair housing policies by private and public actors; and the reduction of racial isolation and increase in racial diversity by neighborhoods, census tracts, and cities. Intangible factors include greater public awareness of the problem of racial discrimination in housing and increased public support for open housing policies. HUD developed an evaluation methodology for rating fair housing agency performance according to the first category of indicators (HUD, 1985).

While the Cuyahoga Plan has received considerable funding over its life from the two leading local philanthropic foundations (Cleveland and George Gund), it has increasingly had to rely on governmental support. It was informed by the foundations, after its initial funding, that they would not continue to support it at those levels. The Cuyahoga Plan's originators did not want to have to rely on funding from cities within Cuyahoga County because few indicated their interest in the organization and it might be in conflict with many of these suburbs over fair housing issues.

The Cuyahoga Plan's initial contract with local government came in 1977 and was with the city of Shaker Heights. This partnership was expanded eventually into the Metropolitan Open Housing Program (MOHP), under which the Cuyahoga Plan contracted both with individual cities (e.g., Cleveland, Cleveland Heights, Euclid, Lakewood, Parma, and Shaker Heights) and with Cuyahoga County (which then allowed the Cuyahoga Plan to provide assistance to smaller cities, townships, and villages). The MOHP arrangement made the Cuyahoga Plan a partner with these cooperative governmental bodies, which were supportive of investigations of fair housing discrimination. By its tenth year (1984), the Cuyahoga Plan derived the majority of its funding from local governments through the MOHP, amounting to $378,089. The remainder of its funding in 1983–1984 came from real estate education programs ($73,253), special service contracts ($26,723), and grants ($3,125) (Cuyahoga Plan, 1984).

Over the period spanning 1974 to 1990, the cumulative total budget for the Cuyahoga Plan was $6,148,931. Much of the Cuyahoga Plan's funding has been targeted to conduct particular programs. Examples include the Crisis Intervention and Prevention Program, the New Resident Survey Project, and the School/Housing Integration Linkage Project, all funded by the Cleveland and George Gund foundations; and a discrimination complaint hotline, funded by the Greater Cleveland Roundtable.

The Cuyahoga Plan's staff peaked at a total of twenty-four in

1985 (sixteen full-time staff and eight part-time staff). By 1990 its staff had declined to thirteen, only eight of whom worked full time). The Cuyahoga Plan's budget in 1990 was $495,732. However, of this total only $174,987 came from the MOHP; almost as much income came from grants ($162,095). The real estate education program ($77,152), special service contracts ($72,998), and fund-raising ($8,500) accounted for the remainder (Cuyahoga Plan, 1991).

Over its life, the Cuyahoga Plan has had six directors. Each has had to deal with the difficult problems facing an agency addressing a most difficult social issue. The critical problems faced by and the program accomplishments of four of these directors are examined in detail in the sections below.

Kermit Lind (1977–1985)

Kermit Lind took over as the Cuyahoga Plan's second director in April 1977. Lind, a former history teacher at Cleveland State University, had previously been the director of the Heights Community Congress (HCC), a major grass-roots force that supported pro-integrative housing policies in Cleveland Heights. Lind's hiring as Cuyahoga Plan director was opposed by several realtists (black real estate brokers) who were outspoken in their opposition to the integrationist policies espoused by HCC. They feared the negative economic consequences to themselves of an opening of the suburban housing market to blacks, who might be more likely to seek housing through white real estate firms already entrenched in the suburbs if the discriminatory practices of the white firms were ended. However, the protests of the realtists did not succeed in preventing Lind's hiring, and he reinforced the integrationist aims of the Cuyahoga Plan.

Lind's immediate problem was financial, because the support from the philanthropic foundations that had helped to launch the Cuyahoga Plan was being reduced. He turned to the city of Cleveland and to Cuyahoga County for support through CDBG funding, arguing that the Cuyahoga Plan could assist local governments in meeting their fair housing obligations. The Northeast Ohio Areawide coordinating Agency and the director of Cuyahoga County's Community Development Department were supportive, but the city of Cleveland's Community Development Department, under the embattled administration of Mayor Dennis Kucinich (1977–1979), was not cooperative.

From 1978 to 1980, the Cuyahoga Plan received fair housing contracts from Cuyahoga County and from some suburbs (e.g., East Cleveland in 1978; Cleveland Heights, Euclid, and Lakewood in 1979; and Bedford Heights in 1980). In 1981, under Kucinich's successor, Mayor George Voinovich, the city of Cleveland also contracted with the Cuyahoga Plan for fair housing services. Meanwhile, foundation support for the organization continued.

Lind also began to develop the research and educational program in order to monitor the patterns of real estate practices, detail patterns of racial segregation and isolation, hold CDBG recipients accountable for their use of federal funds spent on housing, and provide a basis for arguing for reforms in planning and public policy to promote fair housing. As the program developed, it became possible to market its services for fees, primarily to real estate organizations and local governments, as another way to increase income. In 1984 the research and educational program became the affiliated Center for Open Housing Research and Education, which provided training for real estate firms and boards (both within Ohio and nationally) and for other fair housing organizations and which published fair housing workbooks and audiovisual guides. The center generated $73,253 in income in the year it was formed.

Under Lind, the Cuyahoga Plan matured and established a track record in its major activities. It handled an increasing number of housing discrimination complaints. It used testers to conduct housing audits throughout the county. In Lind's last year (1985), the Cuyahoga Plan received 251 complaints. Of those, it investigated 218 cases and found probable cause in 34. In its investigations it conducted ninety-eight audits, finding probable cause in twelve audits.

The Cuyahoga Plan also greatly expanded its research and education publications under Lind's direction. The research reports of the Cuyahoga Plan became one of its greatest accomplishments. They provided the public, the media, local governments, and housing organizations with critical information about patterns of residential segregation through regular reports on "Population and Race." Analysis was done on such issues as home ownership, housing price

appreciation and race, race and conventional lending, rental housing, real estate advertising, and racial patterns of school enrollment.
The Cuyahoga Plan's mapping of residential racial patterns has been
especially informative.

Information generated by the Cuyahoga Plan has also been
important in fair housing litigation and legislation. One striking
example was the analysis done on the racial patterns of home
purchases in Cuyahoga County by participants in the Ohio Housing
Finance Agency (OHFA) mortgage incentive program. The Cuyahoga
Plan analysis showed that prevailing patterns of housing segregation were being reinforced (Cuyahoga Plan, 1985a). This information
played an important role in the development of the OHFA pro-
integrative set-aside program in 1985, which was designed to change
this pattern. Another example was the Cuyahoga Plan's research on
mortgage redlining, which called attention to the inadequacy of
conventional housing financing in many neighborhoods in the city
of Cleveland (Cuyahoga Plan, 1989). This kind of data has been
important to the efforts of the countywide Financial Institutions
Advisory Committee, formed to study concentrations of federally
insured high-risk mortgages in minority neighborhoods.

Lind had to deal with the sensitive issue of litigation and the
filing of complaints with HUD against suburban cities accused of
neglecting their fair housing responsibilities. He could not support
having the Cuyahoga Plan become actively involved in such litigation while under contract to provide fair housing services to local
governments, and so he left the litigation activity to the Citizens
Coalition for Block Grant Compliance, which filed a complaint
against the city of Euclid in 1978. Instead, Lind sought cooperative
arrangements with suburban governments in an effort to win their
support for fair housing and the Cuyahoga Plan.

Judy Airhart (1985–1988)

Lind left in 1985 to become director of Cleveland's Citizens League
and later became an attorney affiliated with Housing Advocates, a
public interest law firm long involved in fair housing litigation. He
was succeeded by Judy Airhart, an associated director of the Cuyahoga Plan. A former schoolteacher, she had overseen all three

component programs of the Cuyahoga Plan during the course of her nine years with the organization.

Airhart's term saw the Cuyahoga Plan become involved with the implementation of the OHFA pro-integrative mortgage incentive program. An internal dispute arose in the Cuyahoga Plan over the wisdom of this approach. Black realtists had opposed OHFA adoption of the pro-integrative policy and, having lost this battle, convinced OHFA to create a separate minority set-aside program.

Within the Cuyahoga Plan, Jan Kearny-King, associate director and an attorney, supported the black realtists' viewpoint. When her position did not prevail, she left the Cuyahoga Plan in 1985 and established an organization called Professional Housing Services (PHS) to promote what she termed "freedom of choice" for minorities. She became a prominent critic of "integration maintenance policies," which she characterized as illegal quotas. PHS dissolved in 1990 and Kearny-King went to work for HUD.

Susie Rivers (1988–1991)

When Judy Airhart left in 1988, she was succeeded by Susie Rivers, the agency's first black director. Rivers, a social worker, had been director of the five-county Area Agency on Aging before she became the first fair housing officer for Associated Estates, a major real estate management firm. She had joined the Cuyahoga Plan in 1985 as its director of education and directed its real estate training activities.

Rivers had experienced racial discrimination in housing firsthand in 1973, when a west-side Cleveland building superintendent refused to rent to her. After complaining to the landlord, she got an apartment. Rivers became a checker for the Cuyahoga Plan and the Heights Community Congress (Torassa, 1989). In 1989 she successfully sued a Beachwood couple for citing a higher price to her than to a prospective white buyer for a house that she was considering purchasing for relatives.

As director, Rivers found herself involved in internal debates over the future direction of the Cuyahoga Plan, as well as struggling to save the Cuyahoga Plan as it faced increased competition from other fair housing groups for limited funding. These debates and struggles, in turn, led to protracted discussions about the future coordination of fair housing activities in metropolitan Cleveland and the Cuyahoga Plan's role. In June 1991, Rivers announced the closing of the Cuyahoga Plan's research division, by then reduced to only one staff person. However, the Cuyahoga Plan was able to obtain funding from HUD for fair housing enforcement through HUD's Fair Housing Initiative Program, and it did continue its enforcement activities.

Rivers also had to deal with Parma in attempting to continue a contractual agreement to assist that city in its court-ordered advertising and outreach program for minorities. There was disagreement between the city and the Cuyahoga Plan over the use of the OHFA pro-integrative mortgage incentive approach. In 1989, Parma terminated its agreement with the Cuyahoga Plan for pro-integrative marketing and educational services (Perry, 1989).

Despite these problems, Rivers maintained the presence of the Cuyahoga Plan and kept its funding largely intact, even while seeing the number of full-time staff decline and the organization's future role in fair housing thrown into doubt.

Stuart Wallace (1991–1992)

In August 1991, Stuart Wallace became the fifth director of the Cuyahoga Plan. A realtor, Wallace has long been a fair housing activist. He came to Cleveland in 1963 to direct Fair Housing, Inc. (FHI), a real estate brokerage firm that was formed to sell homes to blacks in predominantly white suburbs and to whites in racially mixed areas. After eight years, Wallace left FHI to form his own firm (Lubinger, 1991).

At age sixty-eight and a semi-retired real estate broker with Realty One's Shaker Heights office, Wallace took the directorship vowing to revive the Cuyahoga Plan. He emphasized working with the private sector, expanding enforcement efforts, and reviving a research program. He was almost immediately faced with an announcement by the city of Cleveland that it was going to shift the use of most of its CDBG fair housing funds from the Cuyahoga Plan to the city's community relations board (Russell, 1991). This was another indicator of the Cuyahoga Plan's problems in sustaining its funding support from local governments. However, in the fall of 1991 the

Cuyahoga Plan was named to take over the role of the East Suburban Council for Open Communities' (ESCOC's) now defunct Hillcrest Housing Service, a very familiar approach to Wallace.

By the late 1980s, the Cuyahoga Plan and the fair housing movement in greater Cleveland was engaged in an extended dialogue about its problems and future directions. Since 1984 the Metropolitan Strategy Group had served as a public forum for the discussion of fair housing issues, programs, and policy developments. However, its monthly meetings were largely informational.

At the behest of philanthropic funders concerned about "turf wars" among the fair housing groups they funded, and with ESCOC experiencing internal disputes and the Cuyahoga Plan seeing its influence seemingly wane, the first of several fair housing summits was convened in October 1990. The convener was the Greater Cleveland Roundtable, which had been organized in 1981 and had become the forum for Cleveland's governmental, corporate, labor, civic, and religious leadership to address race-related issues. The summit agenda was a broad attempt to resolve organizational and policy differences, to avoid duplicative services, and to arrive at a consensus about an approach to fair housing.

This proved to be extremely difficult. The model of a single, metropolitan-wide agency to deal with fair housing, which could conceivably have been the Cuyahoga Plan, was not acceptable to the participating organizations. Given the plethora of municipal fair housing agencies; municipally supported subregional (e.g., ESCOC), citywide (e.g., Heights Community Congress), and neighborhood-based groups; and private, nonprofit organizations, predictably none was interested in ceding its autonomy, much less in being incorporated into a single entity.

At succeeding fair housing summits held in June and November of 1991, the discussion centered on the notion of a better-coordinated metropolitan federation of fair housing organizations, which would include the Cuyahoga Plan. Lengthy dialogues as to what this would mean for participating organizations, how it would be organized, and how it would affect funding from public and philanthropic sources have not yet produced agreement.

In April 1992, the Cuyahoga Plan was threatened by a crisis that jeopardized its very future. Wallace announced that the entire

Cuyahoga Plan staff was being laid off in the face of a staff protest, led by the manager of the agency's discrimination complaint service (Lubinger, 1992a). The protest was over Wallace's instruction that the Cuyahoga Plan not pursue an investigation of a racial discrimination complaint filed by Yasmine Suliman against the city of Shaker Heights in October 1991. Suliman had claimed that she was not given satisfactory advice in her search for an apartment because she identified herself as black. She later filed a complaint with HUD and sued the city (Drexler, 1992). Ironically, she is the daughter of Shane Suliman, the first director of Open Door West, an organization created in 1989 (and supported with a three-year, $250,000 grant from the Cleveland and George Gund philanthropic foundations) to promote greater racial diversity in the west side of Cleveland and Cleveland's western suburbs.

Wallace took the position that the Cuyahoga Plan could not properly pursue such a complaint against one of its own funders, that is, the city of Shaker Heights. This underscores two continuing problems of the Cuyahoga Plan: first, its fragile relationship with its own municipal funders; and second, continuing disagreement over whether its main purpose is to enforce antidiscrimination in housing laws or to promote greater racial diversity through pro-integrative, race-conscious programs.

The laid-off staff of the Cuyahoga Plan filed a discrimination complaint with the Ohio Civil Rights Commission. Within a short time, Wallace resigned. Amid these considerable difficulties, Eleanor Ramsay Dees, the chairwoman of the board of trustees of the Cuyahoga Plan, became the organization's director and hired a replacement staff in the summer of 1992.

The Record of the Cuyahoga Plan

As of Wallace's resignation and Dee's appointment in 1992, the Cuyahoga Plan had been in existence for eighteen years. Its record has been mixed. Certainly, its housing audits and investigations of complaints have contributed to achieving its original goal of a reduction in racial discrimination in housing rentals and sales. Its research findings and their publication and use by fair housing advocates have also contributed to increased public awareness of the problem of racial discrimination in housing. However, discriminatory practices continue, often in a much more subtle manner than they did earlier. In 1990 the Cuyahoga Plan's Discrimination Complaint Service, which received supportive funding from HUD's Fair Housing Initiative Program, received 279 complaints and found probable cause of racial discrimination in 23 (compared to 152 with no probable cause found, 67 deemed inconclusive, and 34 referrals). It conducted fifty-two audits, finding probable cause in three, no probable cause in forty-two, and seven inconclusive (Cuyahoga Plan, 1991).

The Cuyahoga Plan itself has made no pronouncements on its overall success in achieving its other two original goals, namely, reduction of the pattern of racial segregation in housing and encouragement of patterns of permanent integration. The 1990 U.S. Census data does not indicate great increases in racial diversity in very many suburbs, particularly in the west side of Cuyahoga County. To the extent that the 1980 census and the Cuyahoga Plan's own studies in the 1980s indicated great racial diversity (2 to 5 percent black or more), the Cuyahoga Plan periodically announced that some progress was being made. Public opinion polls done by the Greater Cleveland Roundtable, the *Cleveland Plain Dealer*, and the Citizens League Research Institute during the period from 1982 to 1991 generally indicated greater tolerance for open housing and racial diversity in the greater Cleveland area.

However, statistically Cleveland remains one of the most racially isolated metropolitan areas in the United States. What progress has been made toward reversing this pattern cannot be attributed necessarily, much less solely, to the efforts of the Cuyahoga Plan. Rather, the many fair housing organizations, including the cities of Cleveland Heights and Shaker Heights, active in Cuyahoga County share in what has been achieved to date. Although it is probably too harsh to judge the Cuyahoga Plan a failure in reaching its second and third goals, it has hardly succeeded in either respect. What limited gains it has helped to achieve reinforce the need for a countywide organization to promote fair housing.

ESCOC: An Innovative Interjurisdictional, Regional Experiment

The East Suburban Council for Open Communities (ESCOC) represented an innovative approach in promoting racial diversity in a
subregion of suburban Cleveland. What made ESCOC unique was
that it was organized and funded by three suburban cities (Cleveland Heights, Shaker Heights, and University Heights) and their
public school districts (the Cleveland Heights–University Heights
district and the Shaker Heights district) to target six neighboring
jurisdictions as a housing market that minorities should seriously
consider. The six suburbs are located in what is known as the
Hillcrest area and had minuscule numbers of minority residents in
1983, at the creation of ESCOC (Table 17).

The Hillcrest communities vary in their profile (population,
income, housing prices, and housing mix) (Table 18). But it was
generally felt that the Hillcrest communities represented a likely
major path for future black migration to Cleveland's eastern suburbs
(other than the magnet cities that already had a large black population).

Formation, Purpose, Organization, and Funding

A predecessor of ESCOC was the 1967 effort in Shaker Heights to give
blacks housing choices in addition to Shaker Heights in the eastern
suburbs. Named "Suburban Citizens for Open Housing" (SCOH), it
grew out of the neighborhood-based organizing for stable, racially
diverse neighborhoods, which were the focus of community groups

Table 17. Nonwhite Population in the Six
Hillcrest Suburbs, 1983

City	Nonwhite (%)
Highland Heights	2
Lyndhurst	1
Mayfield Heights	3
Mayfield Village	3
Richmond Heights	4
South Euclid	3

Source: Cuyahoga Plan

Table 18. Profile of the Six Hillcrest Suburbs, 1980

City	Population	Median Income	Median Housing Value	Owner-Occupied (%)
Highland Heights	5,700	$26,200	$80,000	96
Lyndhurst	18,100	$25,400	$67,700	84
Mayfield Heights	21,600	$17,700	$60,700	50
Mayfield Village	3,600	$33,300	$91,700	74
Richmond Heights	10,100	$21,800	$73,000	59
South Euclid	25,700	$22,400	$59,500	89

Source: U.S. Census, 1980

concerned about resegregation in Shaker Heights. Black prospects would be provided with escorts who would show them housing available in other eastern suburbs.

In 1971, SCOH opened an office in South Euclid and sought to introduce the Hillcrest area to black prospects (*Cleveland Plain Dealer*, October 10, 1971). SCOH also investigated complaints of racial discrimination and gained notoriety in 1972 when it was named to oversee the compliance with open housing law of a Lyndhurst landlord who had refused to rent to blacks (*Sun Press*, October 20, 1972). SCOH made little progress in changing the racial composition of the Hillcrest community, however, and disbanded in 1973, its open housing goals assumed in 1974 by the Cuyahoga Plan.

Fair Housing, Inc., an interracial real estate firm formed in 1963, had attempted to open up the Hillcrest suburbs to minority homebuyers. Operation Equality (1966–1973) and the Cuyahoga Plan, both efforts to document racial discrimination in housing in metropolitan Cleveland and to enforce fair housing legislation to give minorities greater access and choice, also emphasized the need for interracial housing in Hillcrest. Despite the efforts of then mayor Oliver Schroeder of Cleveland Heights, however, Hillcrest mayors declined an invitation to join in support of the Cuyahoga Plan.

In 1983, Hillcrest Neighbors was formed to encourage a peaceful, gradual transition to racial diversity in the Hillcrest area. The Heights Community Congress assisted in its creation. The organization has received funding from foundations and, more recently, from Mayfield Village and South Euclid (Hoke, 1993). In 1991, Hillcrest Neighbors had thirty-seven individual supporting members (Hillcrest Neighbors, 1992). Hillcrest Neighbors provides support for fair housing, but, like Euclid Community Concerns, its impact on the policies of the six Hillcrest cities has been marginal to date.

February 1983 marked the beginning of the effort to address the question of racial diversity in the eastern suburbs beyond Cleveland Heights, Shaker Heights, and University Heights. The Cuyahoga Plan convened a meeting, which resulted in a task force consisting of elected officials and staff from the Cuyahoga Plan, the three suburban cities, and their school boards. The task force met regularly during the next several months to discuss a regional strategy to promote broader racial diversity and prevent the resegregation of racially diverse communities. A model considered by the group was a similar interjurisdictional effort in the southern Chicago suburbs (which did not involve public school districts).

In December 1983, five jurisdictions (the three suburbs and their two school districts) approved an agreement to establish ESCOC. The council's mission was to encourage open and interracial housing and school patterns throughout Cleveland's eastern suburbs. ESCOC contacted twenty-nine other eastern suburban governments and school districts to invite them to join. None chose to do so, a repetition of the experience of the founders of the Cuyahoga Plan in 1974.

As its (part-time) executive director, ESCOC chose Winston Richie, a former Shaker Heights City Council member and a longtime community activist for racial integration in housing. The Cuyahoga Plan provided technical and administrative assistance to ESCOC in its formative stage. The council was initially funded with an annual budget of $100,000 by the participating public bodies.

ESCOC's challenge was twofold, and both goals were equally difficult: first, to persuade minority home seekers to consider buying and renting in Hillcrest; and, second, to gain the acceptance of, in addition to Hillcrest Neighbors, the Hillcrest governments, residents, and real estate brokers and landlords.

ESCOC's Hillcrest Campaign

ESCOC's first undertaking was a media and public relations campaign designed to establish its identity and to raise awareness about its concerns. This effort was designed and carried out by local advertising and public relations firms.

In 1985 two full-time staffers were hired to develop ESCOC's planned housing service. ESCOC's Hillcrest office, located in Lyndhurst, opened in March–April 1985. Lyndhurst had gained unwanted notoriety in November 1983 when a newly arrived black family's home was bombed, and it was hoped that the presence of the housing service would alleviate racial tensions and negative publicity. Hillcrest elected officials and realtors were invited to visit ESCOC's Housing Service Office. The council's strategy was to involve local leaders and real estate brokers in eventually promoting its pro-integrative goals by persuading them that the policy was sound. ESCOC adopted a financial incentive program for prospective black homebuyers interested in Hillcrest. Funded by grants from the Cleveland Foundation and the George Gund Foundation, the council offered five-year deferred loans of up to $3,000 to reduce the interest on a first mortgage. Its first loan was approved that same month. In 1985, ESCOC was contacted by approximately 450 black home seekers and gave Hillcrest tours to about 100. Of these prospects, twenty-one were known to have rented in the Hillcrest area and sixteen purchased homes. It was estimated that another twenty-five black families moved into Hillcrest without ESCOC's direct assistance (ESCOC, 1985).

Having opened its Lyndhurst office, ESCOC held its 1985 annual meeting in Mayfield Heights (in contrast to 1984, when its first annual meeting was held in Shaker Heights). However, no public support from Hillcrest elected officials was forthcoming. The council attributed this in part to the fact that 1985 was an election year. In the same year, ESCOC's budget doubled. Of its annual budget of $204,247, 51 percent came from the five sponsoring governmental bodies and 47 percent was provided through foundation grants (ESCOC, 1985). Local foundations continued their funding of ESCOC through its life. The council would also be supported by major corporations such as British Petroleum (BP) America and TRW.

Unlike past pro-integrative efforts in the eastern suburbs through SCOH, Operation Equality, and the Cuyahoga Plan, ESCOC featured gentle persuasion. It did not undertake audits to document discrimination; nor did it engage in public criticism of the Hillcrest municipal governments. It did not litigate against realty firms or landlords for violation of fair housing law. As a publicly supported, "outside" intervenor, it tried to woo voluntary support rather than threaten any potential allies.

Nevertheless, 1986 proved no different from 1985 in garnering the overt support of elected officials. The one significant opening was the proposal in July 1986 by the president of the city council of South Euclid to join ESCOC as a voting member and to appropriate $20,000 to support it (*Sun Press*, July 1986). The proposal drew considerable criticism from opponents, who included South Euclid's major. The city council president subsequently withdrew his proposal in lieu of the city creating a citizen's advisory committee on community relations. This committee reported in November 1987, recommending the creation of the post of community relations director to address such issues as enforcement of fair housing laws and encouragement for minority homeowners to locate in predominantly white neighborhoods and to prevent racial imbalance in Lowden Elementary School (which borders Cleveland Heights). A community relations director was subsequently hired in the fall of 1988. However, South Euclid does not have its own affirmative programs to promote pro-integrative housing and rentals.

In December 1987, South Euclid formally rejected membership in ESCOC (*Sun Press*, December 17, 1987). And in 1989 another city council member who had openly called for the city to address the issue of gradual racial transition lost his seat on the city council, after serving for sixteen years.

Community opposition to South Euclid membership in ESCOC was fanned by the "Richardson controversy." An interracial couple, the Richardsons were one of the first recipients of an ESCOC pro-integrative loan to move into South Euclid. Unfortunately, soon after their late 1986 move they became notorious because of the publicity surrounding the "swinging" couples club that they ran in their home. This created considerable opposition from neighbors and led to a riotous city council confrontation in 1987 (Breckenridge, 1987) and the passage of a municipal ordinance regulating brothels, which the Richardsons were then charged with violating (Sawicki, 1987). The criminal complaint ultimately was dismissed and the ordinance was eventually declared unconstitutionally vague (*City of South Euclid v. Richardson*, 49 Ohio St.3d 147, 551 N.E.2d 606 [1990]). This inflammatory incident and its attendant publicity (including exposure on Phil Donahue's national TV show) were a setback for ESCOC's outreach efforts in South Euclid. Nevertheless, by 1990, 9 percent of South Euclid's population was black (although blacks were concentrated in certain areas).

The city of Lyndhurst did not join ESCOC, but in 1986 it did create a new post of director of community relations that was to address issues related to racial "integration," a term downplayed by the mayor and the newly hired community relations director (*Sun Press*, February 11, 1986). In 1990, Lyndhurst's black population was still less than 0.5 percent.

In 1986, ESCOC's Housing Service handled 423 inquiries, three-fourths of which involved rentals. It claimed credit for ten new black renters and eighteen new black homeowners, raising its cumulative totals to thirty-two renters (out of 203 "active" prospects) and thirty-one homeowners (out of 168 active prospects) for the period 1985–1986 (ESCOC, 1986). To further assist prospective homebuyers, the pro-integrative mortgage incentive program was revised to allow for reducing closing costs, "points," and down payments. The repayment deferral period was reduced from five to three years in order to increase the use of available funds. During 1985–1986, ESCOC provided mortgage assistance to eleven homebuyers (ESCOC, 1986). The council was also able to use the OHFA pro-integrative mortgage program for first-time homebuyers, created in 1985.

The years 1987 and 1988 saw ESCOC gain further acceptance. In 1988, Harvard University's John F. Kennedy School of Government gave an Innovations in State and Local Government Award to Shaker Heights. This was accompanied by funding from the Ford Foundation, part of which supported ESCOC. The council joined with other metropolitan fair housing organizations in promoting local, regional, state, and national fair housing and pro-integrative housing policies.

ESCOC's Housing Service served 569 rental and sales prospects in 1987 and 727 in 1988. In 1987, fifty-one decided to move to Hillcrest. The number of prospects moving to Hillcrest increased to sixty-six in 1988 (ESCOC, 1988).

Transition and Termination: 1989–1991

After a four-year period of establishing itself, ESCOC underwent major transition over the next few years, ending in its sudden termination in 1991. In 1989 its two original staffers left for other positions. Another resignation came in 1990—that of ESCOC Director Winston Richie (now sixty-five and still active in fair housing).

Richie resigned in August, with the resignation effective in January 1991. While reinforcing the importance of ESCOC's achievements, he emphasized his frustration at the inability of ESCOC and other fair housing agencies to make fundamental changes in patterns of residential segregation in most of metropolitan Cleveland (*Sun Press*, October 25, 1990; *Cleveland Plain Dealer*, October 26, 1990). Richie wanted to address fair housing issues throughout Cuyahoga County (which was the purpose of the Cuyahoga Plan), not only in the six-city Hillcrest area.

In the wake of Richie's resignation, ESCOC's board and funders decided to continue its housing service in Hillcrest, but in late 1991 the Cuyahoga Plan took over its management (*Cleveland Plain Dealer*, December 1, 1991). The Heights Fund assumed management of the council's outstanding loan portfolio (*Sun Press*, January 17, 1991). ESCOC had made approximately sixty pro-integrative loans over its lifetime.

ESCOC's Impact

What has ESCOC's impact been? It was certainly greater than that of its predecessor organizations in Hillcrest in the 1960s and 1970s. It gained greater visibility than has the local fair housing group, Hillcrest Neighbors, and it did achieve at least limited success in opening up the Hillcrest community to minority renters and homebuyers.

In contrast, ESCOC failed to achieve a very important goal, at least during the period from 1984 to 1990, namely, persuading the six Hillcrest city governments and school districts either officially to join ESCOC or separately and independently to emulate its programs. Only South Euclid and Lyndhurst took even the modest and tentative step of creating the posts of community relations directors, and neither went beyond this. The other four communities did nothing publicly to support ESCOC. Their black populations in 1990 were:

Highland Heights	0.3 percent
Mayfield Village	0.3 percent
Mayfield Heights	1.9 percent
Richmond Heights	7.7 percent

The heaviest black influx in the Hillcrest area in the 1980s was into the cities of Richmond Heights and South Euclid.

The reason for ESCOC's failure to win the overt support of Hillcrest suburban governments is hardly a mystery. White suburban politicians who espouse fair housing policies are politically vulnerable to constituencies that are not favorably disposed toward racial integration or at least toward affirmative housing policies designed to attract blacks to their suburban communities. This was the sentiment expressed by South Euclid's city council president in the face of the opposition to his 1986 proposal to have South Euclid join ESCOC. The political danger was demonstrated in South Euclid in 1989, when another longtime council member lost his seat over racial issues, and in the neighboring city of Euclid in 1979 with the defeat of pro–fair housing candidates for city council and mayor.

Without a strong internal constituency pressuring a suburb to address racial transition, the policy of most suburban governments has been to try to ignore a lack of racial diversity or initial racial transition in their neighborhoods. An alternative that may be taken with suburbs resistant to affirmative fair housing approaches is direct external pressure on predominantly white suburbs to promote fair housing. However, the example of Parma and its experience for more than a decade under a federal court order does not give great hope for this approach.

The final posthumous chapter cannot yet be written on ESCOC. It may have planted the seeds for a more orderly racial transition in Hillcrest. More pessimistically, if resegregation eventually does occur, the council's epitaph may be a monument to the failure of the regional, voluntary, educational approach to expanding racial diversity as sponsored by pro-integrative suburban governments.

The Metropolitan Strategy Group

Cleveland's Metropolitan Strategy Group (MSG) was an outgrowth of National Neighbors (NN). NN began with a national organizing meeting in Dayton, Ohio, which was preceded by an initial 1969 meeting of representatives of twelve integrated communities, including Shaker Heights (Saltman, 1990: 313–14). NN was a national coalition of municipalities, fair housing organizations, and pro-integrative neighborhood organizations. Its first president was black Cleveland real estate broker Joseph Battle, the director of Operation Equality (Milgram, 1977).

NN has had a difficult history, marked by such issues as developing a working definition of "integration" by which to define membership. Dedicated to the promotion of open housing, the organization has been plagued throughout its life by meager financial support. Although it did obtain Ford Foundation support early in its history, it has been unable to develop sustained funding to finance a national office, its newsletter, and an annual meeting. In 1989, NN changed its name to the "National Federation for Neighborhood Diversity" (NFND).

In 1982, Clevelander Charles "Chip" Bromley became NN's president. In 1983, he became its executive director and chief fund-raiser in an untiring effort to keep the organization alive. Bromley has been involved in fair housing efforts since he joined the Heights Community Congress in 1972 as a community organizer in Cleveland Heights, where he resides and where the Midwest office of NN was opened in 1983 (Saltman, 1990: 330–31).

The purpose of NN's Midwest office was to develop a regional program. As a result, the Cleveland MSG—a coalition of municipalities, fair housing organizations, and other agencies, groups, and individuals interested in promoting fair housing, primarily in metropolitan Cleveland—was formed in 1984 and received modest foundation support (Saltman, 1990: 352). The MSG conducts monthly public forums at which issues related to fair housing are discussed.

MSG, its director, and its members have played an active role in advocating for greater support for fair housing in the Cleveland metropolitan area, the state of Ohio, and nationally. In 1990, MSG was a local co-sponsor for the NFND's twenty-first annual national conference, held at Case Western Reserve University in Cleveland. MSG has played a key role in the creation of such organizations as ESCOC, the (Cuyahoga) County-wide Financial Institutions Advisory Committee, and Greater Cleveland Community Shares (an alternative to the United Way, providing funding to fair housing organizations, among others) (MSG, 1990). The group provides a network for fair housing organizations in metropolitan Cleveland and northeastern Ohio and has provided leadership in advocacy for fair housing in the state capital, for example, before the Ohio Civil Rights Commission.

MSG's greatest achievement has been its successful advocacy for the creation of the Ohio Housing Finance Agency's pro-integrative mortgage set-aside program, initiated in 1985 (Husock, 1989; Saltman, 1990: 353). When this program was challenged, MSG led its successful defense (Bromley, 1992). In 1990 the group received funding from HUD to provide outreach to housing consumers and the real estate industry about the pro-integrative mortgage incentive program, in cooperation with several other Ohio fair housing organizations. MSG carried out its varied functions in 1990 on a budget of $56,251, $50,000 of which came from three foundations (Cleveland, George Gund, and British Petroleum), $3,944 of which came from the Greater Cleveland Community Shares, and $2,000 of which came from the city of Cleveland Heights (MSG, 1990).

Conclusion

The development and activities of fair housing organizations have been very important in the efforts to promote greater racial diversity in metropolitan Cleveland. The most successful have been those with the broadest constituency and financial support, for example, the Heights Community Congress. The least successful have been those operating without a strong constituency within their own communities, for example, Hillcrest Neighbors. The attempts to influence predominantly white suburbs by organizations not supported by targeted communities (e.g., PATH, SCOH, and ESCOC) have encountered the greatest opposition. A pro–fair housing group has not yet emerged in Parma.

The Cuyahoga Plan is the longest-lived metropolitan fair housing organization in the state. Although it has survived for two decades, it still struggles to define its role and to win support among suburban governments in Cuyahoga County. Aside from the city governments of Shaker Heights and Cleveland Heights and the Cleveland and George Gund foundations, the most important organizations that have supported fair housing have been religious denominations.

PART III

Fair Housing: Policies, Programs, Legality, and Prospects

11

Open Housing Policies
and Programs

There is a long history of racial discrimination and bigotry in the
United States. African Americans, more than any other racial minority, have suffered from white hostility and fear. The causes for white
discrimination against blacks in housing are well documented. They
fall into two categories: first, the prejudices of individual whites;
and, second, systematic racial discrimination in the housing market.

Causes of White Bigotry and Discrimination
against Racial Minorities

There has long been prejudice by white Americans against those
whom they considered inferior, dangerous, or just different. This has
included many ethnic and racial groups, from the German and Irish
who led the European mass migration to the United States, to the
Chinese and Japanese who led the Asian migration to the West
Coast, to the Mexicans who led the Hispanic migration to the
Southwest. The native American population, largely confined to
rural reservations until the mid-twentieth century, has also experienced tremendous discrimination.

However, the black experience is different because only blacks
experienced slavery in the United States. The effects of slavery,

abolitionism, and emancipation during the Civil War, Reconstruction, and the civil rights movement are still felt today. Except for native Americans, African Americans still experience the worst poverty, unemployment, education, health care, environmental pollution, and racial discrimination.

Charles Abrams, in writing about *Forbidden Neighbors* (1955: 263–64), discussed seven important fallacies in white assumptions about the undesirability of having black neighbors and living in racially mixed neighborhoods:

1. Negroes and whites do not mix.
2. Negroes (or other nonwhites) are dirty and will spoil the neighborhood.
3. Entry of minority families into a neighborhood hurts social status.
4. The minority always goes where it is not wanted.
5. Once the minority establishes a beachhead, many more will soon follow and displace the once dominant majority.
6. Values go down wherever a minority moves into a neighborhood.
7. Homogeneity stabilizes value.

Abrams refuted these seven myths as false generalizations.

Nevertheless, hostility, fear, and suspicion among the races remain all too prevalent in the United States in the 1990s, fueled by repetitive incidents with racial overtones (Hacker, 1992; Terkel, 1992). The popular perception is that race relations in the United States have improved over the past three decades, heralded by the U.S. Supreme Court's historic 1954 school desegregation decision and the civil rights gains of minorities following the mass protests of the 1960s. Recent evidence suggests otherwise. For example, a survey of racial attitudes conducted by the University of Chicago's National Opinion Research Center (Smith, 1990) found that a majority of whites considered blacks to be more likely than whites:

- to prefer living off welfare and less likely to prefer to be self-supporting (78 percent);
- to be lazy (62 percent);

- to be more violence-prone (56 percent);
- to be less intelligent (53 percent);
- to be less patriotic (51 percent).

Whites' belief that a black presence in their neighborhood will inevitably result in the depreciation of property values remains an enduring myth. In *The Negro Ghetto* (1948), Robert Weaver listed this first, among eight reasons, for white opposition to black neighbors. In his 1950s research on the relationship between the racial mix of neighborhoods and housing values in seven cities (not including Cleveland), culminating in his report to the national citizens' Commission on Race and Housing, Luigi Laurenti (1960) empirically refuted this myth. Yet the belief persists.

It was this belief that led the real estate industry, beginning in Chicago, to develop such devices as restrictive convenants and racial steering to maintain racially separate neighborhoods, in order to protect property values in white neighborhoods. These private practices were adopted by the federal government—for example, by the Federal Housing Administration (FHA)—in the 1930s and reinforced the patterns of racial discrimination in housing practiced by realtors, lenders, developers, and insurers (Abrams, 1955). Systematic racial discrimination, aided and abetted by the housing industry and the FHA, shaped American suburbs from their inception (Jackson, 1985).

Fair Housing Legislation

Racial discrimination in housing seemingly was banned by the radical Reconstruction Congress when it enacted the Thirteenth Amendment to the U.S. Constitution in 1866. This amendment outlawed slavery and was accompanied by the Civil Rights Act of 1866, which guaranteed all citizens (including the freed slaves) property rights. Unfortunately, though the statute survived a veto by Abraham Lincoln's successor, Andrew Johnson, it was rendered impotent by rulings of the U.S. Supreme Court, which negated its impact on private accommodations (Metcalf, 1988: 31–36). The statute would not be revived until a 1968 U.S. Supreme Court decision (*Jones v. Mayer*, 392 U.S. 409) that recognized the intent of Congress to ban racial discrimination in housing (Metcalf, 1988: 37–42). This decision was handed down shortly after Congress enacted the Fair Housing Act of 1968.

After a protracted debate and a southern filibuster in the Senate, Congress hurriedly enacted the Fair Housing Act during the week following the assassination of Martin Luther King, Jr. The act broadly banned racial discrimination in housing in the United States, including such discriminatory practices as blockbusting, racial steering, and redlining. However, it did not cover all privately owned housing (Metcalf, 1988: 85–86).

Even more critical was the inadequacy of the legislation's enforcement mechanism. Complaints about fair housing violations were to be investigated by HUD or, in the alternative, by state and local fair housing agencies, where they existed. HUD itself had no direct enforcement power; it could only refer cases involving probable cause to the U.S. Justice Department for prosecution. This proved to be a very ineffective system of enforcement (Metcalf, 1988: 114–16; Armstrong, 1991). Filing deadlines for complaints, long investigatory delays, and relatively infrequent governmental prosecution discouraged many prospective complainants. In many of the most successful cases, complainants simply bypassed HUD and went directly to the courts. Litigation, however, while often successful and resulting in major damages assessed against the guilty party, has proven to be extremely time-consuming and expensive. After several years of debate, the federal Fair Housing Act was finally amended in 1988. HUD was given the power to initiate complaints, and administrative law judges can now render judgment. The coverage of the law was also broadened (Kushner, 1989).

What still haunts enforcement of federal fair housing law and policy is a debate over its purpose and differing interpretations of the meaning of the legislative history of the 1968 act. One view is that Congress intended that federal policy should be to promote racially integrated living patterns in housing (including federally assisted and insured units, buildings, and development projects) and neighborhoods. The opposing viewpoint is that Congress intended only to ban racial discrimination in housing. This disagreement has never been resolved. Courts have differed in their interpretation, and

Congress did not further clarify the purpose of federal fair housing policy in its 1988 amendments.

State and local fair housing laws, similar in structure to federal law, first made their appearance in the 1960s, with California leading the way. These laws were opposed generally by the lobbying arms of the realtors' and lenders' associations. As enacted (notwithstanding this opposition), the laws were often weak, with the investigatory agency often lacking any enforcement authority if its investigation resulted in a finding of racial discrimination in housing.

In Ohio the college town of Oberlin, with a reputation for addressing racial issues since its leadership in the pre–Civil War abolitionist movement, was the first locality to enact a fair housing ordinance. The constitutionality of this 1961 ordinance was challenged by realtors and lenders, but in 1965 the Ohio Supreme Court upheld its validity (Reich, 1968).

Beginning with the issuance of a 1961 report on housing discrimination by the Ohio Civil Rights Commission, there had been an effort to persuade the legislature to pass a state law. In the face of opposition by the real estate and lending industries, the legal uncertainties raised by the challenge to the Oberlin ordinance, and the attempted override of an Akron ordinance enacted in 1964 (later ruled unconstitutional by the U.S. Supreme Court in *Hunter v. Erickson*, 393 U.S. 385 [1969]), it was not until 1965 that Ohio passed its own fair housing law (Hale, 1968). It authorized the Ohio Civil Rights Commission to investigate complaints of racial discrimination in housing, but like many similar laws it gave the commission no enforcement powers. It took until 1992 for Ohio to amend its law to bring it into conformity with the 1988 federal fair housing amendments.

The Extent of Racial Discrimination in Housing

Despite the existence of municipal, state, and federal fair housing legislation for the past three decades and considerable litigation, racial discrimination against blacks in the housing market remains a serious problem. Both covert and overt discrimination, particularly against blacks, is still practiced in the United States.

G. C. Galster (1990a) reviewed seventy-one fair housing audits conducted during the 1980s. Black auditors seeking homes for sale faced a one-in-five chance and black auditors seeking rental units faced a one-in-two chance of being discriminated against. The most recent national data compiled by HUD in 1989 housing audits presented a pattern of significant unfavorable treatment of minorities in local housing markets (HUD, 1991).

In 1991 the Cuyahoga Plan of Cleveland received 314 complaints of race-based housing discrimination and investigated 264; the Fair Housing Center of Toledo received 257 complaints, 60 percent of which were race-based; the Fair Housing Contact Service of Akron received 107 complaints, 46 percent of which were race-based; and Housing Opportunities Made Equal of Cincinnati received 1,097 complaints, 75 percent of which were race-based (MSG, 1992). These data confirm the reality that racial discrimination in housing continues to be a problem for many minority home seekers in Ohio.

Attitudes toward Racial Integration in Housing and Neighborhoods

Over the past several decades, attitudes toward racial integration in housing and neighborhoods, particularly those of whites, have changed. Howard Schuman, Charlotte Steeh, and Lawrence Bobo (1985) analyzed data from surveys conducted by the National Opinion Research Center and the Institute for Social Research from the early 1960s through the early 1980s. Their analysis focused on responses to questions related to residential choice, support for open housing laws, and acceptance of neighbors of another race.

In analyzing the responses of whites, Schuman, Steeh, and Bobo concluded that the trend during this period has been one of increasing white acceptance or support for racial integration in housing. However, they qualify this finding:

> This acceptance [by whites] of integration goes beyond the single black individual, and similar answers would be given if the questions involved almost any number of blacks, so long as the number represented a clear minority.

But as soon as questions indicate that blacks might constitute a sizable proportion of the neighborhood (or school), open white objection becomes more pronounced. In addition, a large proportion of whites object to any governmental action that might facilitate a change from white preponderance, and, so far as we can tell, this opposition has decreased very little over the past four decades. In sum, the change . . . has been away from . . . absolute segregation . . . but it has not been clearly toward full integration. (Schuman, Steeh, and Bobo, 1985: 162–63)

Based on national telephone survey data from 1985 to 1987, Schuman and Bobo (1988) found that there was still considerable white opposition to open housing laws, with white support nationally in 1986 still at only 48 percent. In trying to understand the increasing white support for open housing and nondiscrimination, on the one hand, and the continuing patterns of racial segregation in housing, on the other, they analyzed three possible reasons for the dichotomy: (1) lip service to democratic platitudes, (2) symbolic racism, and (3) superficial tolerance. They also analyzed the importance of distrust of the federal government, white perceptions of class differences between themselves and potential black neighbors, and white concern about sweeping neighborhood racial changes. Schuman and Bobo concluded that:

- general resistance to government coercion is one important factor in white opposition to open housing laws;
- personal prejudice is an important element in white opposition to open housing laws; and
- some white personal objections to blacks are based on perceived class differences rather than on race differences.

The issue of open housing is not the same when blacks are questioned. Several studies demonstrate that most blacks prefer to live in racially mixed neighborhoods, rather than in predominantly or all-black neighborhoods (Darden, 1987).

W.A.V. Clark (1991) argues that individual white preferences for predominantly white neighborhoods cumulatively explain the pattern of predominantly white neighborhoods. His finding is based on telephone survey data related to school desegregation cases in five cities (including Milwaukee). Clark concludes that "some degree of racial integration is acceptable [to whites] but it is unrealistic to expect large levels of [racial] integration across neighborhoods in view of the [white neighborhood] racial preferences reported here and known differences in income and wealth [between whites and blacks]" (Clark, 1991: 17).

In order for this trend to change, there must be affirmative housing policies designed to change white attitudes.

Regulation of the Real Estate and Lending Institutions

As the case studies of the suburbs of Cleveland Heights and Shaker Heights demonstrated, those communities that aim to promote greater racial diversity in a housing market dominated by private actors have regulated the practices of key sectors of the housing industry, that is, real estate brokers and lenders, in order to prevent racial discrimination and to promote integration. These communities have gone beyond the limited confines of national policy.

Since 1968, federal fair housing legislation has outlawed racial discrimination in housing. In the case of real estate firms and their employees (brokers and agents), any discriminatory behavior related to race in the listing or showing of real estate is prohibited. Racial steering and blockbusting are outlawed. Since the passage of the federal Fair Housing Act, there have been numerous cases in which the courts have found realtors guilty and imposed fines (Metcalf, 1988). The same standard has been applied to other actors, for example, landlords and developers. Institutional lenders are prohibited from discriminatory lending (popularly known as "redlining"). If they are subject to federal regulation, they are also covered by the Home Mortgage Disclosure Act and the Community Reinvestment Act. This legislation provides the basis for challenges if federally regulated lenders are suspected of discriminatory lending practices that redline inner-city neighborhoods (Metcalf, 1988).

Municipal fair housing regulation in pro-integrative communities has primarily addressed the activities of real estate firms and their employees (brokers and agents). There are three typical forms of regulation. The first is regulation of "for sale" signs. In the past, blockbusting or panic selling related to racial transition has been spurred by the appearance of abnormally high numbers of these signs in areas undergoing racial transition. To prevent this, some communities have imposed bans on the signs. Both Cleveland Heights and Shaker Heights have long had such bans in place. Where the communities can show that there is evidence of block-busting and white flight induced by realtors, the courts have upheld this policy. However, "for sale" signs are considered by the courts to be a form of commercial free speech, subject to the protection of the First Amendment. The U.S. Supreme Court has ruled that without evidence of discriminatory practices by realtors, absolute bans are unconstitutional (*Linmark Associates v. Town of Willingboro*, 431 U.S. 85 [1977]). In addition to preventing illegal blockbusting, such sign regulation may also be justified by zoning and building regulations to regulate the appearance and protect the stability and value of residential neighborhoods.

The second type of ordinance regulates solicitation of homesell-ers, again in order to prevent blockbusting and white flight. This type of ordinance prohibits realtors from contacting potential cus-tomers who have placed their names on a list circulated by a city, indicating that they do not wish to be solicited by realtors. Several Cleveland suburbs have such ordinances.

The third type of ordinance requires those realty firms wishing to do business in the city to register with the city and cooperate in complying with any local policies and programs to promote fair housing. In the case of Cleveland Heights, preferred realty firms are registered, agree to comply with the city's fair housing programs and policies, and report on their pro-integrative activities quarterly. The firms' activities are subject to review by a citizens board, which is empowered to hear complaints concerning any alleged violations.

As long as a community has a desirable housing market, there should be no insurmountable difficulty in persuading private realty firms to cooperate with such policies. Many, if not all, are likely to cooperate. For example, in the case of Cleveland Heights, seven realty firms in 1992 cooperated with the city and its pro-integrative housing programs; these included Realty One, Smythe–Cramer, and Coldwell Banker Hunter Realty, ranked in 1992 as the tenth, six-teenth, and seventy-fourth largest residential realty firms, respectively, in the United States (Lubinger, 1992c). In 1991 there were 642 recorded sales of single-family houses in Cleveland Heights, mostly involving real estate agents.

Given the dominance of the private real estate market and the involvement of private realty firms in American suburbs, it is hard to imagine suburban communities successfully implementing pro-integrative housing policies without the cooperation of key elements of the real estate industry, especially realty firms and institutional lenders.

Pro-integrative Mortgage Incentives

One of the more promising approaches to affirmative marketing has been the use of pro-integrative mortgage incentives. These are financial incentives to induce homebuyers to purchase houses in areas where their race is underrepresented.

Metropolitan Cleveland

Pro-integrative mortgage incentives in suburban Cleveland originated in the Shaker Heights neighborhood of Ludlow. Created in 1957 to stabilize a neighborhood in racial transition, the Ludlow Community Association (LCA), as one of its pro-integrative efforts, formed a corporation in 1961, sold shares ($22,000 worth of $100 shares), and then lent this money to prospective white homebuyers in the form of below-market second mortgages (ranging from $1,000 to $5,000 per loan) (Blank, 1968). The purpose of providing this financial incentive was to maintain white demand in a previously all-white neighborhood that had become increasingly attractive to black home seekers and that white realtors were either steering whites away from or ignoring. It was also feared that institutional lenders would withdraw from a racially mixed neighborhood.

In 1968 the Lomond Association, formed in 1963 to stabilize racial transition in that neighborhood, emulated the LCA's example and began its own neighborhood-based, pro-integrative mortgage incentive program for prospective white homebuyers (Alfred and

Marcoux, 1970). Undoubtedly, both of these programs helped to prevent the rapid resegregation of these two Shaker Heights neighborhoods. In 1990 their black populations were 77 percent (Ludlow) and 68 percent (Lomond).

In 1986 the Fund for the Future of Shaker Heights (FFSH) was created to provide pro-integrative mortgage incentives for both white and black homebuyers in racially imbalanced Shaker Heights neighborhoods. The FFSH provides loans of up to $5,000 for either down payments or mortgage interest reductions and loans of up to $6,000 to supplement first mortgages, repayable over six years at 6 percent (simple interest). The FFSH is privately funded, with significant support from philanthropic foundations. By early 1991, the fund had made approximately one hundred loans. There are no income or housing-price eligibility restrictions. The majority of loans have been made to whites purchasing homes in the Lomond neighborhood. An econometric analysis of the impact of this program in the Lomond neighborhood in its early stages concluded that the fund had a positive impact in stabilizing the neighborhood and contributed to appreciation of property values (Cromwell, 1990).

The second major pro-integrative mortgage incentive program was initiated in 1971 in Cleveland Heights by the Heights Area Project (HAP). HAP was created in 1969 and funded by the Jewish Community Federation to prevent an accelerated exodus of the Jewish population from Cleveland Heights as blacks increasingly moved into neighborhoods with concentrated Jewish populations. One HAP response was the creation of a mortgage assistance program, which provided up to $1,500 in interest-free loans for young Jewish couples purchasing houses in Cleveland Heights and in neighboring communities that had a significant Jewish population and were undergoing racial transition (e.g., University Heights and Shaker Heights). Initially funded with a $50,000 endowment, HAP has over two decades provided loans to more than four hundred Jewish homebuyers. The only requirement is that the home purchaser must be Jewish and must buy in the designated Heights communities. Currently, recipients receive low-interest loans of up to $5,000, repayable over a maximum six-year period.

In 1987 the cities of Cleveland Heights and University Heights created the Heights Fund, virtually identical in purpose and structure to the FFSH. Through early 1991 this fund made seventy-two loans.

The East Suburban Council for Open Communities (ESCOC) initiated its housing service in 1985 and offered mortgage incentives to black homebuyers interested in purchasing in the six east-side Hillcrest suburbs. Until 1991, when ESCOC was terminated, fifty-nine homebuyers received second mortgage loans ranging from $3,000 to $5,000 at 3 percent (simple) interest. The ESCOC's Housing Service was revived as the Hillcrest Housing Service in 1992 and is now being operated by the Cuyahoga Plan.

Finally, the most recognized pro-integrative mortgage incentive program is the set-aside program of the Ohio Housing Finance Agency (OHFA). From its beginning in 1983, OHFA has provided below-market mortgages to first-time, moderate-income homebuyers throughout Ohio. Fair housing activists became concerned that this OHFA program, operated through private realtors and lenders, was reinforcing segregated housing patterns in metropolitan Cleveland. In 1985 the Cuyahoga Plan released an analysis of more than two thousand OHFA loans in Cuyahoga County. It documented the lack of participation by blacks and a pattern of purchases in keeping with Cleveland's dual, segregated housing market.

Fair housing groups then successfully lobbied OHFA, with the eventual support of liberal Democratic governor Richard Celeste, to create a special bonus program for participants willing to make voluntary pro-integrative moves within Cuyahoga County. The state's real estate lobby unsuccessfully opposed this policy, which was approved in July 1985. However, the pro-integrative bonus mortgage set-aside program was temporarily inoperative in 1986 and 1987, due to uncertainty over the extension of the federal income tax exemption for state mortgage revenue bond programs and the opposition of a conservative state representative (whose district includes Parma), who demanded an opinion by the state attorney general verifying the legality of this race-conscious program. The verifying opinion was issued in December 1987.

Opposition to revival of the program then emerged from black real estate interests (who were not on the state real estate boards) and a breakaway fair housing group in Cleveland, led by a former Cuyahoga Plan staffer, that opposed integration maintenance. The resolution in 1988 was a new round of OHFA funding for the pro-integrative bonus program and the creation of a separate bonus set-aside program for minority homebuyers without any restrictions as to the location of their moves (Husock, 1989; Chandler, 1992; Bromley, 1992).

Cumulatively, during the period from 1989 to 1991, OHFA set aside $14.6 million for these programs, primarily in Cuyahoga County but also in a few other metropolitan areas in Ohio. In its September 1991 set-aside program, eligibility was limited in Cuyahoga County to home purchasers whose annual income was no more than $38,100 for a family of one to two persons or $43,815 for a family of three to four persons. The down payment on these loans can be as low as 3 percent (compared to a minimum of 5 percent in the other programs). The ceilings on housing prices were $77,130 for a one-family house and $86,848 for a two-family house. OHFA also allows non-first-time homebuyers to participate in specially designated "distressed" low-income areas certified by HUD. Currently, the OHFA program requires that whites purchase homes in areas that are at least 40 percent nonwhite and that blacks purchase homes in areas that are at least 90 percent white. Through early 1991, the Cuyahoga Plan had processed 115 OHFA pro-integrative loans in suburban Cuyahoga County.

Other United States Examples

Formed in 1975, the Fund for an Open Society, or "OPEN," has provided pro-integrative mortgage incentives to homebuyers in several metropolitan areas, most notably Philadelphia and Washington, D.C. (Silverman, 1977: 374). Its president is Morris Milgram, a prominent advocate of racially integrated housing (Milgram, 1977). As of January 1991, OPEN had granted or guaranteed a total of 150 mortgages, primarily for the purchase of single-family homes, with a total investment of $4.5 million (OPEN, 1991).

As a result of the settlement of a court order to desegregate the Milwaukee schools, the Milwaukee Fair Housing Council since 1989 has operated a Center for Integrated Living (CIL) to provide pro-integrative mortgage incentives through a program called "Alternative Financing for Opening Residential Doors." Funded by the

Wisconsin Housing and Economic Development Authority, CIL provides below-market mortgage financing (subsidized mortgage interest rates and down payments) to homebuyers willing to make pro-integrative moves in metropolitan Milwaukee. Eligible neighborhoods are defined as either areas where minority buyers are underrepresented (i.e., where their racial group constitutes under 15 percent of the neighborhood's residents) or selected racially transitory neighborhoods in the city of Milwaukee (Thomas, 1991).

Evaluation of Pro-integrative Mortgage Incentives

In 1991 an evaluation was conducted of four of the five pro-integrative mortgage incentive programs in suburban Cuyahoga County (all but the HAP program). The evaluation was based on two surveys: the first of participants themselves, and the second of a cross-section of suburban residents (Keating, 1992).

The mail survey of a combined total of 358 recipients of pro-integrative mortgage incentives drew an overall response of 52.5 percent (188 responding homebuyers) and 50 percent or better for each of the four programs. In three programs, a majority of the responding participants were white: Heights Fund (90 percent), FFSH (87 percent), and the Cuyahoga Plan (65 percent). The ESCOC program was limited to minorities (86 percent of whom were black). Over one-third (38 percent) of all respondents had purchased their homes in 1990. Altogether, more than two-thirds of all the respondents had purchased their homes in either Cleveland Heights (38 percent) or Shaker Heights (33 percent); this result was largely due to the fact that the FFSH requires participants to purchase in Shaker Heights and the Heights Fund requires a purchase in either Cleveland Heights or University Heights. A total of sixty-eight participants (sixty-seven of whom were white) already lived in either Cleveland Heights (20 percent) or Shaker Heights (18 percent), and forty-four of these (65 percent of this subgroup) purchased homes in these two pro-integrative communities. Three-fourths of all participants listed Cleveland Heights or Shaker Heights as either their first or only choice in their housing search. Among participants in the OHFA bonus program, operated by the Cuyahoga Plan, 43 percent chose to purchase a house in Cleveland Heights.

The most important sources of information for participants on the pro-integrative mortgage incentive programs were realtors (37 percent) and fair housing agencies (28 percent). Other sources included advertisements, news articles, and friends.

Given their voluntary participation and the financial benefit derived, it was assumed that the participating homebuyers would be supportive of this approach (unless, possibly, they had a negative experience). The following were tested as indicators of the success of pro-integrative mortgage incentives:

1. continued support for this approach by the participants;
2. participant satisfaction with their chosen neighborhood and neighbors; and
3. the extent to which participants did not experience racial problems.

By these three standards, the programs surveyed have been successful. Virtually all of the 188 participants were supportive. Most were either "very satisfied" or "satisfied" with their neighborhoods, based upon their rating of five factors: public services, safety (crime), schools, housing, and location. The highest rates of dissatisfaction were with safety (crime)—only 8 percent—and schools—also only 8 percent. This pattern was similar to that in a comparable survey of suburban homebuyers in Cuyahoga County in which 98 percent expressed satisfaction with their neighborhoods, regardless of their race (Keating, Pammer, and Smith, 1987).

Most of the participants in the 1991 four-program evaluation reported either regular or at least occasional contact with their neighbors. Interracial social contact is an important goal of fair housing programs. Only 5 percent of the participants expressed dissatisfaction with their neighbors.

Asked how important the pro-integrative mortgage incentive was in their decision to make a pro-integrative move, almost three-fourths (73 percent) responded that they would have made this type of move anyway. One-fourth responded that they would not have made a pro-integrative move without the mortgage incentive.

It should be noted that this group of respondents was not a

representative cross-section of greater Cleveland homebuyers. More than half (54.5 percent) of the participants indicated that they had previously lived in racially diverse neighborhoods (those either populated mostly by members of another race or not dominated by any one race). This reflects the overrepresentation of participants who already resided in the racially diverse suburbs of Cleveland Heights and Shaker Heights.

Even so, almost half (47 percent) of those who had previously lived in racially diverse neighborhoods viewed the pro-integrative mortgage incentives as "very important" financially to their moves. This was truer of participants in the OHFA program, which has income ceilings, than of participants in the other three programs, which have no income restrictions. These data can be interpreted as meaning that the availability of pro-integrative mortgage incentives reinforced many such moves by those already favorably inclined to living in racially mixed neighborhoods.

Participating homebuyers who had not previously lived in a racially diverse neighborhood (i.e., who had lived in a neighborhood populated mostly by members of their own race) can be divided into two groups. The first group (9 percent) comprises those who responded that they would have made a pro-integrative move in any event. The second group (consisting of twenty homebuyers, or 91 percent of the subgroup) constitutes a key target group. It represents those homebuyers who would not have made the move from a non–racially diverse to a racially diverse neighborhood without the pro-integrative mortgage incentive. Most were white and already lived in Cleveland suburbs. Three-fourths (fifteen) purchased homes in Cleveland Heights and Shaker Heights.

The second part of the 1991 four-program evaluation was a telephone survey of 385 randomly selected residents of suburban Cuyahoga County. Of these, 118 lived in Cleveland Heights and 99 in Shaker Heights, with the remainder (44 percent) living in other Cuyahoga county suburbs. More than four-fifths (83 percent) were homeowners. About one-fourth lived on the same street or in the same neighborhood as a participant in one of the four programs studied.

The key question in this attitudinal survey was "Do you support a government policy of mortgage incentives to willing homebuyers to promote greater racial diversity in neighborhoods?" Overall, 55 percent were supportive, 20 percent were opposed, and 25 percent expressed no opinion. Opinions differed according to the race and residency of the suburban respondents. Whereas blacks were over-whelmingly supportive, just about one-half (49 percent) of whites were supportive. The highest levels of white support were in Shaker Heights (71 percent) and Cleveland Heights (58 percent), compared to 37 percent in the county's other suburbs. The highest level of white opposition (34 percent) was expressed by whites living on the same street or in the same neighborhood as program participants.

When asked whether they were supportive of a homebuyer of a different race who had received a pro-integrative mortgage incentive moving into their neighborhood, overall 57 percent of residents surveyed supportive, 9 percent were opposed, and 34 percent expressed no opinion. The highest levels of white support were in Cleveland Heights (66 percent) and Shaker Heights (60 percent), compared to 44.5 percent in the county's other suburbs. The levels of black support were higher than those of whites. The highest level of white opposition (16 percent) came from those living on the same street or in the same neighborhood as program participants. Yet 47 percent or three times as many whites in these areas were supportive (Keating, 1992).

Other surveys have shown that most white Americans do not expressly oppose having a black neighbor. For example, based on three national telephone polls conducted in the period from 1985 to 1987, Schuman and Bobo (1988: 290, table 6) found that 73 percent of whites would not mind having a black neighbor, compared to 15 percent who said that they would "mind a little," 7 percent who said that "it would depend," and 5 percent who said that they would "mind a lot."

Racial discrimination persists in Cuyahoga County, as is reflected in complaints of racial discrimination in housing reported to the Cuyahoga Plan, which investigated 160 such complaints in 1990 (Cuyahoga Plan, 1991). A 1991 survey of greater Clevelanders found that 4 percent (2 percent of whites and 8 percent of blacks) reported racial discrimination in their attempts to buy or rent housing (CLRI, 1991). This finding is similar to those of national studies based on housing audits, which show that racial discrimination in housing continues (e.g., Galster, 1990a). Of all participants in the four programs studied, 9 percent reported encountering racial discrimination. Blacks (27 percent) experienced a much higher rate of racial discrimination that whites (5 percent), but no black homebuyers reported such racial discrimination in 1990, compared to four white homebuyers who did (Keating, 1992).

The 1991 four-program evaluation of pro-integrative mortgage incentives in Cuyahoga County suggests that there is not a high level of overt resistance to such incentives. However, except in pro-integrative suburbs such as Cleveland Heights and Shaker Heights, there does not appear to be majority white support. Much educational work remains to be done to convince white suburbanites and their elected representatives of the acceptability of the pro-integrative mortgage incentive approach.

As long as racial rather than class differences are the issue, these data give hope that whites are indeed more tolerant today than they were. Schuman and Bobo (1988: 290–91, table 6) found that when whites were asked about the acceptability of a black neighbor of the same social status, the results were not significantly different from responses when similar social status was not addressed. In the metropolitan Cleveland programs, the homebuyer participants purchased in neighborhoods assumed to be composed typically of homeowner residents with similar income levels. If, as in the regional housing mobility and fair-share experiments, the purpose was to integrate suburban neighborhoods both racially and economically, then the likelihood of suburban opposition would be much higher than in the pro-integrative mortgage incentive programs.

Comparative Suburban Case Studies

The suburbs of Cleveland Heights and Shaker Heights are not alone in their long-term efforts to promote stable racial diversity; there are other examples in the United States. Those municipalities, mostly suburban, that have adopted affirmative fair housing policies have joined together in National Neighbors, a national organization formed in 1969 (Saltman, 1990) and renamed the "National Federation for Neighborhood Diversity" in 1989. Five suburbs in Illinois, Michigan, and New Jersey that have gained reputations similar to those of Cleveland Heights and Shaker Heights for their long-term efforts to promote stable racial diversity are profiled here.

Oak Park, Illinois

The village of Oak Park lies directly west of Chicago, about nine miles from the Chicago Loop. Most of it was developed in the late nineteenth century. It is known as the site of the first home and studio of famous architect Frank Lloyd Wright, who designed many buildings in Oak Park, and as the birthplace of novelist Ernest Hemingway.

During the 1960s, Oak Park became concerned about the racial transition underway in the neighboring Chicago section of Austin. In 1960 there were no whites living in Austin; by 1970, five census tracts in south Austin had become nearly all black, and blacks had moved to the eastern border of Oak Park. Despite efforts by the Organization for a Better Austin and the Town Hall Assembly to maintain stable racial diversity, by 1980 three-fourths of the Chicago neighborhood's population was black and the area was highly segregated. By the mid-1980s, only one section of Austin was still predominantly white (Berry, 1979; Goodwin, 1979; Squires, Bennett, McCourt, and Nyden, 1987: 118).

In 1963, Oak Park created a community relations commission. Fair housing efforts were supported by the Oak Park-River Forest Citizen's Committee for Human Rights. In May 1968, following the assassination of Martin Luther King, Jr., and after considerable debate, Oak Park enacted a comprehensive fair housing ordinance. The suburb banned racial discrimination in housing, including blockbusting and racial steering.

In 1970 only 132 of Oak Park's population of 62,506 were black. However, concern that black in-migration was being directed to the southeastern corner of the suburb, adjacent to Austin, which was undergoing rapid racial transition, and commitment to the social goal of long-term racial diversity led to the creation of a private, nonprofit Oak Park Housing Center (OPHC) in 1972 (Berry, 1979; Berry, Goodwin, Lake, and Smith, 1976: 237; Goodwin, 1979: 166–78;

Saltman, 1990: 305). OPHC's purpose was affirmative marketing to ensure racial diversity without racial resegregation. It engaged in what some observers termed "reverse steering" (Berry, 1979). White homebuyers and renters were encouraged to consider living in Oak Park's southeastern area, while blacks were encouraged to look elsewhere in Oak Park, where they were underrepresented. Housing audits to test for racial discrimination began in 1973, when Oak Park officially adopted a policy of "maintaining diversity" (Goodwin, 1979: 156–57). The Oak Park Citizens' Action Program took the lead in fighting redlining by lenders, a practice banned in Oak Park in 1972 as its black population increased (Goodwin, 1979: 179–88).

In 1973, Oak Park invoked the "exempt location" clause of its 1968 fair housing ordinance. The village exempted one block and one apartment building from possible enforcement of the fair housing ordinance in order to permit pro-integrative efforts to continue in the face of racial transition, which had resulted in black populations of over 50 percent in some areas of the suburb (Goodwin, 1979: 158).

An even more controversial proposal emerged in December 1973, when a village trustee proposed to legislate racial quotas in southeastern Oak Park by limiting black occupancy of residential blocks to no more than 30 percent. This proposal represented a prevailing fear that once such a racial "tipping point" was reached, whites would begin to leave or would refuse to consider entering that part of the village. The racial housing quota proposal provoked tremendous controversy and debate. The Oak Park Community Relations Commission rejected it, but only by the margin of eight to seven in February 1974. In the face of opposition by community organizations, questions as to its legality, and adverse publicity, the proposal was tabled and died (Berry, Goodwin, Lake, and Smith, 1976: 237–38; Goodwin, 1979: 159–60; Vodar, 1975).

Instead, Oak Park embarked on different approaches to promoting dispersed racial diversity. It promoted strict housing code enforcement and rehabilitation programs to maintain the quality of the housing stock. In 1978, Oak Park initiated a unique "equity assurance" program, under which participating single-family homeowners would be guaranteed 80 percent of the difference between the pre-sale assessed valuation of their house and the actual sale price (within five years after an appraisal). This program was designed to counteract white fears that an increasing black presence would lead to the depreciation of housing values (Vodar, 1975; McNamara, 1984; Lauber, 1992). Very few residents have participated in this program, and no claims have ever been filed (Goel, 1990: 379).

Subsequently, Oak Park also developed an innovative program of providing financial incentives to apartment owners who would agree to increase racial diversity in their buildings (Squires, Bennett, McCourt, and Nyden, 1987: 119; Lauber, 1992). Unique in the United States, this program, operated by the OPHC, provides grants of up to $1,000 per rental unit to participating landlords, who must provide matching funds for improvements. In 1991 the OHPC assisted 261 renters to make pro-integrative moves into fifty-five buildings whose landlords participated in this program. Since the program's inception, the village has provided $770,531 cumulatively in grants, with private landlords providing matching funds amounting to $2,689,000.

The OPHC has concentrated its efforts on rental housing. Of the 23,571 housing units in Oak Park, 44 percent are rental units. Much of this rental housing, particularly the larger buildings, is concentrated in the southeastern part of Oak Park, where much of the black population is concentrated. Home purchasers are referred to private real estate brokers.

Oak Park is an acknowledged leader among pro-integrative suburbs. In 1977 it initiated an annual Oak Park Congress Exchange, during which other municipal governments and fair housing organizations that promoted racial diversity could meet to discuss their experiences (Saltman, 1990: 308). The village and the OPHC cooperated in the formation of the Near West Suburban Housing Center to expand the housing choices of black home seekers in Chicago's western suburbs (Saltman, 1990: 307–8). In 1991 the OPHC served 4,686 clients, including 2,236 whites and 1,957 blacks. It located housing for 1,272 renters (867 white and 261 black). Its budget was $390,000, including municipal support from its Community Development Block Grant and a marketing contract for the "diversity assurance" program for landlords, which provided about 70 percent of its funding; the remainder came from corporate and foundation support, membership dues, and benefits. The OPHC staff of ten full-time and four part-time persons was assisted by volunteers, who acted as escorts for prospective residents (OPHC, 1992). In 1990, 18.3 percent of Oak Park's population of 53,648 was black.

In marked contrast to Oak Park, its neighboring blue-collar, working-class town of Cicero has gained a national reputation for its resistance to racial diversity. In 1951 residents of Cicero violently forced out a black veteran who attempted to rent an apartment. In 1966 the town turned back a civil rights march headed by Martin Luther King, Jr., who termed Cicero "the Selma of the North." In 1980, Cicero had no black residents, despite being bordered by Chicago's all-black Lawndale neighborhood. It was subsequently sued by the U.S. Department of Justice for fair housing and employment violations (Squires, Bennett, McCourt, and Nyden, 1987: 120). In 1990 only 141 (0.002 percent) of Cicero's population of 67,436 were black. However, Cicero is beginning to have a significant influx of Hispanics.

To the west of Oak Park and Cicero is the suburb of Maywood, which underwent racial transition beginning in the 1960s. However, unlike Oak Park, Maywood could not maintain racial diversity and gradually resegregated into a predominantly black suburb. By 1980, 75 percent of its population was black (Squires, Bennett, McCourt, and Nyden, 1987: 120–21). In 1990, 83.8 percent of Maywood's population of 27,139 was black. However, there is still white demand for older housing in Maywood that is less expensive than neighboring Oak Park and River Forest.

Park Forest, Illinois

Park Forest is an example of a privately planned suburb. The village of Park Forest is located south of Chicago, whose South Shore neighborhood unsuccessfully attempted to maintain racial diversity in the late 1960s (Berry, 1979; Molotch, 1972). The developer-planners had been previously associated with the federal "greenbelt" planned suburban experiments and early public housing during the 1930s. Unlike these projects, Park Forest was developed privately for profit after World War II (Teaford, 1986: 103). A middle- and moderate-income, mostly residential, commuter suburb, Park Forest gained fame as the setting for William Whyte's *The Organization Man*.

Although the village created the Park Forest Commission on Human Relations in 1951 to study racial discrimination, its first black family did not move in until 1959 (Helper, 1986). By 1965, the village became concerned about the clustering together of black residents, steered by real estate brokers. Park Forest encouraged the brokers instead to support white home purchases where blacks lived. In 1968 the village adopted a comprehensive fair housing ordinance. By 1970, only about 2.4 percent of Park Forest's population of 30,638 was black (Berry, Goodwin, Lake, and Smith, 1976).

However, by 1973 the black population had more than doubled to about 7 percent. Concern also grew about the impact of the development of hundreds of federally subsidized homes in an adjacent area called Beacon Hill–Forest Heights, whose population was predominantly black and whose children were within the Park Forest school district. In order to meet state school desegregation guidelines, the school district in which Park Forest was located voluntarily began school busing in September 1972. White residents in the Eastgate neighborhood of Park Forest, immediately adjacent to Beacon Hill–Forest Heights, felt most threatened by these developments (Berry, 1979; Berry, Goodwin, Lake, and Smith, 1976).

In 1973 the concerns about possible white flight and racial resegregation led Park Forest to adopt several ordinances for the purpose of "integration maintenance." They included the prohibition of racial steering of prospective homebuyers and redlining by lenders, establishment of a fair housing review board to regulate real estate brokers, and empowerment of the village manager and the human relations commission to review complaints of racial discrimination in housing (Helper, 1986; Berry, Goodwin, Lake, and Smith, 1976). Opposed to this policy, a black member of the human relations commission resigned in protest. His wife later filed a complaint of racial discrimination against the village's affirmative marketing program, but the complaint was rejected by HUD (Hayes, 1990).

In 1977, Park Forest adopted a comprehensive pro-integrative policy titled "Integration in Housing: A Plan for Racial Diversity" (Onderdonk, DeMarco, and Cardona, 1977). Through its affirmative marketing program, the village sought to make white homebuyers aware of those areas with a sizable black population. A key administrator of Park Forest's integration maintenance program was Don DeMarco, who left in 1982 to assume a similar position in Shaker Heights, Ohio.

The Park Forest affirmative marketing program became the target of a major legal challenge brought by real estate organizations in 1987 (Squires, Bennett, McCourt, and Nyden, 1987: 123–24). Concerned that white homebuyers, influenced by real estate brokers, were shunning Apache Street in the Eastgate section (which in 1980 had a black population of 56 percent) and in response to the complaints of the neighborhood's white residents that racial steering was occurring, Park Forest purchased three vacant, HUD-foreclosed houses in the Apache Street neighborhood during 1979–1981 and sold them to the South-Suburban Housing Center, a fair housing agency that operates in many Chicago suburbs. The agency then marketed the houses to white buyers. Spurred by this success, Park Forest in 1982 purchased and rehabilitated another three vacant houses whose previous owners had their mortgages foreclosed and again contracted with the South-Suburban Housing Center to market them, to attract white prospects as part of Park Forest's affirmative marketing program (Hayes, 1990). In 1991 the U.S. Seventh Circuit Court of Appeals upheld the 1988 trial court decision in favor of this race-conscious, affirmative marketing program in the face of real estate organization claims that it amounted to unconstitutional racial discrimination (*South-Suburban Housing Center v. Greater South-Suburban Board of Realtors*) (935 F.2d 868 [7th Cir. 1991] (Thomas, 1991: 973). The U.S. Supreme Court declined to hear an appeal.

Park Forest has collaborated with real estate brokers through a realtor liaison program. Realtors must register with the village and comply with its nonsolicitation ordinance. This has resulted in realtor cooperation with the village's fair housing goals. Park Forest also monitors racial occupancy patterns in rental housing (Lauber, 1992).

In 1990 nearly one-fourth (24.6 percent) of Park Forest's population of 24,656 was black. Over almost two decades, Park Forest's integration maintenance policies and programs have resulted in a racially diverse suburb. A 1981 study by L. F. Heumann concluded that a majority of the residents were supportive of these policies and programs, although many newer residents were not familiar with their details, and that the policies had been effective in maintaining racial diversity.

Two Detroit Suburbs: Southfield and Oak Park

Detroit is ranked as the third most racially isolated metropolis in the United States, behind only Chicago and Cleveland. The city of Detroit has also lost is population steadily the past three decades, as the black population became a majority. Suffering from deindustrialization and the flight of the middle class and much of the working class, especially whites since the 1967 riot and the election of black mayor Coleman Young in 1973, Detroit has become an ever poorer and more racially polarized city (Darden, Hill, Thomas, and Thomas, 1987).

The city's suburbs are also almost entirely racially segregated. Dearborn, the headquarters of Ford Motor Company and a white, working-class enclave, has, like Cicero, overtly resisted black suburbanization (Darden, Hill, Thomas, and Thomas, 1987: 119–25). In 1990 less than 1 percent (494) of Dearborn's population of 89,286 was black. The blue-collar suburb of Warren gained national notoriety in 1971 when it rejected federal housing aid in a referendum because then HUD secretary (and former Michigan governor) George Romney insisted that Warren act affirmatively to comply with federal fair housing policy in order to obtain urban renewal funding (Danielson, 1976: 223–27). In 1970 only five black families lived in Warren, even though 30 percent of the work force was black (Darden, Hill, Thomas, and Thomas, 1987: 142). In 1990 less than 1 percent (1,047) of Warren's population of 144,864 was black.

One of the few examples of support for racial diversity in suburban Detroit is Southfield. Southfield has long been considered the primary Jewish suburb of Detroit (Chafets, 1990: 138). The Jewish population of Detroit has been more tolerant of blacks than any other white ethnic group. Such Jewish support for racial diversity also has played a role in the case of the Detroit suburb of Oak Park.

In 1970, Southfield only had 102 black residents. In the face of the possible resegregation of its Magnolia subdivision in the wake of the 1967 Detroit riot, the suburb enacted an antisolicitation ordinance in 1971. Subsequently, Southfield adopted an eight-point policy to promote stable racial diversity and to prevent resegregation. The city created its own Southfield Housing and Neighborhood Center and supports the Oakland County Center for Open Housing.

Like its counterparts in suburban Chicago and Cleveland, Southfield has made overt efforts to recruit whites in order to maintain white demand for housing and to prevent becoming a magnet for black suburbanization, which could in turn eventually lead to resegregation (Chafets, 1990: 140–42). This policy has proved controversial, and the city does not provide pro-integrative mortgage incentives. However, the Jewish Community Council provides its own mortgage incentive program to Jewish homebuyers.

A prosperous suburban city, Southfield is home to the huge Northland shopping center and one of the most rapidly growing suburban office centers in metropolitan Detroit. In 1990, 29 percent of its population of 75,728 was black, more than three times the 1980 level. The black population is concentrated in the southern part of Southfield, which is also home to most of the city's Orthodox Jewish residents and to a growing Middle Eastern (primarily Chaldean Christian) population.

In a 1985 survey, metropolitan Detroit residents were questioned about their racial attitudes. A majority (75 percent) of whites in Southfield indicated that they preferred to live in racially mixed neighborhoods, compared to only 53 percent of all white suburbanites surveyed. Only 16 percent of Southfield's white population indicated a preference for an all-white neighborhood, compared to 35 percent of all white suburbanites surveyed. Almost all (96 percent) of Southfield's black population indicated a preference for living in racially mixed neighborhoods, with none preferring all-black neighborhoods. When asked if "most of the people in your neighborhood are of your own race," 68 percent of Southfield's whites responded affirmatively, compared to 87 percent of suburban whites generally. In contrast, only 32 percent of Southfield's blacks responded affirmatively, compared to 62 percent of suburban blacks generally (Bell and O'Connor, 1985). This indicates that Southfield's white population is generally supportive of racially diverse neighborhoods, although two-thirds in 1985 lived in mostly white neigh-borhoods in the suburb.

Like Southfield, its neighbor Oak Park continues to stand out as a Detroit suburb tolerant of racial diversity. Oak Park is home to the area's largest Orthodox Jewish population, as well as to numerous ethnic groups, most notably Middle Eastern Chaldeans. Beginning in 1973, Oak Park adopted a ban on "for sale" signs (Darden, Hill, Thomas, and Thomas, 1987: 147). In 1990 about one-third of Oak Park's population of 30,462 was black.

Teaneck, New Jersey

Teaneck township gained fame as one of the first suburban commu-nities in the United States voluntarily to integrate its public schools (Damarell, 1968). Black migration to this formerly all-white suburb began in the 1950s. Teaneck's growth occurred mostly between World Wars I and II. Its population peaked at about forty-two thousand in 1960.

There was considerable white resistance to black settlement in Teaneck. A buffer zone created by Teaneck to separate itself from a predominantly black section of neighboring Englewood failed to keep black homebuyers out. Blockbusting led to white panic selling. This in turn led to the formation in 1955 of the Teaneck Civic Conference. It supported school desegregation, which was ap-proved in 1964 in the face of considerable white opposition.

In 1966, Teaneck passed an antisolicitation ordinance to prevent blockbusting. In 1972, "Teaneck Together" was formed to promote Teaneck as a community attractive to white homebuyers. The suburb funded a housing center in 1977 to promote the city as an interracial suburban community (Lake, 1981: 81–86; Saltman, 1990: 302–5).

In 1990, 26 percent of Teaneck's population of 37,825 was black. However, the suburb has faced increasing problems. By 1990 it no longer had a municipal housing center. In the same year, Teaneck's reputation as an example of a harmonious, interracial suburb was damaged by the controversy over the killing of a black teenager by a white police officer. Controversy and conflict arose again over the officer's acquittal in 1992 (*New York Times*, February 9, 1992).

Conclusion

Through the examples herein of the municipal pro-integrative housing policies and the suburbs in several metropolitan areas, it is evident that sustained affirmative policies to promote racially diverse suburban housing and neighborhoods are possible. Though white resistance to such policies remains, this is not an insurmountable obstacle. However, the goal of racial diversity must be kept separate from the goal of greater economic integration of the suburbs, because the latter raises far more opposition.

12

The Legal Status
of Race-conscious, Pro-integrative
Housing Policies and Programs

Race-conscious policies and programs, including housing, in the United States not only have been politically controversial but also have been subjected to legal attack. They have been challenged as violative of the prohibition against racial discrimination in housing that is embodied in the 1968 federal Fair Housing Act and similar state and federal legislation. Opponents have also contended that race-conscious policies have denied members of racial minority groups constitutional guarantees of equal protection, as provided by the Fourteenth Amendment to the U.S. Constitution.

In a nondiscriminatory society, race-conscious policies would not be necessary to promote greater racial harmony and neighborhood racial diversity and to reduce racial discrimination in housing. However, as demonstrated previously, there continues to be considerable racial separatism and housing discrimination in the United States, despite the passage of national, state, and local fair housing legislation.

Proponents of the necessity of using race-conscious policies argue that there must be affirmative action taken to overcome the problems that have prevented the realization of the goals of fair housing legislation. Whether it is to persuade whites to remain when minorities move into their neighborhoods or to move into neighbor-hoods with a substantial minority, to persuade blacks to move into predominantly or all-white neighborhoods, or to stabilize racially balanced neighborhoods, race is to be taken into consideration.

A. J. Goel (1990) argues that the "anti-subjugation" principle, rather than ideals of color blindness or integration, must govern how race-conscious policies are viewed. By this he means that practices that aggravate or perpetuate the subordinate position of a specially disadvantaged group are unconstitutional. Race-neutral or color-blind policies that result in racial segregation or resegregation violate this principle.

Proponents of affirmative action argue that only by taking race into account can past racially discriminatory practices be overcome. This seemingly contradictory position has been long accepted by the courts in fashioning remedial orders where alleged racial discrimi-nation has been proven.

Opponents argue that the goal of national policy is to achieve race-neutral housing markets. The use of race-conscious policies *ipso facto* violates both this national policy and, it is argued, the prohibi-tion against racial discrimination embodied in fair housing legisla-tion. R. A. Smolla (1985) proposes a four-step test to judge race-conscious policies:

1. should one always act in a colorblind fashion?
2. may race-conscious governmental actions include classifica-tions, or only persuasion?
3. may racial classifications in order to integrate burden any-one?
4. if racial classifications may burden anyone, may they burden minority group members or majority group members only?

Legal Standards for Proof of Racial Discrimination in Housing

The statutory standards for determining whether racial discrimina-tion in housing has occurred are found in Title VIII of the U.S. Code (Fair Housing Act) and in court decisions, which derive from similar legislation (Title VII) and legal precedents concerning racial discrimination in employment. Title VIII prohibits "treating a person differently because of race."

A violation occurs if it can be proven that there is discriminatory intent. A prima facie case can be established by evidence that:

1. the complainant is a member of a racial minority;
2. the complainant applied for and was qualified to rent or purchase the housing unit sought;
3. the complainant was rejected by the defendant; and
4. the housing continued to be available after rejection of the complainant.

The defendant must rebut such a case by showing a legitimate, nondiscriminatory purpose for the denial of housing to the minority complainant. In the absence of supportive witnesses, intentional discrimination can be very difficult to prove if a defendant has a plausible reason for rejection of the complainant.

Even if intentional discrimination cannot be proven, establishment of discriminatory effect by a defendant can lead to a decision that there has been a violation of fair housing law. A prima facie case of discriminatory effect can be shown by evidence that an apparently race-neutral policy either has a disparate impact on a protected minority group or perpetuates the effects of racial segregation. The former claim is often supported by statistical evidence, for example, that minorities have a much higher housing rental or purchasing rejection rate than whites. This can be rebutted by a showing that there is a legitimate nondiscriminatory reason for the practice, despite its effect (e.g., business necessity). The latter claim typically involves rejection of housing projects that would likely have racial mix of occupants in a predominantly or all-white community. In this context, a community that denies approval of such a project must prove that its reasons are legitimate and nondiscriminatory (Zimmerman, 1992).

If a claim of racial discrimination is made against a public entity under the Fourteenth Amendment's guarantee of equal protection, the courts have applied similar tests. Assuming that a complainant establishes a prima facie case, the courts will apply a "strict scrutiny" test, meaning that the accused has the burden of proof to rebut the accusation.

There has been a quarter-century of experience with litigation under Title VIII. The U.S. Supreme Court and the lower federal courts have clarified many fair housing law questions, for example, who has standing to sue, what the standards of proof are, and what reasonable remedies, including damages, are (Metcalf, 1988). Numerous precedents provide guidance on what usually constitutes racially discriminatory behavior in housing.

Access Quotas versus Ceiling Quotas

In order to end racial segregation in housing, race-conscious policies have been used on occasion. These have sometimes involved "quota" systems. In a supposedly meritocratic society, quotas, especially those based on race (or, previously, on ethnicity and religion), have been anathema. Despite their past exclusionary use, in the context of promoting greater racial integration in housing they have been called "benign" quotas.

One version is the "access" quota, which is intended to guarantee minimum minority representation (Ackerman, 1974; Bishop, 1988; Kushner, 1988; Potter, 1990). Access quotas have been used in employment and education under the rubric of "affirmative action" to ensure that minorities have the opportunity for improved schooling and job opportunities. Whites who claim that these quotas have cost them similar opportunities have challenged these controversial policies, claiming that they amount to reverse discrimination (Glazer, 1987).

The other version is the "ceiling" quota. Associated with "integration maintenance" programs, this quota places a limit on the number of minorities to be allowed to live in a housing project (building or development), in order to prevent racial "tipping" should this ceiling be exceeded. The rationale is to prevent white flight and resegregation of racially diverse housing developments (Gelber, 1985; *Harvard Law Review*, 1980; *Yale Law Review*, 1980).

Integration maintenance policies have proven to be particularly vulnerable to legal challenge. Goel argues that integration maintenance programs that restrict minority access through ceiling quotas may stigmatize minorities as being inferior, noting that the Thirteenth Amendment to the U.S. Constitution prohibits the "badges of slavery" (Goel, 1990: 400). He concludes the ceiling quotas impose a heavy burden on minorities by limiting their access to housing, thus appearing to subjugate minorities by making them unacceptable (Goel, 1990: 406). Smolla brands ceiling quotas "morally and legally wrong" (Smolla, 1985: 1015).

Integration Maintenance in Public and Federally Subsidized Housing

Despite federal antidiscrimination law, much of the low-income public housing built in the United States has become racially segregated. This has led to litigation aimed at forcing federally assisted local housing authorities (LHAs) to comply with Section 808 of the federal fair housing statute, which requires that federal agencies affirmatively further the purposes of that law. The best known of these lawsuits is certainly the decades-long *Gautreaux* case brought against the Chicago Housing Authority, which eventually led to the experimental use of federal rent subsidies to allow poor, minority Chicago tenants to move into privately owned rental housing in predominantly white Chicago suburbs (Polikoff, 1988). A similar case (*Banks v. Perk*) brought against Cleveland's public housing authority resulted in only a small number of "scatter-site" units being occupied by minorities in predominantly white neighborhoods on the city's west side.

Another approach has been to force LHAs to integrate their projects building by building as units become vacant. After vacancy, units in predominantly white buildings would be assigned only to minorities and vice versa until a satisfactory racial balance was achieved. This requires the institution of a racial quota. In three instances federal courts have ruled that this race-conscious approach violates federal fair housing law.

In *Williamsburg Fair Housing Committee v. New York City Housing Authority* (493 F. Supp. 1225 [S.D.N.Y. 1980]), a federal district court rejected a housing developer's policy of maintaining racial occupancy quotas—75 percent white, 20 percent Hispanic, and 5 percent black—to preserve integration. Separate lists were kept for access by members of each group to units allocated to their race. The court ruled that a prima facie case of racial discrimination was made and that the defendant-owner had failed to rebut it by showing the necessity for the policy. The defendant did not invoke the probability of racial tipping in the absence of such quotas to justify integration maintenance.

In *Burney v. Housing Authority of the County of Beaver* (551 F. Supp. 746 [W.D. Pa. 1982]), a local housing authority sought to achieve racial parity in long-segregated public housing. In this case, the federal district court reviewed the intent of Congress in passing fair housing legislation. Although it found that Congress had both antidiscrimination and pro-integrative goals, it concluded that integration was ancillary to the central congressional purpose of banning racial discrimination in housing. Therefore, the court ruled that the imposition of racial quotas to ensure black–white parity in public housing projects was prohibited.

In *United States v. Charlottesville Redevelopment and Housing Authority* (718 F. Supp. 461 [W. D. Va. 1989]), a federal district court similarly ruled that a race-conscious tenant selection policy aimed at ending a twenty-five-year policy of racial discrimination and achieving a fifty-fifty racial mix in public housing was invalid.

The leading case is *United States v. Starrett City Associates* (640 F. Supp. 668 [E.D. N.Y. 1987], *affirmed* 840 F.2d 1096 [2d Cir. 1988], *cert. denied*, 488 U.S. 946 [1988]). Starrett City is a privately owned housing development of almost six thousand rental units in forty-six high-rise buildings, housing approximately twenty thousand residents, in Brooklyn, New York. Built in the 1970s using federal and state subsidies, Starrett City is surrounded by mostly racially segregated neighborhoods. Racial strife in sections of Brooklyn and other areas of New York City during the past several years has received extensive national publicity and was dramatized in Spike Lee's movie *Do the Right Thing*. To prevent segregation and racial tipping, resulting in white flight and ultimate resegregation, the management of Starrett City instituted a racial quota policy that limited minority occupancy to between 30 and 40 percent.

A lawsuit was brought on behalf of black members on the waiting list for Starrett City units, challenging this ceiling quota system as racially discriminatory. Because of the great black demand and consequently long waiting list, prospective minority tenants had a much longer waiting period for places in those apartments designated for minority occupancy than whites did for other units. At the trial there was expert testimony that racial tipping resulting in white flight can occur from a low black population of 1 percent to a high of 60 percent, with most experts agreeing that it occurs when the black population in predominantly white areas ranges from 10 to 20 percent (*United States v. Starrett City Associates*, 660 F. supp. 668 at 674).

In its defense, the management invoked the decision of the Second Circuit Court of Appeals in *Otero v. New York City Housing Authority* (484 F.2d 1122 [2d Cir. 1973]). In that case, the New York City Housing Authority refused to abide by its own policy of providing displaced residents (predominantly black) first priority to return to replacement housing built in an urban renewal project. It did so to prevent the resegregation of the area and instead rented about half of the units to nonformer site residents, most of whom were white. The district court in *Otero* (354 F. Supp. 941 [S.D.N.Y. 1973]) had ruled that affirmative action by the Housing Authority to achieve a racially balanced community was precluded by a policy that would deny minority residents scarce public housing. But the federal Second Circuit Court of Appeals reversed. Like the federal district court in *Burney*, it reviewed the twin purposes of the federal fair housing law. However, it came to the opposite conclusion, that is, that the Housing Authority did indeed have an affirmative duty to achieve racial integration in public housing. It ruled that the Housing Authority could meet its heavy burden of proof required to justify a race-conscious policy by its convincing evidence that adherence to a race-neutral policy would lead to the destruction of racial balance.

Nonetheless, the district court ruled against Starrett City by finding that its race-conscious tenant selection policy violated the fair housing law and by disallowing a defense based on the *Otero* precedent because it involved a governmental entity, whereas Starrett City was a private developer. A compromise settlement was apparently reached when Starrett City agreed to admit a small number of minorities in excess of its existing quota system on an accelerated basis. However, the Reagan administration intervened to challenge this settlement, claiming that it amounted to reverse discrimination.

The Second Circuit Court of Appeals then upheld the district court decision (although by a split two-to-one vote). It based its decision on a threefold test applied to integration maintenance, which would be upheld only if (1) such maintenance was temporary in nature, (2) the community had a past history of racial discrimination, and (3) minorities would be provided with access to housing. Starrett City failed all three tests. First, its policy, in effect for a decade and envisioned to remain in effect for another fifteen years, was not considered "temporary," thus distinguishing this case from the singular policy challenged in *Otero*. Second, because it was a newly constructed project (built on landfill), it had no prior history. Patterns of racial segregation in nearby Brooklyn neighborhoods were not considered in determining whether increased minority access would lead to racial tipping, white flight, and eventual resegregation. Third, because the racial quotas were ceiling rather than access quotas, they did not enhance minority access.

The dissenting judge agreed with the interpretation of the primary goal of federal fair housing law made in *Otero* but did not interpret that precedent as limiting the duration of race-conscious affirmative policies to temporary measures. The U.S. Supreme Court refused to review this decision: therefore, there is not yet any binding U.S. Supreme Court precedent involving integration maintenance policies. Under different circumstances, it is conceivable that, applying the appeals court's three-part test, racial quotas would be justifiable, at least temporarily.

In the wake of this 1988 decision, the white proportion of the Starrett City project's approximately twenty thousand residents declined from 62 percent to 50 percent in 1992. The minority population increased from 38 to 50 percent, including 35 percent black and 11 percent Hispanic (Roberts, 1992). Only time will tell whether, in the absence of rigid racial quotas, racial parity will be replaced with a predominantly or all-minority population as a result of racial tipping.

"For Sale" Sign Restrictions

Most housing in American suburbs is privately owned, and most, whether for sale or rent, is marketed by private realty firms (with some owners marketing on their own). Although the firms use a variety of marketing techniques, real estate "for sale" signs are usually prominently displayed to advertise houses for sale.

Many suburban communities regulate the appearance of residential neighborhoods, invoking their zoning and land use powers. The primary purpose of "aesthetic zoning" is to protect property values. "Signage" regulations routinely restrict the place, size, and number of commercial advertising signs. Furthermore, those municipalities experiencing white flight have resorted to absolute bans on real estate "for sale" signs in an attempt to remove the most visible signs of panic selling. Several suburban Cleveland communities, the earliest being Shaker Heights, have resorted to such bans. Euclid is the latest Cleveland suburb to enact this type of policy, banning lawn (but not window) "for sale" real estate signs in 1992.

Absolute bans on advertising have been challenged on First Amendment grounds. The U.S. Supreme Court has ruled in several cases that commercial advertising is a protected form of free speech. The leading case is *Linmark Associates, Inc. v. Willingboro* (431 U.S. 85 [1977]). Willingboro, New Jersey, was one of several Levittowns, originally developed in the 1950s and almost exclusively white. In 1960 only sixty (0.005 percent) of its residents were nonwhite. However, in the following decade, as Willingboro grew rapidly, so did its minority population, increasing to 11.7 percent of its forty-four thousand residents in 1970. By 1973 the minority population had increased to 18.2 percent of the township's population, while the white population dropped by 5 percent between 1970 and 1973.

The city council, alarmed by these trends, conducted public hearings in early 1974, culminating in the passage of an absolute ban on "for sale" signs. This measure was first suggested in a 1973 town meeting. During the public hearings, there was widespread support expressed for the ban, although it was based largely on concern for aesthetics and real estate values, rather than fear of white flight.

In ruling that Willingboro's sign ban violated the First Amendment, the federal district court judge determined that there was no evidence of white flight but rather resident concern about a decline in property values due to an influx of minorities. Although the federal Third Circuit Court of Appeals upheld the ban, a unanimous U.S. Supreme Court agreed with the trial judge, reversing the court of appeals decision. The U.S. Supreme Court based its ruling (authored by liberal black justice Thurgood Marshall) primarily on the absence of convincing evidence of the necessity of such a sign ban, despite recognizing a legitimate public purpose, namely, promoting a racially integrated community. The court distinguished this case from *Barrick Realty v. Gary* (Indiana) (491 F.2d 161 [7th Cir. 1974]), in which a similar sign ban was upheld because there was convincing evidence of white flight, triggered in part by "for sale" signs. By 1990, 80 percent of Gary's population was black.

Seemingly, this decision could have left racially transitory suburbs without the use of a sign ban as defense against blockbusting and white flight until after substantial and perhaps irreparable damage had been done. The U.S. Supreme Court did advise that Willingboro continue to educate its residents about the problem and create inducements to persuade potential homesellers not to leave.

As it has turned out, municipalities were not denied the right to regulate signs after all. Such communities as Cleveland Heights and Shaker Heights, with long-standing bans on "for sale" signs in residential neighborhoods, have been able to justify this policy, as long as it applies consistently to all commercial signs (excepting perhaps political advertising), on the ground that it was designed to protect the aesthetic appearance of residential neighborhoods. This was illustrated in the real estate board challenge to fair housing policies in south suburban Chicago. Four suburbs that were sued, including Park Forest, had a variety of restrictions on the size and placement of "for sale" signs, none having banned the signs altogether. All of the ordinances justified the signage regulations on aesthetics. The district court judge upheld the legality of these ordinances under the Fair Housing Act, based on findings that realtors did not prove any significant loss of income resulting from the regulation, any racially discriminatory impact on minority home seekers, or any denial of housing access. The ordinances also met the constitutional free speech tests applied to regulation of commercial advertising, namely, they were narrowly tailored to meet a significant governmental purpose, they did not regulate speech content, and they left open ample alternative channels of communication (*South-Suburban Housing Center v. Greater South-Suburban Board of Realtors*, 713 F. Supp. at 1090–93). This ruling was upheld on appeal

(*South-Suburban Housing Center v. Greater South-Suburban Board of Realtors*, 935 F. 2d at 876 and 896–97).

After Euclid, Ohio, adopted its ban on lawn "for sale" signs in 1992, the Cleveland Area Board of Realtors challenged the suburb on First (free speech) and Fifth (taking of private property) Amendment grounds (Heider, 1992b). The sponsor of the ban admitted that the city could not document the assertion that such lawn signs constituted a blight on residential property values.

In the case of a fifth Chicago suburb that had enacted a total "for sale" sign ban in 1972, but which had suspended it following the 1977 *Willingboro* decision, the suburb decided to revive its enforcement in 1984. When challenged, however, it repealed the ban again prior to trial.

These cases still leave open the circumstances under which the courts will accept or reject the legality of a total ban on "for sale" signs, especially if the specific or primary basis for the adoption of such a ban is racial transition rather than simply aesthetics.

Antisolicitation Policies

Another regulatory policy aimed at preventing illegal blockbusting is the prohibition of unwanted solicitations of homeowners by realtors. The types of solicitation banned include written materials (mailed or otherwise delivered) and telephone calls. Some municipalities keep lists of those residents who indicate that they do not wish to be solicited and then provide these lists to realty firms operating within their housing market. The avowed purpose of this type of ordinance is to maintain a stable housing market and racial stability, as well as to protect homeowners' right to privacy.

Municipal antisolicitation policies were challenged in the *South-Suburban Housing Center* case. The district court judge ruled that these ordinances were violative of commercial free speech as protected by the First Amendment and were also unconstitutionally vague (713 F. Supp. at 1095–96). However, the judge also ruled that there was no evidence that these ordinances violated the Fair Housing Act (by depriving black home seekers of housing available for sale).

On appeal, the Seventh Circuit Court of Appeals agreed that there was no proven violation of the Fair Housing Act (935 F.2d at 888). The appeals court reversed the district court judge's other conclusions by finding that there was no First Amendment violation, holding that homeowner's right to privacy was properly protected in a manner least restrictive of commercial free speech and that the ordinances were not unconstitutionally vague (935 F.2d at 894–95). Thus the legality of antisolicitation policy, if it is properly enacted, stands confirmed.

Affirmative Marketing Strategies

Affirmation marketing has been viewed differently by the federal courts than rigid racial admission and occupancy quotas, which are vulnerable to legal challenge. In two cases, both involving nonprofit fair housing agencies in Chicago, the legality of race-conscious, affirmative marketing has been upheld.

In *Steptoe v. Beverly Area Planning Association* (674 F. Supp. 1313 [N.D. Ill. 1987]), the Beverly Area Planning Association (BAPA) Housing Center engaged in what has been termed "benign steering." Operating in a southwest Chicago neighborhood, BAPA encouraged whites and minorities to make nontraditional moves into areas where their race was underrepresented. Blacks and other minorities seeking housing were given information only about predominantly white (i.e., nonintegrated) areas of the neighborhood. This policy was made known to the association's clients, who were provided this information by volunteers without charge. BAPA was not a realty firm and did not actually rent or sell housing itself. Based on evidence obtained by checkers confirming this practice, BAPA was accused of racial steering in violation of the Fair Housing Act (Section 3604[a]).

Relying on the "plain meaning" rule, that is, relying upon the language of the statute, and on the facts, the court concluded that BAPA was not guilty because it had not made housing unavailable. First, because it did not actually rent or sell housing, it could not deprive anyone of housing based on their race. Second, because it encouraged nontraditional moves rather than denied available housing information, it was actually increasing housing information. The court concluded that BAPA was furthering a worthy purpose of the fair housing legislation, namely, "the maintenance of integrated residential neighborhoods." However, the court refused to grant a blanket exemption to all affirmative marketing organizations, which could mean that those organizations that actually engage in the rental or sale of real estate could be found guilty of housing discrimination. This, in turn, could deter for-profit realty firms that engage in the same affirmative marketing policy.

The leading precedent regarding the legality of affirmative marketing is *South-Suburban Housing Center v. Greater South-Suburban Board of Realtors* (935 F.2d 868 [7th Cir. 1991]) (Thomas, 1991; Zimmerman, 1992). This case represents a challenge against the affirmative marketing policies of both a nonprofit fair housing agency—South-Suburban Housing Center (SSHC—and the village of Park Forest, Illinois, a south Chicago suburb (profiled in Chapter 11). The case was occasioned by the action of a realtors board in response to the village's affirmative marketing plan.

The case resulted from the Park Forest's decision to try to promote greater racial diversity on a particular street (Apache Street) that comprised forty-seven homes where blacks had first moved in during the 1970s. Bounded by a newer subdivision that became occupied almost entirely by blacks by 1972 and in a school district that changed from 25 percent black to 90 percent black during the decade of 1970–1980, Apache Street by 1980 had a black population of 56 percent. Park Forest feared that, if white demand on this street was nil, with realtors not showing any housing to whites, the street would eventually become predominantly or all black. Therefore, as part of its integration maintenance policy, the village sought to promote white demand on Apache Street.

In 1982, Park Forest purchased three abandoned houses from HUD and the Veterans Administration, which had foreclosed the mortgages. Then the village sold them to SSHC for rehabilitation and resale. SSHC, in turn, agreed to affirmatively market the three houses to whites, using a realtor who promised to make special outreach efforts to attract potential white homebuyers. This included advertising in newspapers with predominantly white circulation and contacting employers and landlords with potential white clientele.

However, the listing agreement with the village forbade "any action which prohibits, restricts, narrows or limits the housing choice of any client on the basis of race."

The Greater South Suburban Board of Realtors (GSSBR), which operates a multiple listing service (MLS), decided that the affirmative marketing listing constituted illegal "benign steering" because of its race-conscious nature. It removed the listing from its MLS and filed a complaint against the realtor with the Equal Opportunity Commission of Illinois for violation of the code of ethics of the National Association of Realtors, which forbids racial discrimination. This, in turn, led to a suit brought by the SSHC against, the GSSBR, in which the real issue was whether Park Forest's affirmative marketing plan violates the Fair Housing Act, a charge raised in counterclaims by the realtors.

While the district court did not find that the GSSBR's action violated the Fair Housing Act by interfering with the SSHC's affirmative housing marketing of the Apache Street homes, it also concluded that the affirmative marketing policy of the SSHC (and, in effect, Park Forest) did not violate the Fair Housing Act (713 F. Supp. 1068 [N.D. 1988]). The court rejected the realtor's claim that this type of affirmative marketing amounted to a racial quota and distinguished it from the quota system invalidated in *Starrett City*. Citing the *Steptoe* precedent, the court found that there was no adverse impact on any racial group with regard to the availability of housing. It interpreted several U.S. Supreme Court and circuit court precedents as supporting a fundamental national policy of promoting long-term racial diversity, which reinforced the validity of the efforts of the SSHC.

The Seventh Circuit Court of Appeals upheld this decision. It too did not view the affirmative marketing plan under review as similar to the racial quotas invalidated in the *Starrett City* and *Charlottesville Redevelopment and Housing Authority* cases. In analyzing the potential violation of the Fair Housing Act, the court did not see a conflict between the goal of furthering integration and providing equal opportunities to homebuyers of all races. It concluded that, although whites might be especially attracted through the SSHC's outreach efforts, there was no evidence that blacks would be denied access to information about the houses for sale or the right to buy. Therefore Park Forest's affirmative marketing policy (and that of the private, nonprofit SSHC) was found to be legal, even in the absence of any showing of past racial discrimination in the village. The U.S. Supreme Court declined to review this decision, leaving it as the leading legal precedent to date.

M. W. Zimmerman (1992) argues that a significant shortcoming of the Seventh Circuit Court's analysis is its conclusion that private realtors have no duty under the fair housing law to affirmatively promote greater racial integration. This reasoning upheld GSSBR's right to remove an affirmative marketing listing from its MLS rather than considering this as a violation of the Fair Housing Act, as claimed by the SSHC. If the courts had interpreted the Fair Housing Act as implying an obligation affirmatively to promote integration, then all private actors in the real estate market would at least have to cooperate with race-conscious, pro-integrative efforts. As long as this cooperation remains voluntary, it is likely to be limited, at best, to the handful of suburbs that are committed to such policies, where it is in the interest of realty firms to cooperate.

There was also a legal challenge mounted against Cleveland Heights's similar affirmative marketing policy. Although a district court dismissed the case for lack of a valid legal claim by a black resident who was not actually seeking to buy or rent, the legal "standing" of the plaintiff to bring such a challenge was upheld by the Sixth Circuit Court of Appeals (*Smith v. City of Cleveland Heights*, 760 F.2d 720, *cert. denied*, 474 U.S. 1056 [1986]). Thus there is no substantive legal opinion on the validity of the Cleveland Heights approach, including its pro-integrative mortgage incentive program.

When the legality of the Ohio Housing Finance Agency pro-integrative mortgage incentive program was challenged by a conservative state senator in 1986, the attorney general of Ohio issued an opinion upholding its legality (Bromley, 1992; Thomas, 1991: 946–47). The program's legality has never been challenged in the courts.

Finally, the legality of Oak Park, Illinois's equity assurance plan, which is not race-conscious, was upheld by the courts as not violating the fair housing laws (McNamara, 1984).

Conclusion

Race-conscious policies that were designed to redress past racial discrimination and to prevent race discrimination and segregation in the future have been politically controversial and subject to legal challenge. In the case of housing, racial quota systems, however benign, have been deemed politically unacceptable and have been extremely difficult to defend legally.

In contrast, while the primary purpose of federal fair housing law is somewhat ambiguous, the courts have recognized that furthering racial integration is a legitimate aim. Although the U.S. Supreme Court has yet to rule on race-conscious affirmative marketing policies, the courts have upheld the legality of carefully constructed and justifiable policies regulating "for sale" signs and solicitation of homeowners, as well as marketing policies designed to maintain a racial balance in designated areas. These policies, unlike racial quotas or metropolitan-wide subsidized housing, seem to be the most viable ways to further the goal of racially mixed communities.

13

Toward Greater Racial Diversity
in the Suburbs

The struggle for racially diverse suburbs in metropolitan Cleveland
has been waged for three decades. If this were to be considered a
war, some battles have been won, many have been lost, the trends
have not been encouraging, and the outcome remains unknown.
Although Cleveland was considered the second most racially isolated metropolis in the United States in 1990, it has also been the site
of some of the most innovative and persistent pro-integrative efforts
in the United States. Important lessons have been learned that can
contribute to greater progress in the future in the struggle for a more
tolerant and racially mixed society.

The Cleveland experience also parallels that of the fair housing
movement in other metropolitan areas such as Chicago and Detroit.
A fair housing movement persists in the United States, despite the
indifference or even hostility of national administrations over most
of the past twenty-five years. Although occasional legislative victories have been won, such as the 1968 federal Fair Housing Act, the
Home Mortgage Disclosure Act in 1975 and the Community Reinvestment Act in 1977 regulating lenders, and the 1988 strengthening
of federal fair housing law, the battle has mostly been waged at the
municipal and metropolitan level, as well as in the courts. What has
been attempted and accomplished during this period?

Fair Housing Policies and Programs in Metropolitan Cleveland

Several different approaches have been tried in metropolitan Cleveland over the past three decades. One approach has been on a person-to-person level, within the context of neighborhood organizing in a city undergoing racial transition. The Shaker Heights neighborhoods of Ludlow, Lomond, and Moreland pioneered this approach through community associations formed in the late 1950s and early 1960s. In Cleveland Heights in the 1960s, white residents were organized by the Heights Citizens for Human Rights and the Heights Area Project of the Jewish Community Federation. Organizers sought to allay the fears of white residents and to persuade them of the benefits of racially integrated neighborhoods and public schools. The Heights Community Congress continued this organizing in Cleveland Heights in the 1970s, focusing on block clubs and neighborhood organizations. Such organizing efforts have succeeded in preventing blockbusting and white flight and have contributed to the development of citywide, pro-integrative, multiracial policies and programs that resulted in long-term racial diversity in many of the neighborhoods of these two suburbs. This diversity has gained these two suburbs their reputation as vigorous proponents of racial diversity.

This type of organizing has been tried elsewhere in Cleveland suburbs but often has failed to stem the tide of resegregation (e.g., East Cleveland and Warrensville Heights in the 1960s and 1970s and Bedford Heights in the 1980s). Pro-integrative community organizations in suburbs such as Euclid (Euclid Community Concerns, organized in 1981) and South Euclid (Hillcrest Neighbors, organized in 1983) have survived but to date have had only minimal impact in influencing their municipal governments to adopt affirmative, pro-integrative policies. One likely reason for the difficulties experienced by these groups in trying to convert white residents to such policies is that many of these residents had previously fled ethnic neighborhoods in Cleveland that were undergoing racial transition. Many residents particularly elderly residents now in retirement, may fear experiencing yet another racial transition.

Another form of person-to-person advocacy has been the use of pro-integrative mortgage incentives to persuade white and black homebuyers to consider neighborhoods where their race is under-represented. Beginning in Shaker Heights in the 1950s and continuing into the 1990s in Cleveland Heights, Shaker Heights, University Heights, and the Hillcrest suburbs, fair housing organizations, both municipal and regional (e.g., the East Suburban Council for Open Communities and the Cuyahoga Plan), have tried to convince individuals to make this very important, personal decision, sometimes making these residents pioneers in the fair housing movement. This approach has been successful, but, because fewer than a thousand homebuyers have received these mortgage incentives over a quarter-century, it has made only a marginal impact on Cleveland's suburban racial patterns (Keating, 1992). A study of the Lomond neighborhood of Shaker Heights did indicate that the use of pro-integrative mortgage incentives after the 1985 creation of the Fund for the Future of Shaker Heights did have a positive impact on racial diversity and contributed to stable housing values (Cromwell, 1990).

A second approach to integration has been the effort to change municipal housing policies to embrace affirmative, pro-integrative policies and programs. Certainly, the cities of Cleveland Heights and Shaker Heights have been the leaders and most successful in their efforts. Their policies have been a combination of regulatory ordinances (e.g., banning "for sale" signs, monitoring the conduct of real estate firms, and strictly enforcing housing codes); incentives (e.g., pro-integrative mortgage incentives and housing rehabilitation loans); and civic promotion (e.g., creation of municipal housing offices and support for fair housing groups). These kinds of policies came too late in East Cleveland to prevent resegregation. Court imposition of fair housing policies in Parma (underway since the early 1980s) has so far had only marginal impact in changing that city's racial composition. The majority of suburbs in Cuyahoga County have taken no affirmative actions, mostly limiting their "action" to the mere adoption of a fair housing resolution (Cuyahoga Plan, 1989).

A third approach has been to promote affirmative fair housing policies at metropolitan and subregional levels. Efforts at the former level have been represented by Operation Equality, Plan of Action for Tomorrow's Housing (PATH), and the Cuyahoga Plan. Operation

Equality (1966–1973) pioneered in promoting black migration to Cleveland's suburbs, supported by Fair Housing, Inc., the interracial real estate brokerage firm established in 1963 to serve pro-integrative suburban moves by homebuyers. After passage of the federal fair housing legislation in 1968, Operation Equality was the most visible vehicle for the enforcement of the antidiscrimination legislation in Cuyahoga County. However, its role was superseded by the Cuyahoga Plan after the latter's creation in 1974.

Like its counterparts in other metropolitan areas, the Cuyahoga Plan has over its life mainly been a vehicle for the investigation of racial discrimination and the documentation of patterns of racial segregation and isolation in housing and neighborhoods throughout its metropolitan area. While it has enjoyed fairly consistent support from several cities, Cuyahoga County, and philanthropic foundations, it has not converted a majority of the county's suburbs to support of its efforts or initiation of their own programs. The Cuyahoga Plan, from its beginnings in the mid-1970s to its most recent crisis in 1992, has never been able fully to resolve the tension between the freedom of choice approach (i.e., mere enforcement of antidiscrimination laws) and the affirmative, pro-integrative approach, featuring race-conscious policies.

PATH, during its brief life (1967–1974), was notably unsuccessful in its efforts to lobby for and litigate dispersion of federally subsidized public housing throughout Cuyahoga County's suburbs. The effort to promote a countywide fair-share plan for low-income housing, at least partially successful in a few metropolitan areas (e.g., Dayton, Minneapolis, and Washington, D.C.) in the 1970s, met heavy resistance from suburban officials, which PATH could not overcome.

A subregional approach to promotion of affirmative fair housing policies has been to form organizations to try to attract blacks to the Hillcrest suburbs (six cities) on Cleveland's east side, in part to relieve the pressure on pro-integrative suburbs such as Cleveland Heights and Shaker Heights. This approach was pioneered by Suburban Citizens for Open Housing in the late 1960s, in tandem with Operation Equality and Fair Housing, Inc. However, all three of these organizations disappeared in the early 1970s, having made only a minor impact.

In 1984 this approach was renewed, supported by the cities of Cleveland Heights, Shaker Heights, and University Heights and their school boards. The East Suburban Council for Open Communities (ESCOC), working with cooperative realty firms and landlords, using advertising and an escort service, and providing pro-integrative mortgage incentives to black homebuyers, did make progress, although the number of its clients who chose to live in Hillcrest was relatively small. Its efforts to enlist the support, overt or unofficial, of the six municipalities in the Hillcrest area were unsuccessful. When it dissolved in 1990 over differences concerning its future direction, its efforts seemingly ended. However, with the continuation of its housing service, now administered by the Cuyahoga Plan, hope remains that it can continue to attract at least small numbers of blacks to the Hillcrest communities and contribute to greater racial diversity in an area where such efforts are now more than two decades old.

Open Door West, active only since 1990, has adopted a much less visible approach to facilitating greater racial diversity in the west side of the city of Cleveland and the western suburbs of Cuyahoga County. It has not yet made a noticeable impact in changing suburban housing patterns.

A fourth approach to integration in the Cleveland metropolitan area has been litigation. This has taken different forms.

First, individuals (e.g., landlords and homesellers) and organizations (e.g., realty firms) have been sued for alleged violations of applicable fair housing law. These lawsuits have certainly created a better public understanding of fair housing law, but the approach does not seem to have deterred altogether those determined to discriminate. Second, key real estate industry agencies (e.g., HGM–Hilltop Realty) have been sued (e.g., by the Heights Community Congress and the city of Cleveland Heights) for alleged systematic violations of fair housing law. These two types of litigation have influenced the real estate industry to accept greater education of real estate brokers and agents about fair housing law.

Third, suburban municipalities have been sued for alleged exclusionary practices, that is, practices designed to exclude the poor, including racial minorities. In the case of East Cleveland, the U.S. Supreme Court struck down a strict interpretation of the city's housing code that arbitrarily excluded certain blood relatives from living with other family members (*Moore v. East Cleveland*, 431 U.S. 494 [1977]). In contrast, PATH's attempt to force suburban municipalities to provide public housing and to have the federal requirement for cooperation agreements between suburbs and the Cuyahoga Metropolitan Housing Authority (CMHA) invalidated was rejected by the federal courts. Likewise, in a challenge to a mandatory referendum requirement, affecting subsidized housing, that had been enacted by the Lake County suburb of Eastlake, the U.S. Supreme Court upheld this democratic version of land use planning in the absence of proof that it had an intended or disparate exclusionary racial impact. Mandatory referenda regulating land use and development were subsequently widely adopted by Cuyahoga County suburbs.

Fourth, one suburb, Parma, was sued by the U.S. Department of Justice and found guilty of a long-standing pattern of fair housing violations. The tangible results of a remedial court order to promote greater racial diversity remain minimal after more than a decade. The city's black population is still below 1 percent. Despite similar patterns of racial segregation (or non diversity) in many other predominantly white suburbs, no other suburb in Cuyahoga County has been similarly sued.

Barring the advent of a much different national administration, one determined to attack suburban residential segregation in the courts as violative of federal fair housing law, it is most unlikely that the courts can be a vehicle for systematically addressing suburban integration problems. Without the involvement of the federal government, it is very unlikely that fair housing advocacy groups will be able to afford to engage in such costly and time-consuming litigation. The Parma litigation took seven years from the filing of the lawsuit by the U.S. Justice Department to the trial, and a decision and an appeal lasted another two years. A countywide fair housing organization such as the Cuyahoga Plan, which has been heavily dependent on suburban governments for financial support, is not in a position to engage in litigation against those same suburban municipalities. The history of fair housing litigation suggests that the role of the courts will continue to be that of a mostly passive forum where individual complaints of racial discrimination in housing can be heard, if administrative attempts to resolve them fail.

Three Decades of Racial Transition in Metropolitan Cleveland: Progress or Not?

The post–World War II racial patterns of metropolitan Cleveland have been in transition for more than three decades. Based on indexes of dissimilarity derived from decennial census data, the ranking of the Cleveland metropolitan area as one of the most racially isolated or segregated in the United States, second only to Chicago in 1990, would seem to indicate that little or no progress has been made with regard to race relations in housing. Sporadic but regular racial incidents and confrontations, mostly occurring in the city of Cleveland, have underscored the continued racial tension in the metropolis.

Black suburbanization has continued to increase, as it has elsewhere in the United States, but resegregation has occurred, most notably in the surburbs of East Cleveland and Warrensville Heights and also in neighborhoods of cities such as Euclid, Maple Heights, and South Euclid. But for the efforts of the many fair housing organizations that have struggled to eliminate racial discrimination and to promote greater racial diversity, there undoubtedly would be even less racial diversity in 1992 than does exist.

Due to the efforts of the fair housing organizations and changing social attitudes, the white population of metropolitan Cleveland and its suburbs has shown an increasing awareness of the problem of racial discrimination in housing, has supported enforcement of fair housing legislation, has indicated an increasing tolerance for racially mixed neighborhoods, and has shown very little preference for all-white neighborhoods. However, these attitudinal changes have not been translated into changed residential patterns. Whites have not, by and large, sought out racially diverse neighborhoods.

The exceptions have been those few suburbs, such as Cleveland Heights and Shaker Heights and their counterparts in suburban Chicago, Oak Park and Park Forest, that have adopted pro-integrative housing policies and implemented them over a long period. The experience of these Cleveland and Chicago suburbs has demonstrated that there are significant numbers of whites interested in living in racially diverse communities. The participation and leadership of interfaith clergy and churches; neighborhood-based community organizing; and the support of municipal government, the public schools, and philanthropic foundations have all been critical to these suburbs' success. Their experience gives support to the possibility of promoting and sustaining racially integrated living patterns on a much broader scale throughout the Chicago and Cleveland metropolitan regions. The continuation of white demand in now predominantly black neighborhoods in Cleveland Heights, Shaker Heights, Oak Park, and Park Forest has shown that the "tipping point" phenomenon is not inevitable (Galster, 1990a). To achieve sustained racial diversity, however, much different public policies, particularly as implemented by predominantly white suburban municipalities, will be required.

In the suburbs of metropolitan Cleveland, responses to the experience of racial transition have been mixed. Among those suburbs experiencing a noticeable growth of black population, some have supported the activities of the Cuyahoga Plan and designated their own staff to deal with race-related issues (e.g., Euclid). Others have not gone this far and have rejected overtures to join or support ESCOC's activities (e.g., South Euclid). Those suburbs with a negligible black population have mostly done nothing, with few exceptions (e.g., Lakewood). If the pattern of the past three decades continues, more of Cleveland's inner-ring, older suburbs will experience the black suburbanization that has already occurred in cities such as Euclid, South Euclid, Bedford Heights, Garfield Heights, and Maple Heights (all of which are on the east side). If they adopt pro-integrative policies, it is conceivable that they may successfully promote long-term, stable racial diversity in their communities. But if they choose not to act unless problems arise, it is entirely likely that some of their neighborhoods will resegregate, as many whites leave when the black population rises above what they consider to be acceptable levels.

The 1991 Citizens League Research Institute survey indicated that if nonwhite (e.g., black) in-migration numbered "only a few," then only a small percentage of whites would merely consider moving out. This reflects the willingness of most whites to have black neighbors (Schuman and Bobo, 1988). If black in-migration were to grow, then the rate of possible white flight would increase (Table 19). A similar pattern emerged when whites were asked if

Table 19. Whites Considering Out-Migration
with Black In-Migration, Cleveland, 1991

Black In-Migration	White Out-Migration (%)
Only a few	15
About one-quarter	20
About one-half	38
Most	54

Source: CLRI, 1991: 53, graph V–3

they would actually move out in the face of black in-migration
(Table 20).

If whites perceive that white demand for housing is rapidly
declining or disappearing, increasing numbers indicated that they
would either consider moving or would actually move out.

This response pattern seems to confirm the tipping point theory,
although it also demonstrates that total resegregation is not inevitable. An orderly transition to a racially mixed neighborhood does not
inexorably lead to resegregation. Rather, long-term, stable racial
diversity is possible, particularly if affirmative, pro-integrative policies are in effect. Contrary to W.A.V. Clark's (1991) conclusion,
long-term, stable racial diversity is possible, difficult as this has been.
Beyond prejudicial white attitudes, what must change is behavior in
the housing market.

What can be done in metropolitan Cleveland and other, similar
metropolitan areas to encourage greater racial diversity while preventing resegregation?

Table 20. Whites Planning Out-Migration with
Black In-Migration, Cleveland, 1991

Black In-Migration	White Out-Migration (%)
Only a few	7
About one-quarter	14
About one-half	35
Most	49

Source: CLRI, 1991: 54, graph V–4

A Metropolitan Perspective, Metropolitan Strategies

The Cleveland experience shows that "gradualism," that is, the piecemeal migration of blacks to suburbs and subsequent inaction by suburbs, is not leading to greater racial diversity. Instead, blacks will likely gravitate to those suburbs and suburban neighborhoods with the highest proportional black populations, where they will feel most "comfortable," and whites will continue to gravitate to predominantly white suburbs and white suburban neighborhoods. The exception, as shown in the 1987 study of suburban Cleveland homebuyers (Keating, Pammer, and Smith, 1987), consists of those white and black homebuyers and renters who wish to live in a racially diverse community and who are aware of the affirmative, pro-integrative policies of such suburbs as Cleveland Heights and Shaker Heights. However, while this provides these suburbs with a special market, it does not broaden the number of pro-integrative suburbs and, insofar as blacks are attracted to these magnet, racially diverse suburbs, could actually threaten the racial diversity that these suburbs have worked so long to maintain.

If most surburban municipalities will not adopt pro-integrative, affirmative policies voluntarily, then only two options exist: these policies can be mandated by higher levels of government (regional, state, and federal) or incentives can be provided to those suburbs willing to cooperate. The former policy is more likely to have the greater impact but is politically less feasible. The latter policy may have a greater possibility of acceptance but is likely to have much less impact, either because most suburbs will decline to participate or because recipients of pro-integrative incentives may still gravitate toward the few pro-integrative magnet suburbs that exist, as long as their housing is affordable to them.

Governmental Mandates for Pro-integrative, Affirmative Housing Policies and Programs

A federal mandate could conceivably make the most impact. As George Galster (1990b) has suggested, federal aid to state and local governments could require the creation and implementation of affirmative fair housing plans by jurisdictions receiving federal aid, whether by entitlement or discretion. An example would have been requiring this in the Comprehensive Housing Assistance Strategy, which is a prerequisite for use of HUD funding under the 1990 housing act. However, reflecting the conservative nature of contemporary national politics, this requirement was not made or even discussed in Congress. In the face of White House opposition to affirmative action, which the Bush administration chose to characterize as racial quotas, the Democratically controlled Congress had difficulty in overriding a presidential veto of civil rights legislation. Internally, the Democrats themselves are divided on the politically volatile issue of making federal aid contingent on the institution of affirmative, pro-integrative programs. Federal social policy mandates also fly in the face of the continuing strong trends to deconcentrate federal regulatory control and to institute additional block grant funding without too many strings attached.

Finally, with the continued existence of huge federal budget deficits, absent a peace dividend devoted to domestic social spending, there is little new federal funding available to all states and localities to which such a mandate could be tied. The most likely general funding would be for infrastructure improvements, education, and environmental and anticrime programs. Politically, it would be very difficult to attach fair housing mandates to federal support to state and local governments for these purposes. Tying fair housing requirements to federal lower-income housing assistance is not likely to work because most suburbs do not seek such aid, even if available, because they do not want below-market housing in the community.

Although federal mandates can require local funding for implementation, it is most unlikely that a Congress increasingly influenced by suburban representatives would mandate fair housing opposed by their suburban constituents (even with federal subsidies provided to help achieve compliance). The fair-share housing plans supported by the federal government in the 1970s were not mandated by Congress. Given the drastic reductions in newly constructed, federally subsidized housing since the election of Ronald Reagan in 1980 and the suburban resistance to regional fair-share housing plans, it is not likely that such a policy could be revived and receive the support of the federal government. Politically, it is unclear that the representatives of central cities, which are increasingly composed of a majority of minority residents, would even support such a federal policy if it were proposed. Thus what is left is the uncontroversial funding by HUD of fair housing organizations to assist in the enforcement of antidiscrimination legislation. In the 1992 federal budget, HUD's funding of its Fair Housing Initiatives Program amounted to only a few million dollars.

If federal mandates are not likely options, then another possibility is state-mandated fair housing policy. No state has yet adopted such a policy. One state, New Jersey, has mandated regional fair-share housing, but only because of state supreme court rulings based on an interpretation of New Jersey's constitution as guaranteeing a right to housing. Implementation of the *Mt. Laurel* decision, ongoing since the initial decision in 1975, could change exclusionary racial patterns. However, the impetus for the case was primarily economic, rather than racial, discrimination. The ability of suburbs since 1985 to "sell" part of their fair-share obligation to central cities, where the poorer minority population is concentrated, will undoubtedly reduce the pro-integrative impact of the future implementation of the order (Seton Hall University Colloquium, 1991). Other states, such as California, Massachusetts, and Oregon, that have legislatively required that local land use plans allow for broad housing opportunities for all income groups have not linked this policy to affirmative municipal action to promote greater racial diversity in housing.

While states are involved in the enforcement of anti–housing discrimination laws, in tandem with federal and local government, this has not led to greater racial diversity. One of the few hopeful signs has been the designation of a percentage of first-time homebuyer mortgage subsidies by the Ohio Housing Finance Agency for pro-integrative moves. If this policy were incorporated into all state—as well as federal and municipal—home purchase programs, then the states could take the lead in promoting greater racial diversity. This would require considerable political pressure on state housing finance agencies by fair housing advocates, as occurred in Ohio in the 1980s (Thomas, 1991: 944–48; Bromley, 1992). The alternative would be court-mandated state programs to promote greater residential racial integration, such as occurred in Wisconsin and greater Milwaukee in the late 1980s (Thomas, 1991:

948–50). However, there is little prospect that either political or legal pressure will persuade or force states to take the lead in promoting greater racial diversity, especially in the suburbs of metropolitan areas. In proposing state legislation requiring a set-aside for racial minorities of at least 25 percent of the units in any new housing development of five or more units, M. F. Potter (1990) conceded that adoption of such legislation was not politically feasible.

The final possibility for government-mandated, pro-integrative, affirmative housing policy lies at the metropolitan level. Regional fair-share housing plans, which could include affirmative pro-integrative policies, could be mandated by a metropolitan government, if one exists, or agreed upon voluntarily, as happened in a few metropolitan areas such as Dayton in the 1970s through councils of governments (COGs). As Glaster argues, it is critical that all, or at least most, of the local governments in a region comply; otherwise, progress toward greater racial integration will be piecemeal (Galster, 1990b: 149). Unfortunately, regional government does not exist in most of the United States, and there is little prospect of any change in this regard. Single-purpose metropolitan agencies with jurisdiction over housing also do not exist, with the exception of a few public housing authorities such as Cleveland's Cuyahoga Metropolitan Housing Authority (CMHA). However, as the history of CMHA and the short-lived efforts of PATH demonstrate, most suburbs will not cooperate with a regional public housing authority, leaving most public housing concentrated in the central city. In the case of CMHA, its central-city public housing is racially segregated for the most part.

The alternative is a consensual agreement among cooperating municipalities in a metropolitan region operating through a COG. If a consensus like that achieved in Dayton, Ohio, in 1970 could be voluntarily attained, then the mandate problem could be avoided. But the dilemma is that there is little indication of any interest in such a policy by most predominantly white suburbs. The fact that most of Cuyahoga County's predominantly white suburbs have not financially supported the activities of the Cuyahoga Plan since its creation in 1974 is an indication of this prevailing attitude. This disheartening pattern is even more discouraging because the Cuyahoga Plan primarily confined its activities to assisting in enforcement of antidiscrimination laws and has not taken the lead in promoting pro-integrative policies. And even if some form of a consensus could be reached by some municipalities in a region, COGs have no power to enforce such a policy. COGs have been weakened since the Reagan administration began to reduce federal mandates and eliminated much of federal support for regional planning (Ross, Levine, and Stedman, 1991: 296).

Incentives for Pro-integrative, Affirmative Housing Policies

The alternative to a mandatory policy approach is to provide financial incentives to promote racial integration in housing, "carrots" instead of "sticks." Anthony Downs (1973: 161–62) proposed providing financial assistance to cooperating suburbs, lower-income central-city residents willing to move to the suburbs, and housing developers who build subsidized housing in the suburbs. Ronald Silverman (1977) proposed similar policies and also advocated providing cash awards to residents of "receiving" suburban neighborhoods to prevent their moving out and resegregation occurring. He admitted the offensive appearance of subsidizing tolerance (Silverman, 1977: 488–91) but advocated this approach, at least on an experimental basis.

A weaker version of this notion is to guarantee property owners in racially transitional neighborhoods that their property values will remain stable, a policy adopted by Oak Park, Illinois, which has an "equity assurance" program available to concerned homeowners (Goodwin, 1979). When a similar program was enacted for white neighborhoods in Chicago, black mayor Eugene Sawyer vetoed the ordinance. Subsequently, the Illinois State Legislature adopted similar legislation applicable to Chicago (Goel, 1990: 379).

Elements of the incentives approach have been tried with some success. The court-ordered remedies in the *Gautreaux* (Chicago) and *Mt. Laurel* (New Jersey) cases have led to the suburban entry of a few thousand lower-income minority residents through federal, state, and local housing subsidies. The use of pro-integrative mortgages in Ohio (beginning in metropolitan Cleveland), Milwaukee, Philadelphia and Washington, D.C., has proven successful in persuading or reinforcing the decision of voluntarily participating homebuyers to choose homes in racially mixed neighborhoods.

With the massive reduction of federal subsidy programs for new housing under the Reagan and Bush administrations, there is little prospect in the near future for even debating the efficacy of the Downs and Silverman recommendations. They assumed the availability of large-scale federal housing subsidy programs that would be applicable to the suburbs, such as briefly existed during the period from 1969 to 1972, before Richard Nixon's moratorium on federal housing subsidy programs in January 1973. The 1990 revival of federal funding authority for new below-market housing programs is modest, and metropolitan dispersion of this housing was not a goal of its proponents.

There is virtually no chance, given federal fiscal problems, of federal funding being made available to reward suburban communities that are willing to participate in pro-integrative housing programs. The same is true for fiscally strapped states, which were cutting back on social welfare programs in 1992 to eliminate growing budget deficits.

Whether such race-conscious governmental policies would be politically feasible, even if funding could be made available, is highly debatable. There has been opposition, mostly from black real estate interests, to Ohio's pro-integrative mortgage program, resulting in the creation of a separate minority homebuyers program, which has no geographical restrictions as to where participants purchase. There was also some conservative opposition to the idea of race-based incentives. In a conservative political climate in which affirmative action policies have been under threat of elimination and attacked as unjustifiable racial quotas, the question of winning public support for pro-integrative policies is a most difficult political issue.

The 1991 survey of suburban Cuyahoga County residents indicated that a majority (54 percent overall, including 49 percent of whites) supported a policy of providing pro-integrative mortgage incentives to voluntarily participating homebuyers, and only a fairly small minority (20 percent) opposed this type of program (Keating, 1992). White support was much higher in the suburbs of Cleveland Heights and Shaker Heights than in predominantly white suburbs, especially the western suburbs. A 1992 survey of the opinions of greater Clevelanders showed less support for this approach. When asked whether "housing incentives (for example, lower mortgage rates) should be offered to homebuyers who move into neighborhoods which are mostly of a different race," only 43 percent either agreed or strongly agreed. While a majority of blacks (60 percent) and Hispanics (50 percent) agreed with this policy, only 35 percent of whites were supportive. Only 38 percent of suburbanites interviewed were supportive.

In contrast, just over one-half (52 percent) of all interviewed (city and suburban residents) agreed that "there should be government programs to help integrate neighborhoods." However, only 43 percent of whites were supportive, compared to 78 percent of blacks. Just under one-half (46 percent) of suburbanites were supportive (CLRI, 1991). This indicates that there is not yet majority white and suburban support for affirmative governmental policies, including pro-integrative mortgage incentives, to promote racially integrated neighborhoods.

Whether broad political consensus for a much more visible program of pro-integrative mortgage incentives, with greatly increased public funding, could gain support and whether this support would continue if most predominantly white suburbs were targeted is unknown. Polls indicate that white tolerance for greater racial diversity, especially if a minority presence is relatively small, has increased since the dawning of the civil rights era, despite the backlash that has occurred since the 1970s.

Legally, the 1992 refusal by an increasingly conservative U.S. Supreme Court to review the decision upholding the validity of the voluntary race-conscious policies that were challenged in *South Suburban Housing Center* indicates that pro-integrative housing programs can avoid the fatal claim that they are the type of illegal racial quotas found to have violated the equal protection clause and fair housing law in *Starrett City* (Simon, 1991; Thomas, 1991).

The Viability of a Metropolitan Strategy

What is the answer to the dilemma that a metropolitan pro-integrative housing strategy is imperative but a viable metropolitan strategy dependent on public approval and funding seems to be highly unlikely? The answer must be a quasi-governmental strategy. Short of court-ordered regional or state mandates, the remaining alternative is to develop the type of metropolitan strategy represented by ESCOC. While ESCOC affected only six of fifty-eight Cuyahoga County suburbs, it could be applied to virtually all of Cleveland's suburbs. Of course, to make any impact there would have to be much more funding than has been available to date to ESCOC and its successor agency to provide pro-integrative mortgage incentives. Unless there are pro-integrative suburban municipalities such as Cleveland Heights, Shaker Heights, and University Heights (and, preferably, their school boards) in existence that are willing to provide support, or unless urban counties can be persuaded to provide financial assistance, funding must be obtained from private sources (e.g., philanthropic foundations) and, if feasible, from state housing finance agencies.

If extended to entire metropolitan areas and sustained over long periods of time (and assuming that participants are satisfied and supportive and that there is little active opposition from their neighbors and the municipalities to which they move), this approach represents the best available hope for affecting residential patterns in all of metropolitan America, rather than only a few isolated suburbs. Providing financial incentives for pro-integrative action can affect the behavior as well as the attitudes of whites, not only those participating directly but also their friends and neighbors, giving greater hope for gradually reducing the segregative racial patterns that so characterize the suburbs of metropolitan America.

This modest proposal presumes that there is still a sizable constituency, both white and black, that supports the dreams and ideals of Martin Luther King, Jr., and the civil rights movement, which espoused the goal of a racially integrated society. The Kerner Commission warned that, unless drastic changes occurred, that goal would not be reached and the United States would become even more racially segregated and separated by spatial and political borders. In addition to race, it suggested that Americans would continue to be divided by class, as reflected in income. African Americans on the average still earn far less than whites. To the extent that the black middle class continues to suburbanize, they remain more acceptable to whites, particularly their social peers (according to education, occupation, income and value of their home). However, not all middle-class black suburbanites necessarily adhere any longer to the integrationist ideal, as is illustrated by the attitudes of many black residents in Prince Georges County, Maryland (Dent, 1992). The much more difficult problem is to persuade suburbanites, especially whites, to accept as neighbors those of a lower social status. Economic, as opposed to racial, diversity is perhaps even more difficult to envision in most American suburbs. Therefore, the goals of the fair housing movement are best pursued primarily through the promotion of greater racial diversity among homeowners living in neighborhoods that otherwise are mostly homogeneous.

The goal of racial diversity in housing and neighborhoods can be achieved. But it must be remembered that there is no end to this struggle. With the mobility of Americans and the resultant turnover of houses, their owner-occupants, and residential neighborhoods, there must be a constant educational process reminding suburbanites of the benefits of living in a racially diverse society. Suburban governments must actively support pro-integrative, affirmative housing policies. There must be continuing liaison with the real estate industry and enforcement of antidiscrimination legislation. Those suburbs profiled in this book that have kept alive the goal of racial integration over a long period, despite controversy and setbacks, demonstrate that it is not an idle hope or impossible dream. In all of the case studies of suburbs and fair housing organizations profiled herein, it is a handful of fair housing advocates, many of them clergy or affiliated with religious organizations, who have kept the often flickering flame of interracial community alive. Whether they represent a movement of the past or prologue to the future remains an unanswered question.

References and Index

REFERENCES

Abrams, C. 1955. *Forbidden Neighbors*. New York: Harper & Brothers.

Ackerman, B. L. 1974. "Integration for Subsidized Housing and the Question of Racial Occupancy Controls." *Stanford Law Review*, 26: 245–309.

Alfred, S. J., and C. R. Marcoux. 1970. "Impact of a Community Association on Integrated Surburban Housing Patterns." *Cleveland State Law Review* 19: 90–99.

Armstrong, M. 1991. "Desegregation through Private Litigation: Using Equitable Remedies to Achieve the Purposes of the Fair Housing Act." *Temple Law Review* 64: 909–35.

Auletta, K. 1982. *Underclass*. New York: Random House.

Beard D. 1984. "Parma Gets Fair Housing Lesson." *Cleveland Plain Dealer*, 28 March: 12A.

Bell, D., and L. O'Connor. 1985. "Southfield: A Place to Start Over?" *Detroit Free Press*, 8 Dec.: 5H.

Bellamy, J. S., II. 1990. *Angels on the Heights: A History of St. Ann's Parish, Cleveland Heights, Ohio, 1915–1990*. N.P.

Bernstein, M. 1991. "Minorities 'Welcome' Often Ugly." *Cleveland Plain Dealer*, 24 Nov.: 1A.

Berry, B.J.L. 1979. "Oak Park: Reverse Steering and Racial Quotas" and "Park Forest: A Program of Integration Maintenance." In Berry's *The Open Housing Question: Race and Housing in Chicago, 1966–1976*. Cambridge, Mass.: Ballinger.

Berry, B.J.L., C. A. Goodwin, R. W. Lake, and K.B. Smith. 1976. "Attitudes toward Integration: The Role of Status in Community Response to Racial Change." In Barry Schwartz, ed., *The Changing Face of the Suburbs*. Chicago: University of Chicago Press.

Bier, T. 1989a. *Buyers of Cleveland Homes, 1989*. Cleveland: Maxine Goodman Levin College of Urban Affairs, Cleveland State University.

————. 1989b. *Sellers of Single-Family Homes, City of Cleveland, 1988.* Cleveland: Maxine Goodman Levin College of Urban Affairs, Cleveland State University..

Bishop, D. 1988. "Fair Housing and the Constitutionality of Governmental Measures Affecting Community Ethnicity." *University of Chicago Law Review* 55: 1229–66.

Blank, J. P. 1968. "Ludlow—A Lesson in Integration." *Reader's Digest* 93: 193–98.

Bradburn, N. M., S. Sudman, and G. L. Gockel. 1971. *Side by Side: Integrated Neighborhoods in America.* Chicago: Quadrangle Books.

Brandt, N. 1990. *The Town That Started the Civil War.* Syracuse, N.Y.: Syracuse University Press.

Breckenridge, T. 1987. "Integrators Catch Flak in S. Euclid." *Cleveland Plain Dealer,* 6 Mar.: 1B.

Brilliant, E. L. 1975. *The Urban Development Corporation.* Lexington, Mass. Lexington Books.

Bromley, C. H. 1992. "The Politics of Race Reform of the Single Family Mortgage Revenue Bond Program in the State of Ohio 1983–1988." Paper presented at the annual meeting of the Urban Affairs Association, Cleveland.

Brown, R. 1987a. "Neighbors Battle Maple Heights Exodus." *Cleveland Plain Dealer,* 12 Apr.: 1B.

————. 1987b. "Maple Heights Passes Fair-Housing Law." *Cleveland Plain Dealer,* 25 Mar.: 1B.

Chafets, Z. 1990. *Devil's Night and Other True Tales of Detroit.* New York: Random House.

Chandler, M. 1992. "Obstacles to Integration Efforts." In G. C. Galster and E. Hill, eds., *The City in Black and White.* New Brunswick, N.J.: Center for Urban Policy Research, Rutgers University.

————. Forthcoming. "The Politics and Development of Public Housing." In W. D. Keating, N. Krumholz, and D. C. Perry, eds., *Cleveland: A Metropolitan Reader.* Kent, Ohio: Kent State University Press.

Citizens League Research Institute (CLRI). 1991. *Race Relations in Greater Cleveland: A Report on the Attitudes, Opinions, and Experiences of Greater Clevelanders.* Cleveland: CLRI.

City of Cleveland Heights. 1978. *Report on Housing Services.* Cleveland Heights, Ohio: City of Cleveland Heights.

————. 1983. *Citizen Survey Report.* Cleveland Heights, Ohio: City of Cleveland Heights.

————. 1987. *Analysis of 1987 Citizen Survey Results.* Cleveland Heights, Ohio: City of Cleveland Heights.

------. 1990. *Annual Report.* Cleveland Heights, Ohio: City of Cleveland Heights.

------. 1992. *Annual Report.* Cleveland Heights, Ohio: City of Cleveland Heights.

Clark, W.A.V. 1991. "Residential Preferences and Neighborhood Racial Segregation: A Test of the Schelling Segregation Model." *Demography* 28: 1–19.

Clay, P. L. 1979. "The Process of Black Suburbanization." *Urban Affairs Quarterly* 14: 405–24.

Cleveland Foundation. 1990. *Annual Report.* Cleveland: Cleveland Foundation.

Condon, G. E. 1967. *Cleveland: The Best Kept Secret.* New York: Doubleday.

Cooper, P. J. 1988. "*United States v. City of Parma, Ohio:* Open Housing Conflict in a Cleveland Suburb." In Cooper's *Hard Judicial Choices: Federal District Court Judges and State and Local Officials.* New York: Oxford University Press.

Coulton, C. J., J. Chow, and S. Pandey. 1990. *An Analysis of Poverty and Related Conditions in Cleveland Area Neighborhoods.* Cleveland: Center for Urban Poverty and Social Change, Mandel School of Applied Social Sciences, Case Western Reserve University.

Council for Economic Opportunities in Greater Cleveland (CEOGC). 1991. *Poverty Indicators.* Cleveland: CEOGC.

Cromwell, A. 1990. *Prointegrative Subsidies and Their Effect on Housing Markets: Do Race-based Loans Work?* Cleveland: Federal Reserve Bank (Working Paper No. 9018).

Cuyahoga Plan. 1984, 1985, 1991. *Annual Reports.* Cleveland: Cuyahoga Plan.

------. 1985a. *Preliminary Findings Racial Impact Analysis, Ohio Finance Agency—Single Family Mortgage Program Series 1983A and 1984B, Cleveland and Cuyahoga County.* Cleveland: Cuyahoga Plan.

------. 1985b. *Race and Single-Family Mortgages Made by Major Savings Institutions in the City of Cleveland, 1989.* Cleveland: Cuyahoga Plan.

------. 1985c. *A Report on Population and Race: Estimates of Racial Composition for Cuyahoga County and Select Outlying Communities, 1978–1983.* Cleveland: Cuyahoga Plan.

------. 1987. *A Report on Population and Race: Estimates of Racial Composition for Cuyahoga County, 1980–1985.* Cleveland: Cuyahoga Plan.

------. 1989. *Municipal Approaches to Fair Housing in Greater Cleveland.* Cleveland: Cuyahoga Plan.

Damarell, R. 1968. *Triumph in a White Suburb.* New York: William Morrow.

Danielson, M. N. 1976. *The Politics of Exclusion.* New York: Columbia University Press.

Darden, J. T. 1987. "Choosing Neighbors and Neighborhoods: The Role of Race in Housing Preference." In G. A. Tobin, ed., *Divided Neighborhoods: Changing Patterns of Racial Segregation.* Newbury Park, Calif.: Sage.

Darden, J. T., R. C. Hill, J. Thomas, and R. Thomas. 1987. *Detroit: Race and Uneven Development.* Philadelphia: Temple University Press.

Davidoff P., and L. Davidoff. 1971. "Opening Up the Suburbs." Syracuse University Law Review 22: 509.

Davidoff, P., L. Davidoff, and N. Gold. 1970. "Suburban Action: Advocate Planning for an Open Society." *Journal of the American Institute of Planners* 36: 12–21

Davis, A. J. 1990. *Second Chance: White Pastor–Black Church.* Dayton, Ohio: Landfall.

Delaney, P. 1971. "Outer City: Blacks Find Few Tangible Gains." *New York Times,* 1 June.

DeLater, L. 1987. "Judge Attacks Parma's Pace on Integration." *Cleveland Plain Dealer,* 11 Sept.: 1B.

DeMarco, D. L. 1989. *Pro-Integrative Policy and Program.* Shaker Heights, Ohio. N.P.

DeMarco, D. L., and G. C. Glaster. 1993. "Prointegrative Policy: Theory and Practice." *Journal of Urban Affairs* 15: 141–60.

Dent, D. J. 1992. "The New Black Suburbs." *New York Times Magazine,* 14 June, Sec. 6, p. 18.

Downs, A. 1973. *Opening Up the Suburbs: An Urban Strategy for America.* New Haven: Yale University Press.

Drexler, M. 1992. "Woman Sues over Shaker Housing Policy." *Cleveland Plain Dealer,* 8 May: 5C.

———. 1992. "Policy Directions Concerning Racial Discrimination in U.S. Housing Markets." *Housing Policy Debate* 3: 685–745.

East Suburban Council for Open Communities (ESCOC). 1985, 1986, 1988, 1989. *Annual Reports.* Lyndhurst, Ohio: ESCOC.

Farley, R. 1978. "Chocolate City, Vanilla Suburbs: Will the Trend toward Racially Separate Communities Continue?" *Social Science Research* 7: 319–44.

Forest Hills Church (FHC) Housing Corporation. 1992. *Annual Report.* Cleveland Heights, Ohio: FHC Housing Corporation.

Fox, K. 1986. *Metropolitan America: Urban Life and Urban Policy in the United States, 1940–1980.* Jackson: University Press of Mississippi.

Frey, W. H. 1979. "Central City White Flight: Racial and Non-racial Reasons." *American Sociological Review* 44: 425–48.

Gabe, C. 1985. "'Fair Housing': In Spite of Order, Some Say Parma Not Yet 'open' City." *Cleveland Plain Dealer,* 5 June: 1A.

Gale, D. E. 1987. *Washington, D.C. Inner-City Revitalization and Minority Suburbanization.* Philadelphia: Temple University Press.

Galster, G. C. 1987. "The Ecology of Racial Discrimination in Housing: An Exploratory Model." *Urban Affairs Quarterly* 23: 84–107.

―――. 1990a. "Racial Discrimination in Housing Markets in the 1980s: A Review of the Audit Evidence." *Journal of Planning Education and Research* 9: 165–75.

―――. 1990b. "Federal Fair Housing Policy: The Great Misapprehension." In D. DiPasquale and L. C. Keyes, eds., *Building Foundations: Housing and Federal Policy.* Philadelphia: University of Pennsylvania Press.

―――. 1990c. "Neighborhood Racial Change, Segregationist Sentiments, and Affirmative Marketing Policies." *Journal of Urban Economics* 27: 344–61.

―――. 1991. "Black Surburbanization: Has It Changed the Relative Location of Races?" *Urban Affairs Quarterly* 26: 621–28.

Gans, H. J. 1967. *The Levittowners: Ways of Life and Politics in a New Suburban Community.* New York: Random House.

Garvin, M. 1987. "Inside Cleveland: Can Theater Change the Civic Landscape?" *Cleveland Magazine* 16: 23.

Gelber, B. S. 1985. "Race-conscious Approaches to Ending Segregation in Housing: Some Pitfalls on the Road to Integration." *Rutgers Law Review/Civil Rights Developments.* 37: 921–61.

George Gund Foundation. 1990. *Annual Report.* Cleveland: George Gund Foundation.

Gillmor, D., and S. K. Doig. 1992. "Segregation Forever?" *American Demographics* 14: 48–51.

Glazer, N. 1987. *Affirmative Discrimination: Ethnic Inequality and Public Policy.* Cambridge: Harvard University Press.

Goel, A. J. 1990. "Maintaining Integration against Minority Interests: An Anti-Subjugation Theory for Equality in Housing." *Urban Lawyer* 22: 369–416.

Goering, J. M. 1978. "Neighborhood Tipping and Racial Transition: A Review of the Social Science Evidence." *Journal of the American Institute of Planners* 44: 68–78.

―――, ed. 1986. *Housing Desegregation and Federal Policy.* Chapel Hill: University of North Carolina Press.

Goodwin, C. 1979. *The Oak Park Strategy: Community Control of Social Change.* Chicago: University of Chicago Press.

Governmental Research Institute. 1971. *A Brief History of the Efforts to Reorganize the Cuyahoga County Government.* Cleveland: Governmental Research Institute.

Gray, B. 1989. *Collaborating: Finding Common Ground for Multiparty Problems.* San Francisco: Jossey–Bass.

Greater Cleveland Roundtable (GCR). 1982. *Race and Ethnic Relations in Greater Cleveland.* Cleveland: GCR.

Grossman, J. S. 1966. "Psychological Determinants of Reaction to Neighborhood Racial Change." Ph.D. diss., Case Western Reserve University, Cleveland.

Gruen, C., and N. J. Gruen. 1972. *Low and Moderate Income Housing in the Suburbs: An Analysis for the Dayton, Ohio Region.* New York: Praeger.

Hacker, A. 1992. *Two Nations: Black and White, Separate, Hostile, Unequal.* New York: Scribner's.

Hale, M. Q. 1968. "The Ohio Fair-Housing Law." In L. W. Eley and T. W. Casstevens, eds., *The Politics of Fair-Housing Legislation.* San Francisco: Chandler.

Harris, M. E., and R. M. Robinson. 1963. *The Proud Heritage of Cleveland Heights, Ohio.* Cleveland: Allen.

Hartman, C., D. Keating, and R. LeGates. 1982. *Displacement: How to Fight It.* Washington, D.C.: Legal Services Anti-Displacement Project.

Harvard Law Review. 1980. Comment: "Benign Steering and Benign Quotas: The Validity of Race-conscious Government Policies to Promote Residential Integration." Harvard Law Review 93: 938–65.

Hayes, A. S. 1990. "Is Town's Housing Plan the Key to Integration or a Form of Racism?" *Wall Street Journal,* 4 Oct.: 1A.

Hays, R. A. 1985. *The Federal Government and Urban Housing: Ideology and Change in Public Policy.* Albany: State University of New York Press.

Heider, T. 1991a. "City's Minority Hiring Down Since 1988." *Cleveland Plain Dealer,* 2 Sept.: 2B.

———. 1991b. "NAACP Questions 'Dismal' Minority-hiring Record." *Cleveland Plain Dealer,* 13 Sept.: 2B.

———. 1991c. "Schools Flunk in Minority Hiring." *Cleveland Plain Dealer,* 18 Aug.: 2B.

———. 1992a. "Euclid OKs Ban on Realty Lawn Signs." *Cleveland Plain Dealer,* 17 Nov.: 2B.

———. 1992b. "Agents File Suit against Sign Ban." *Cleveland Plain Dealer,* 24 Dec.: 2B.

———. 1993. "Realtors Say 'White Flight' Fear behind Sign Ban." *Cleveland Plain Dealer,* 5 May: 2C.

Heights Community Congress, (HCC). 1992. *Annual Report.* Cleveland Heights, Ohio: HCC.

Heights Fund. 1991. *Annual Report.* Cleveland Heights, Ohio: Heights Fund.

Helper, R. 1979. "Social Interaction in Racially Mixed Neighborhoods." *Housing and Society* 6: 20–38.

————. 1986. "Success and Resistance Factors in the Maintenance of Racially Mixed Neighborhoods." In J. M. Goering, ed., *Housing Desegregation and Federal Policy.* Chapel Hill: University of North Carolina Press.

Heumann, L. F. 1981. *Integration Maintenance Program Evaluation.* Urbana: Housing Research and Development Program, University of Illinois at Urbana–Champaign.

Hill, E. Forthcoming. "The Restructuring of the Cleveland Economy." In W. D. Keating, N. Krumholz, and D. C. Perry, eds., *Cleveland: A Metropolitan Reader.* Kent, Ohio: Kent State University Press.

Hillcrest Neighbors. 1992, *Peaceful Transitions* 6.

Hoffman, M. C. 190. *Single-Family Homes Sales and Appreciation: Cuyahoga County 1980–1989.* Cleveland: Housing Policy Research Program, Urban Center, Maxine Goodman Levin College of Urban Affairs, Cleveland State University.

Hoke, W. A. 1992a. "Suit Charges Shaker with Discrimination." *Sun Press,* 14 May: 1A.

————. 1992b. "Firings Draw Plan Protests." *Sun Press,* 14 May: 1A.

————. 1992c. "Plan Combines 2 City Divisions." *Sun Press,* 18 June: 1A.

————. 1992d. "Discrimination Suit Ends Out of Court." *Sun Press,* 8 Oct.: 1A.

————. 1993. "United effort begins, sustains integration", *Sun Press,* 25 Mar.: 1A.

Holland, D. 1992. "Euclid Church Reaches Out to Welcome Blacks." *Cleveland Plain Dealer,* 29 Aug.: 5B

HUD (U.S. Department of Housing and Urban Development). 1985. *The Fair Housing Assistance Program Evaluation.* Washington, D.C.: Office of Policy Development and Research, HUD.

————. 1991. *Housing Discrimination Study: Incidence and Severity of Unfavorable Treatment.* Washington, D.C.: HUD.

Husock, H. 1989. *Integration Incentives in Suburban Cleveland.* Cambridge: John F. Kennedy School of Government, Harvard University.

Jackson, K. T. 1985. *Crabgrass Frontier: The Suburbanization of the United States.* New York: Oxford University Press.

Jewish Community Federation of Cleveland (JCF). 1982. *Survey of Cleveland's Jewish Population, 1981.* Cleveland: JCF.

Jordan, F. 1990. *Innovating America.* New York: Ford Foundation.

Jordan, G. 1984. "Euclid: Is It 'White Flight' Revisited?" *Cleveland Plain Dealer,* 30 Dec.: 22A.

Journal of Planning Education and Research 1989. Symposium on Yonkers. *Journal of Planning Education and Research* 167–96.

Kahoun, J. 1988. "Stokes Sees New Image for Parma." *Cleveland Plain Dealer,* 19 Nov.: 3B.

———. 1989. "Parma Can't Shake Whites-Only Image." *Cleveland Plain Dealer,* 19 Feb.: 1A.

Kain, F. J., and J. J. Persky. 1969. "Alternatives to the Gilded Ghetto." *Public Interest* 14: 74–87.

Katz, M. B. 1990. *The Undeserving Poor: From the War on Poverty to the War on Welfare.* New York: Pantheon Books.

Keating, W. D. 1992. *An Evaluation of Pro-Integrative Mortgage Incentives in Suburban Cuyahoga County.* Cleveland: Maxine Goodman Levin College of Urban Affairs, Cleveland State University.

Keating, W. D., N. Krumholz, and J. Metzger. 1989. "Post-populist Public–Private Partnerships." In Gregory D. Squires, ed., *Unequal Partnerships: The Political Economy of Urban Redevelopment in Postwar America.* New Brunswick, N.J.: Rutgers University Press.

Keating, W. D., W. J. Pammer, Jr., and L. S. Smith. 1987. *A Comparative Study of Three Models of Racial Integration in Suburban Cleveland.* Cleveland: Maxine Goodman Levin College of Urban Affairs, Cleveland State University.

Knapp, G. 1990. "State Land Use Planning and Exclusionary Zoning: Evidence from Oregon." *Journal of Planning Education and Research* 10: 39–46.

Krumholz, N. 1990. "Twenty Years after Kerner: The Cleveland Case." *Journal of Urban Affairs* 12: 285–97.

Krumholz, N., and J. Forester. 1990. *Making Equity Planning Work: Leadership in the Public Sector.* Philadelphia: Temple University Press.

Kubasek, R. 1976. *The History of Parma: A Township, a Village, a City.* N.P.

Kushner, J. A. 1989. "The Fair Housing Amendments of 1988: The Second Generation of Fair Housing." *Vanderbilt Law Review* 42: 1049–1120.

Kushner, M. A. 1988. "The Legality of Race-conscious Access Quotas under the Fair Housing Act of 1968." *Cardoza Law Review* 9: 1053–89.

Kusmer, K. L. 1976. *A Ghetto Takes Shape: Black Cleveland, 1870–1930.* Urbana: University of Illinois Press.

Lake, R. W. 1981. *The New Suburbanites: Race and Housing in the Suburbs.* New Brunswick, N. J.: Center for Urban Policy Research, Rutgers University.

Lamar, M., A. Mallach, and J. M. Payne. 1989. "*Mount Laurel* at Work: Affordable Housing in New Jersey, 1983–1988." *Rutgers Law Review* 41: 1197–1277.

Lauber, D. 1992. "Racially Diverse Communities: A National Necessity." In P. W. Nyden and W. Wiewel, eds., *Challenging Uneven Development: An Urban Agenda for the 1990s*. New Burnswick, N. J.: Rutgers University Press.

Laurenti, L. 1960. *Property Value and Race: Studies in Seven Cities*. Philadelphia: University of Pennsylvania Press.

Leigh, W. A., and J. D. McGhee. 1986. "A Minority Perspective on Residential Racial Segregation." In J. M. Goering, ed., *Housing Desegregation and Federal Policy*. Chapel Hill: University of North Carolina Press.

Lemann, N. 1991. *The Promised Land*. New York: Knopf.

Levin College of Urban Affairs Housing Policy Project. 1990. *Toward the Year 2000: Housing Policy Recommendations for Cleveland Metropolitan Area*. Cleveland: Housing Policy Research Program, Urban Center, Maxine Goodman Levin College of Urban Affairs, Cleveland State University.

Lewis, S. 1992. "A Parallel Experience." *Planning* 58 (May): 14.

Listokin, D. 1976. *Fair Share Housing Allocation*. New Brunswick, N.J.: Center for Urban Policy Research, Rutgers University.

Little A. D. 1967. *East Cleveland: Response to Urban Change*. N.P.

Logan, J. R., and M. Schneider. 1984. "Racial Segregation and Racial Change in American Suburbs, 1970–1980." *American Journal of Sociology* 89: 874–89.

Lovejoy, E. 1992. "*Mount Laurel* Scorecard." *Planning* 58 (May): 10–14.

Lubinger, W. 1991. "Housing Group's Director Committed to Cause." *Cleveland Plain Dealer*, 24 Aug.: 355U.

———. 1992a. "Housing Workers Laid Off." *Cleveland Plain Dealer*. 25 Apr.: 1A.

———. 1992b. "Fair-Housing Workers Protest Recent Layoffs." *Cleveland Plain Dealer*, 30 Apr.: 1D.

———. 1992c. "Cleveland-Area Brokers Ranked among Largest in U.S." *Cleveland Plain Dealer*, 14 June: 1G.

McBride, K. 1988. "Homing in on Housing: Parma Taking 2nd Look at New Bill." *Cleveland Plain Dealer*, 22 June: 8B.

McClain, K. 1992. "Regional Housing Mobility: Promoting Housing Choice for Hartford Area Section 8 Tenants." *PRRAC Researchers Report* 1: 5–6.

McMillian, M. 1986. "Euclid Schools Told to Reduce Racial Imbalance." *Cleveland Plain Dealer*, 9 Apr.: 1A.

McNamara, M. A. 1984. "The Legality and Efficacy of Homeowner's Equity Assuance: A Study of Oak Park, Illinois." *Northwestern University Law Review* 78: 1463–84.

Masotti, L. H., and J. R. Corsi. 1969. *Shootout in Cleveland*. New York: Praeger.

Massey, D. S., and N. A. Denton. 1987. "Trends in the Residential Segregation of Blacks, Hispanics, and Asians: 1970–1980." *American Sociological Review*, 52: 802–25.

———. 1988. "Suburbanization and Segregation in U.S. Metropolitan Areas." *American Journal of Sociology*. 94: 592–626.

Metcalf, G. R. 1988. *Fair Housing Comes of Age*. Westport, Conn. Greenwood.

Metropolitan Strategy Group (MSG). 1990. *Annual Report*. Cleveland: MSG.

———. 1992. "Ohio's Fair Housing Agencies in Review." *Metro Eye* 5: 1–3.

Meyerson, M., and E. C. Banfield. 1955. *Politics, Planning, and the Public Interest: The Case of Public Housing in Chicago*. New York: Free Press.

Milgram, M. 1977. *Good Neighborhood: The Challenge of Open Housing*. New York: Norton.

Molotch, H. L. 1972. *Managed Integration: Dilemmas of Doing Good in the City*. Berkeley: University of California Press.

Molyneaux, D. G., and S. Sackman, eds., 1987. *75 Years: An Informal History of Shaker Heights 1912–1987*. Shaker Heights, Ohio: Shaker Heights Public Library.

Myrdal, G. 1944. *An American Dilemma*. New York: McGraw-Hill.

National Advisory Commission on Civil Disorders. 1968. *Report* New York: Bantam Books.

National Commission on Urban Problems. 1968. *Building the American City*. Washington, D.C.: National Commission on Urban Problems.

Nelson, W., Jr. 1987. "Cleveland: The Evolution of Black Political Power." In M. B. Preston, J. Henderson, and P. Puryear, eds., *The New Black Politics: The Search for Political Power*. New York: Longman.

Oak Park Housing Center (OPHC). 1992. *Annual Report*. Oak Park, Ill.: OPHC.

O'Connor, R. 1986. "A City in Chaos." *Cleveland Magazine* 15: 88–94, 126.

O'Donnell, D. 1992. "Fond Memories of 'the Projects.'" *Cleveland Plain Dealer*, 30 Aug., 1B.

O'Hare, W. P., and W. H. Frey. 1992. "Booming, Surburban, and Black." *American Demographics* 14: 30–38.

O'Malley, M. 1991. "Lawyer Lashes out at Citywide Bigotry." *Cleveland Plain Dealer*, 18 July: 1B.

———. 1992. "Lawyer Says Parma Still Discriminates." *Cleveland Plain Dealer*, 23 Apr.: 3B.

———. 1993a. "Don't Expect a Revolt: Suburbs Content with Governments." *Cleveland Plain Dealer*, 22 Mar.: 6B.

———. 1993b. "Black Recruit Hired: Could Be First on Parma Force." *Cleveland Plain Dealer*, 14 Apr.: 4B.

Onderdonk, D., D. DeMarco and K. Cardona. 1977. *Integration in Housing: A Plan for Racial Diversity*. Park Forest, Ill.: Village of Park Forest.

OPEN (Fund for an Open Society). 1991. *Annual Report*. Philadelphia: OPEN.

Orfield, G. 1981. *Toward a Strategy for Urban Integration: Lessons in School and Housing Policy from Twelve Cities.* New York: Ford Foundation.

Orfield, G., and C. Ashkinaze. 1991. *The Closing Door: Conservative Policy and Black Opportunity.* Chicago: University of Chicago Press.

Palen, J. J. 1987. *The Urban World.* New York: McGraw-Hill.

Perry, R. M. 1989. "Cuyahoga Plan Dropped as Housing Consultant." *Cleveland Plain Dealer,* 9 Mar.: 1B.

Perry, S. E. 1987. *Communities on the Way: Rebuilding Local Economies in the United States and Canada.* Albany: State University of New York Press.

Podziba, S. L. 1992. "Consensus-based Planning Helps Transcend NIMBY-ism." In *Land Lines.* (Newsletter of the Lincoln Institute) Cambridge, Mass. Lincoln Institute of Land Policy.

Polikoff, A. 1978. *Housing the Poor: The Case for Heroism.* Cambridge, Mass.: Ballinger.

———. 1988. "*Gautreaux* and Institutional Litigation." *Chicago–Kent Law Review* 64: 451–78.

Potter, M. F. 1990. "Racial Diversity in Residential Communities: Societal Housing Patterns and a Proposal for a 'Racial Inclusionary Ordiance.'" *Southern California Law Review* 63: 1151–1235.

Powers, G. F. 1980. "Under One God: The Catholic Church and Race Relations in Cleveland, 1955–1970." Senior thesis, Department of History, Princeton University, Princeton, N.J.

Preston, M. B., L. J. Henderson, Jr., and P. L. Puryear. 1987. *The New Black Politics: The Search for Political Power.* 2d ed. New York: Longman.

Price, E. L. 1970. *A History of East Cleveland.* N.P.

Reich, D. R. 1968. "The Oberlin Fair-Housing Ordinance." In L. W. Eley and T. W. Casstevens, eds., *The Politics of Fair-Housing Legislation.* San Francisco: Chandler.

Rich, W. 1989. *Coleman Young and Detroit Politics.* Detroit: Wayne State University Press.

Roberts, S. 1992. "White Tilt to Balance a Project in Canarsie." *New York Times,* 3 Aug., Sec. B, p. 3.

Rosenbaum, J. E. 1991. "Black Pioneers—Do Their Moves to the Suburbs Increase Economic Opportunity for Mothers and Children?" *Housing Policy Debate* 2: 1179–1213.

Rosenbaum, J. E., and S. J. Popkin. 1990. "The Gautreaux Program: An Experiment in Racial and Economic Integration." *The Center Report: Current Policy Issues* 2: 1–4. (Report of the Center for Urban Affairs and Policy Research, Northwestern University.)

Ross, H. R., M. A. Levine, and M. S. Stedman, Jr. 1991. *Urban Politics: Power in Metropolitan America.* 4th ed. Itasca, Ill. Peacock.

Rubinowitz, L. S. 1974. *Low-Income Housing: Suburban Strategies.* Cambridge, Mass.: Ballinger.

Russell, M. 1991. "Cuyahoga Plan Objects to City Funding Cut." *Cleveland Plain Dealer,* 24 Oct.: 7B.

Saltman, J. 1971. *Open Housing as a Social Movement: Challenge, Conflict and Change.* Lexington, Mass.: Heath.

———. 1990. *A Fragile Movement: The Struggle for Neighborhood Stabilization.* Westport, Conn.: Greenwood.

Sawicki, S. 1987. "The Maple Grove Affair." *Cleveland Magazine* 16: 94–97, 129–31.

Schuman, H., and L. Bobo. 1988. "Survey-based Experiments on White Racial Attitudes toward Residential Integration." *American Journal of Sociology.* 94: 273–99.

Schuman, H., C. Steeh, and L. Bobo. 1985. *Racial Attitudes in America: Trends and Interpretations.* Cambridge: Harvard University Press.

Segall, G. 1991. "Flier by Mayor Alleged to Fan Racial Tensions." *Cleveland Plain Dealer,* 1 Nov.: 1B.

Selig, J. L. 1984. "The Justice Department and Racially Exclusive Practices: Creative Ventures in Fair Housing Act Enforcement." *University California, Davis Law Review* 17: 445–504.

Seton Hall University Center for Social Justice Affordable Housing Colloquium. 1991. "*Mount Laurel* and the Fair Housing Act: Success or Failure?" *Fordham Urban Law Journal* 19: 59–86.

Shields, G., and L. S. Spector. 1972. "Opening Up the Surburbs: Notes on a Movement for Social Change." *Yale Review of Law and Social Change* 2: 300–327.

Siemon, K. L. 1981. "Settlement Ends Court Fight over Fair Housing in Euclid." *Cleveland Plain Dealer,* 25 Nov.: 18C.

———. 1982. "Euclid Group Tries to Ease Integration Tension." *Cleveland Plain Dealer,* 23 May 25A.

Sigelman, L., and S. Welch. 1991. *Black Americans' Views of Racial Inequality.* New York: Cambridge University Press.

Silverman, R. H. 1977. "Subsidizing Tolerance for Open Communities." *Wisconsin Law Review* 375–401.

Simon, T. W. 1991. "Double Reverse Discrimination in Housing: Contextualizing the *Starrett City* Case." *Buffalo Law Review* 39: 803–53.

Smith, T. W. 1990. *Ethnic Images.* Chicago: University of Chicago National Opinion Research Center.

Smolla, R. A. 1985. "In Pursuit of Racial Utopias: Fair Housing, Quotas, and Goals in the 1980s." *Southern California Law Review* 58: 947–1016.

Squires, G. D., L. Bennett, K. McCourt, and P. Nyden, eds., 1987. *Chicago:*

Race, Class, and the Response to Urban Decline. Philadelphia: Temple University Press.

Stahura, J. M. 1988. "Changing Patterns of Suburban Racial Composition, 1970–1980." *Urban Affairs Quarterly* 233: 448–60.

Stern, J. 1991. "Yonkers Gives In." *Planning* 57: 8–11.

Sternlieb, G. 1971, "The City as Sandbox." *Public Interest* 4: 14.

Stokes, C. 1973. *Promises of Power.* New York: Simon & Schuster.

Taeuber, K. 1983. *Racial Residential Segregation in 28 Cities, 1970–1980.* Madison: University of Wisconsin–Madison Center for Demography and Ecology.

Taeuber, K., and Alma T. Taeuber. 1965. *Negroes in Cities.* Chicago: Aldine.

Teaford, J. C. 1986. *The Twentieth-Century American City: Problem, Promise, and Reality.* Baltimore: Johns Hoplins University Press.

Terkel, S. 1992. *Race—How Blacks and Whites Think and Feel about the American Obsession.* New York: The New Press.

Theiss, E. 1992. "Marchers Hail City's Unity, Diversity." *Cleveland Plain Dealer,* 25 May: 2B.

Thomas, S. A. 1991. "Efforts to Integrate Housing: The Legality of Mortgage-Incentive Programs." *New York University Law Review* 66: 940–78.

Tidwell, B. J. 1992. "Serving the National Interest: A Marshall Plan for America." In J. Dewart, ed., *The State of Black America 1992.* New York: National Urban League.

Tittle, D. 1992. *Rebuilding Cleveland: The Cleveland Foundation and Its Evolving Urban Strategy.* Columbus: Ohio State University Press.

Torassa, U. 1989. "Cuyahoga Plan Chief Wears Many Hats." *Cleveland Plain Dealer.*

U.S. Commission on Civil Rights. 1986. *Directory of Private Fair Housing Organizations.* Washington, D.C.: U.S. Commission on Civil Rights.

Vernarelli, M. J. 1986. "Where Should HUD Locate Assisted Housing? The Evolution of Fair Housing Policy." In J. Goering, ed., *Housing Desegregation and Federal Policy.* Chapel Hill: University of North Carolina Press.

Vincent, S. Z., and J. Rubinstein. 1975. *Jewish Life in Cleveland.* Cleveland: Western Reserve Historical Society and Jewish Community Federation of Cleveland.

Vodar, L. M. 1975. "The Use of Racial Housing Quotas to Achieve Integrated Communities: The Oak Park Approach." *Loyola University of Chicago Law Journal* 6: 164.

Weaver, R. 1948. *The Negro Ghetto.* New York: Harcourt Brace.

Weiher, G. R. 1991. *The Fractured Metropolis: Political Fragmentation and Metropolitan Segregation.* Albany: State University of New York Press.

Wheeler, Michael. 1993. "Regional Consensus on Affordable Housing: Yes in My Backyard?" *Journal of Planning Education and Research* 12: 139–41.

Whelan, E. P. 1985. "Surviving Social Upheaval in Shaker Heights." *Cleveland Magazine* 14: 97–99, 152, 154, 156, 158, 160, 162–65.

Wilkerson, I. 1988. "A City Finds Its Racist Image Is Hard to Shed." *New York Times*, 30 Nov. Sec. I, p. 1.

———. 1991. "One City's 30-Year Crusade for Integration." *New York Times*, 30 Dec., sec. I, p. 1.

Wilson, W. J. 1987. *The Truly Disadvantaged: The Inner City, the Underclass, and Public Policy*. Chicago: University of Chicago Press.

Yale Law Review. 1980. Comment: "Tipping the Scales of Justice: A Race-conscious Remedy for Neighborhood Transition." *Yale Law Review* 90: 377–99.

Yinger, J. 1986. "On the Possibility of Achieving Racial Integration through Subsidized Housing." In J. Goering, ed., *Housing Desegregation and Federal Policy*. Chapel Hill: University of North Carolina Press.

Zannes, E. 1972. *Checkmate in Cleveland*. Cleveland: Case Western Reserve University Press.

Zimmerman, M. W. 1992. "Opening the Door to Race-based Real Estate Marketing: *South-Suburban Housing Center v. Greater South-Suburban Board of Realtors*." *DePaul Law Review* 41: 1271–1367.

INDEX